# In Search of the
# 'Special Relationship'
# with Britain

# In Search of the 'Special Relationship' with Britain

**John A. Ziegler**

The Pentland Press
Edinburgh – Cambridge – Durham – USA

First published in 2000 by
The Pentland Press Ltd
1 Hutton Close
South Church
Bishop Auckland
Durham

ISBN 1–85821-746–6


Typeset in Melior 10/12
by Carnegie Publishing, Carnegie House, Chatsworth Road Lancaster
Printed and bound by Antony Rowe, Chippenham

*To my many mentors but above all the
Political Science professors at Southern
Illinois University, Carbondale, in the 1950s
who guided my search and study at home
and abroad.*

# Contents

# Illustrations and Maps

## Illustrations:

## Maps:

# Preface

*H*ighly autobiographical, this book should be seen as the story of a rather typical member of an American generation that was born in the Great Depression, grew up during World War II, and reached adulthood in the 1950s. With parents often born before the turn of the twentieth century, we had fathers who fought in World War I, but when they returned home from abroad, most of them resumed their lives as before in whatever calling they had followed. So farmers returned to the farms; steel workers returned to the mills; and artisans returned to their trades.

Hence, many of us were the first in our families to attend college after completing high school, something our parents had not done either, and we were often educated by a generation born during and immediately after World War I. Many of these teachers and professors were not merely our role models for a different type of life than our parents followed, but also our heroes because they had struggled through a very difficult adolescence during the Great Depression when jobs were scarce and had fought and won World War II while very young adults. Like ourselves, a large number of them had been first-generation college students, and their higher education had been made possible by the United States Government's GI Bill. Many also endured years of hardships before they were able to enter their professions, and some, the war-wounded, carried heavy burdens for the rest of their lives. This book is dedicated to them.

To recognize the influence of that generation on mine and to describe the world view of people like me, I have written about my experiences in search of the 'special relationship' with Great Britain which serves as the organizing concept. Other concepts could have been chosen, but this one has been central in my personal relations with the outside world. Choosing voluntarily to be engaged with that outside world, something our parents and teachers had not done, is perhaps one of the main differences between my generation and previous ones.

My approach in this book has been to focus on institutions I have come to know well during more than forty years of travel to and periods of residence in Britain as first a college student and later a professor. Hence, the range of topics is very wide, some rather sophisticated – especially in an academic sense – while others much less so.

Recognizing this early on in my writing, I asked some undergraduates at my college to rank order four chapters in terms of readability. To my surprise the class of twenty divided into an almost perfect distribution concerning their preferences for each of the four. My conclusion was that the book seemed to have something for everyone.

Therefore, to provide a guide about content and difficulty, a sentence or two describing each chapter follows. The most autobiographical of all, Chapter I details the context in which I first encountered the 'special relationship' concept, and my ultimate understanding of its meaning in anthropomorphic terms. Chapter II tells about the implementation of the concept through foreign study programs in Oxford and London. One of the more academic chapters, Chapter III recounts key points in several of my lectures at Oxford and Cambridge on 'special relationship' topics. The topics are American isolationism, the decline thesis, and functionalism.

Chapter IV considers some of journalist Alistair Cooke's writings that are representative of my notion of the 'special relationship.' The most sophisticated academically, Chapter V outlines some ideas of two scholars I consider my mentors in the area of comparative British and American political institutions. These men are Woodrow Wilson and James MacGregor Burns, and I have borrowed some of their ideas to argue for change in the American political party system based on British experience.

While three generations of my family history tie this chapter together, Chapter VI focuses mainly on the public lives of these men who were Jurats and Mayors of Dover, Deputies of the Cinque Ports, and Members of Parliament during the reigns of the Tudor monarchs.

Chapter VII describes Wilton Park, a British government conference center in Sussex, that followed for many years an educational philosophy and practices which fostered the 'special relationship.'

Certainly the most impressionistic and mystical of all, Chapter VIII recounts the outcome of my walks on the South Downs and along the Adur River in Sussex. The vehicle of walks is continued in Chapters IX and X which focus on four London themes – churches, theaters, villages, and parks – that offer like the country walks much insight to an American seeking the 'special relationship' with Britain.

# Acknowledgements

*I* would like to thank my daughter Robin E. Ziegler for her cover design and maps and for her suggestions concerning six chapters while the book was being written. Four of these chapters also received excellent scrutiny from students in my American foreign policy course at Hendrix College. In addition, helpful comments about early drafts of the Wilton Park chapter were given by three former and two current members of staff. In particular, I wish to single out Robert S. Sturrock, who knew Heinz Koeppler well, for his many insights about Wilton Park's founder which he shared with me.

# Introduction

$T$his book takes an anthropomorphic approach to understand the special relationship between Britain and the United States. Some readers will no doubt find this approach unsatisfactory, but I offer no apologies for adopting it. In the first place, the review of some literature in Chapter I shows that scholars have found this approach quite useful in their studies.

In the second place, I became convinced of its usefulness as well when seeing a parallel between America's and my own personal experiences in growing up. Passing through adolescence and entering early adulthood just after World War II, I was struck by the thought that I was witnessing America doing the same. In seeing people like myself struggle through this difficult period of development, I came to see America as a reflection of ourselves.

Moreover, as I studied American history at university, I came to believe that the best way to understand our diplomatic experience was to see this country as an immature adolescent male. Hence, our history showed that here was a rebellious youth who had rejected his parents at the time of the American Revolution in the late eighteenth century, and when he struck out on his own at the end of the nineteenth century his 'protest masculinity' got out of hand. His policies of imperialism from 1898 to 1917, of internationalism from 1917 to 1920, and of isolationism from 1920 to 1941 all suggested a behaviour pattern of the immature. In other words, America was in turn a self-assertive bully, a self-righteous moralizer, and a self-indulgent loner. All of us are familiar with these roles played by the immature adolescent.

Specifically, America first bullied a very sick and frail old man in 1898 – that is, the Spanish Empire or what was left of it. Feeling quite macho, as male adolescents are inclined to feel, he quickly knocked this defenseless old fellow to the ground and felt enormous pride and elation in doing so. Who would be next? He turned his attention to a few other easy targets: this time young children (as President Theodore Roosevelt called them) in his own backyard (Colombia and Mexico, among others) and bullied them into submission as well. With buttons virtually popping from his chest now, he felt he was ready to take on the 'big boys' or the real men of the world.

His big chance came with World War I. However, these men of the world (Britain, France, Italy, etc.) were quite clever, very experienced, and therefore could not be bullied like an old man or young children. Hence, America tried another tactic of the immature adolescent male: self-righteous moralizing as expressed by America's 'preacher', President Woodrow Wilson. The real men of the world saw through this device and ignored America's feeble moralizing at Versailles after the war.

His youthful pride now hurt beyond repair, America again behaved like an immature male and ran away to hide from the rest of the world by assuming his isolationist stance during the interwar period. Seeing him on the run, some of the real men of the world, bullies in their own right, knocked him down and almost out at Pearl Harbor and elsewhere. Badly dazed, America got to his feet and with the help of his parents – Britain/Britannia – and a few others, he subdued these bullies in a fight to the death.

As my generation looked at America and of course at ourselves after World War II, we asked some very big questions: Had these experiences made us into mature adults? Had we finally grown up to be men of the world who would now assume our responsibilities. What should our role in the world be?

Perhaps many readers find my brief anthropomorphic interpretation of American diplomatic history unsatisfactory; in fact some, especially American patriots, are probably outraged. Yet, I think this is a fair presentation of the thoughts and concerns of many people my age as we were coming to maturity after World War II. At any rate, I ask readers to keep these ideas in mind as context for what follows in this book.

# Prologue

*I* am a child of the Great Depression and World War II eras, the Age of Franklin Roosevelt, if you will. Although the momentous events of this Age defined the larger context for my youth, I do not want to overstate their significance, especially the Depression's, in the development of my world view. Since my family was no worse off than most other families in our Illinois village in the St Louis area, the Depression did not seem to affect me in any really adverse ways. My father always had a job – in fact his own small business with one employee – and my mother supplemented the family income by working part-time from our home next door to the business. Moreover, the Depression was essentially over when I entered public school.

The war, on the other hand, raged between my sixth and twelfth years and therefore affected me much more significantly, though our family was in no way personally touched by it. Again, we were no more inconvenienced by the war than most other families in New Athens, our village, and its life seemed to go on much as before with the absence of course of some young men, only one of whom failed to return home at war's end. Clearly our community was quite lucky – again.

Yet, for me, the many war movies – and I saw my share of them at the local movie house – the radio news and other wartime broadcasts, and the daily newspapers delivered to our door all helped to make the war somewhat 'real' for me in at least a detached sort of way. Of these means of communication, it was perhaps the radio broadcasts that affected me most because it seemed that the radio was on much of the time from morning to night at our house. While several major St Louis stations got a share of our attention, KMOX, the CBS affiliate, was heard most often, especially during the morning and evening news broadcasts. Although both parents followed the news, my father seemed to be a 'news junkie' and was most certainly a faithful listener of Edward R. Murrow, the great CBS correspondent stationed in London during the war. Like President Roosevelt, Murrow was always welcome as a radio guest in our home. Perhaps, therefore, it was Murrow's dramatic reporting of the Battle of Britain that first stirred my interest in that country. To this day Murrow, who became one of my boyhood heroes, and Britain are inextricably linked in my mind, and I can still hear echoes in my memories of his famous line, 'This ... is London.'

As a result of such powerful communications, my young friends and I played 'war' a great deal throughout the village and in the surrounding pastures and woods as well during the summer months, and we were of course inclined to be the British rather than the German forces. In fact, I well remember my father once raising a disapproving eyebrow and telling us to be less anti-German in our 'war games.'

Yet the lives of elementary schoolboys in 1940 were usually focused on playing sports rather than war. Baseball and basketball filled most of our playtime at school and on weekends. Moreover, we were more likely to daydream about hitting a home run to win a game for the St Louis Cardinals in the last of the ninth inning or hooping a basket at the buzzer for a victory for the 'Fighting Illini' than flying a Spitfire for the RAF. No, it wasn't Britain at war – either heard about or played at – that sustained my youthful interest in Britain itself.

Although I was not an overly bookish child, some of my school books whetted my appetite for things British. Certainly the books containing stories and poems from English literature were important in bringing out the charm of British life and countryside, but they are not as memorable today as the geography books. Those books, though only in black and white, had fascinating pictures of exotic places the world over. All kinds of places vied for attention, but for some reason the firths and lochs of Scotland always won out. Why? I am not sure, but since those were the days before television, when the written and spoken word had not been lost to the picture, the equally exotic names no doubt had something to do with it. My hope was that one day I would see these beautiful places for myself.

Like the experiences of many other Americans, my high school years seemed to produce something like a hiatus rather than a period of substantial growth. I didn't seem to learn very much and spent most of my time engaged in athletics and related school activities. Certainly Britain was put on hold until I got to college.

After a transition period from athletics to academics during my first year or two at college, the latent interest in Britain manifested itself again in my study of international relations, comparative politics, English literature, and history, including one course in English history. Once deciding on those academic paths it seemed almost inevitable that a trip to Britain would be forthcoming, if not sooner, certainly later.

But why those paths? Obviously the factors mentioned before were important, but I think much more intellectual reasons, though ones really grounded in feelings, lay at the root of my choices. Many of my favorite professors at Southern Illinois University, Carbondale, were veterans of World War II or if not were specialists in international relations. If any common, yet simple, idea came from all of them, it was that the world could not afford another war like the last one. This of course was also the prevailing attitude among Americans after World War I, but the United States took the wrong course of action when adopting the policy of isolationism during the interwar period. The same mistake should not be repeated after World War II. Hence my professors argued that we all had an important job to do to keep America involved in world affairs this time. For a young idealistic young man remembering the reports of Murrow and other wartime correspondents who detailed the awful death and destruction of the 1940s, this idea was not difficult to accept.

It was also an idea that was not difficult to develop further, for American policy makers had already committed the United States to a world leadership role by the 1950s when I entered college. NATO and other military alliances – extraordinary policy changes for America – were in the process of being implemented as I pursued my studies. While many countries, especially those of Western Europe, were important in this process, it seemed obvious to me that Britain was the key. She had been the staging area for victory in the European war, and this 'permanent aircraft carrier' off the coast of Europe seemed to be destined to play a similar role in the Cold War.

All of this was grand and glorious stuff for academic discussions, but what would be my role in it, the role of an obscure undergraduate at an equally obscure state university in the Middle West? How should I do 'my bit,' as the ordinary GI of World War II would put it? Should I join the army or one of the other military services? Should I try to become a diplomat or another type of civil servant? What other options were open to me?

Up to that time, I had been leaning in the direction of teaching. During my high school athletic days, I thought mainly about coaching, though teaching academic subjects like history and government had some appeal. The availability at the end of my senior year of what was called at that time an Illinois normal school scholarship seemed to open the door for this interest, but the sudden death of my father, whose business was experiencing difficult times, put entrance to college in doubt. However, my mother, who immediately went to work full-time, insisted that I accept the scholarship and enroll at SIU. Having done so, I felt a moral obligation to study for a secondary school teaching credential, but by my senior year in Carbondale my association with fellow government and history majors and professors convinced me that I should enter graduate school there with the intention of becoming a college professor.

It was my year as a teaching assistant in the Department of Government that helped me decide definitely on an academic career. Of the many factors in my decision-making, the professors in the department were probably the most important. In those days SIU was still small, about 3,000 students when I entered as a freshman, but was growing rather rapidly, and the government faculty reflected this. As I entered graduate school, there were over a dozen professors in government, and most of them were housed in one large open room, desk backed against desk, because of the shortage of individual offices. The five TAs shared two or three desks in the same room. As indicated above many of these professors (there was only one woman among them) were veterans of the war, and perhaps because of that as well as the crowded facilities, they did not fit the professorial stereotype. They were gregarious rather than aloof, informal rather than formal, practical rather than 'ivory tower,' fun-loving rather than deadly serious, and so on. While these professors did some research – and several of them became noted in their fields – they saw themselves as teachers first. And most important for the TAs, they also saw themselves as teachers of would-be teachers and as our friends. During my first term as a TA, several of them gave me opportunities to teach their classes for a couple of days, and beginning my second term, I was given a class of my own. Therefore, I experienced one of the best processes of professional socialization anyone can have.

It is often said that one does not learn a subject well until one teaches it. This was certainly my experience teaching my first college course in American political institutions. Although I thought – in my youthful arrogance – that I had acquired as an undergraduate a rather solid background in that area, I soon learned how little I knew and how urgent additional preparation was needed. My background reading for my lectures convinced me that a good understanding of basic American politics required a solid foundation of many things British. For example, knowledge of the backgrounds of American political thought required a thorough reading of John Locke, and any excursion into American law necessitated some immersion in the common law.

As these and other factors too numerous to mention here came together in my thinking during the 1955–56 academic year, I concluded that now was the time to go to Britain. But how? Since graduate students have little money for such things, I began to look into scholarships. A scheduled visit to my dentist in New Athens provided a good lead. A member of the local Rotary Club, he urged me to apply for a Rotary Foundation Fellowship for Advanced Study Abroad. He thought the local club would support my application. It did, and the Fellowship came my way for a year's study at St Andrews University, Scotland, beginning in September 1956.

Those reading the above very carefully will have certainly noticed that the term 'special relationship' has not as yet been used. The reason is that I do not recall using it or even being familiar with it until my arrival in Britain. It is, in the first place, an essentially British expression, the origin of which is usually attributed to Winston Churchill in the 1940s. Even today Britons rather than Americans are more inclined to use it. Certainly in the early 1950s, as American Presidents like Truman and Eisenhower attempted to be even-handed leaders of the 'Free World,' there were conscious efforts made to maintain some distance between the two countries by avoiding its use, often to the consternation of British leaders like Churchill. In my own case, given the knowledge and attitudes I had of Britain at the time, I certainly stood closer to our own leadership than to Churchill. In addition, from my perspective it was difficult to call the relationship with Britain 'special' in the light of our relationship with such other countries as Canada and Israel which also seemed to have 'out-of-the-ordinary' connections with the United States as well. Hence, the word 'special' did not really seem to apply. 'Different,' yes, but 'special,' no.

Perhaps I would have felt differently had I had contact with some people from Britain during the first twenty-three years of my life. However, New Athens and most of the other communities in the area had been settled by Germans, and their descendants had rather effectively maintained the ethnic character of the villages and towns. Moreover, while these people considered themselves loyal Americans during the two World Wars, their German backgrounds worked against the development of strong British sympathies. Although Carbondale was essentially a Southern town with an Anglo-Saxon past, little influence was apparent because of the distance between town and gown. While some cosmopolitan elements were present at SIU, few of them were British. Even the foreign students – and the university had a rather large number of them, many of whom I knew well – seemed to come from almost everywhere but Britain. No, in those days a British connection seemed to be possible only at the movies, and the occasional Alec Guinness comedy was about all we had to influence us.

So, on the eve of my departure for Britain, how would I describe my state of mind? Obviously I was excited and enthusiastic about going, but intellectual curiosity of a general nature seemed to be my prevailing attitude. I felt that I was going mainly for the purpose of studying a country that was the source of much of America's intellectual and cultural heritage and that had become our leading ally in the Cold War. Having acquired a few tourist books and magazines, I was also determined to see the important sights, especially those Scottish firths and lochs shown in my geography books.

In addition, since one of the obligations of the scholarship was to play the role of an 'ambassador of goodwill' by speaking to Rotary and other civic organizations, I put together a couple of short talks on American politics and culture which I intended to present during my year's stay.

It is also important to remember that in those days few Middle Westerners where I lived, apart from the returning veterans, had ever traveled abroad. Therefore, my family and friends, as well as most members of the New Athens and nearby Rotary Clubs, expected to experience vicariously a representative part of Britain, and perhaps other parts of Europe, through my talks when I returned. Consequently, I was given a new camera and plenty of film with instructions to take 'hundreds' of pictures of everything.

One of my professors at SIU, an air force veteran who had served in Scotland during the war, also gave me an important piece of advice just before I left. He said, 'Don't go over there and spend all your time in the library. Don't take your studies too seriously. Get out and see things and meet people, for this trip might turn out to be the high point of your life.' I departed for Britain with this advice uppermost in my mind.

In the 1950s, the principal means of transportation to Britain – at least for struggling students – was the steamship. For me it was the *Empress of Scotland*, a 26,300 ton Canadian Pacific liner, that made the run from Montreal to Liverpool. There were four of us – three students and a professional hockey player – crowded into a very small room down in the bowels of the ship which had been built around 1930 and had seen wartime service hauling troops across the Atlantic. It was not difficult to see that comfort and spaciousness had never been major considerations in its construction – at least at our level. The initial thought was 'so what' since the room's principal function was that of a dormitory with most hours of the daytime and even the night-time being spent elsewhere on board. Little did I realize how wrong that thought would be.

The journey, which was to take six days, started off well enough. Clear, crisp autumn weather had settled in over the St Lawrence River Valley, and for two days everyone seemed to be having a marvellous time on deck. Cameras clicked constantly as one charming village after another appeared along the shore. The main attraction waited for was, of course, Quebec with the Plains of Abraham and the impressive Old World-appearing Hotel Frontenac. But we passed that landmark very quickly and immediately had the sense, as the weather was indeed beginning to change, that we would soon be out in the north Atlantic.

A raging storm announced our arrival loud and clear. For the next several days the ship was tossed about like a cork, and few people ventured on deck where ropes had been strung to aid walking. One night, so word of mouth said, a crewman was washed overboard and lost. Our crowded room was indeed that as trips outside tended to be short runs to the lavatory and back. I spent a lot of time lying in my bunk thinking that if the ship should go down, I would certainly go with it. If it were true, as I had been told so often, that Britain was a land of sailors, I had my first serious doubts that I would fit in very well.

When the ship finally reached the Irish Sea, a St Lawrence River-type calm returned, and the remainder of the trip was an absolute delight. While little time was spent immediately reflecting on what had happened during the previous days at sea, in hindsight now after many jet flights across the Atlantic, including one on Concorde, it is clear that slow ocean travel is more in keeping with the way in which the mind and body function. The days at sea, though awful in this first instance, allowed time for some easy 'gear-shifting' which does not occur in the jet age. Even though one kind of time has been gained with the jet, another kind has been lost. Like the athlete getting ready for the big game, one needs to prepare both physically and mentally for the upcoming encounter with a different culture. For first impressions, it is far better to see and experience a new culture with a clear mind and an energetic body.

My first glimpse of the Old World was a mixture of the expected and the unexpected. Before the ship docked at Liverpool, it passed what appeared to be an island almost covered by a town. The stone-constructed row houses were expected but the grid-patterned streets were not. None of this, however, was as surprising as my first encounter with Liverpool itself. I had known of course that the city had been heavily bombed during the war, but the war had been over eleven years when I arrived. Yet the dock area was still essentially flat with little evidence of any rebuilding in progress. This was something of a shocking experience – the first of many I was to have during my initial three months in Britain – concerning the country's economic condition. Certainly I had heard about Britain's difficulties immediately after the war, but I had thought that by the middle 1950s she would have recovered rather significantly. Clearly she had not.

Perhaps the most shocking evidence of Britain's appalling condition was to be seen in London at Christmas time. I did not expect to see the area around St Paul's Cathedral, close to the heart of the City of London, still flat from the wartime bombardment. After seeing several German cities including Frankfurt, which had been largely rebuilt, soon thereafter, I kept asking myself whether Great Britain had in fact been on the winning side of the war. At any rate, it seemed clear almost immediately there in Liverpool on my arrival that the 'Great' in her name had been lost – perhaps forever. Hence, my first impression was one that left me asking, 'Oh, Britannia, what has befallen you?'

So my first journey into Britain began not in search of the 'special relationship' but in wondering about the extent of her decline as a great power and perhaps even her impending fall.

# Chapter I

# A Year at St Andrews University

*A*lma Mater. Although I wasn't quite sure what I was searching for in Britain when I arrived for the first time, perhaps it was inevitable that my search for whatever it was would start within the context of the university. While family and church were the most important institutions shaping my life to age eighteen, the university, which was introduced at that time, soon displaced the church, though family continued as an important factor as before. In fact, the university became church and many other things as well in my life as years passed.

The pervasive influence of the university was not felt immediately, partly I am sure, because I lived in private housing rather than in a university residence hall during my years at Southern Illinois University, Carbondale. But over the years as the university became more than just a collection of buildings where classes met, its influence on me grew. Perhaps my first realization of this occurred during the spring break of my freshman year when the SIU baseball team, of which I was a member, traveled down the lower Mississippi River valley to play other college teams in Tennessee, Mississippi, and Louisiana. As rather privileged representatives of the university community, we were expected to do two things: be on our best behaviour and win games for SIU, not necessarily in that order of course.

As I became more involved in academic activities sponsored by the university and its organizations, such as trips to places like the Universities of Chicago and Wisconsin and meetings of the International Relations and Government Clubs, its importance as a source of ideas and values grew in my understanding. The contacts with other like-minded students and faculty stimulated my thought and interest. Probably by the time I was a senior – most certainly at the time I entered graduate school – the university had come to represent a definite way of life, a way of life I wanted to follow.

One of the many great services to that way of life which SIU provided was the recruitment of foreign students to the campus. This was done mainly through the availability of fellowships and teaching assistant-ships for students from abroad by the Graduate School. In view of the large numbers of such students in Carbondale in the early 1950s, SIU must have been one of the leaders in a field that would expand rapidly across the nation in the years ahead with the help of the Fulbright Program and Rotary International, among others. Most of the initiative for this policy at SIU came from two specialists in international relations in the Government Department, Dr Willis G. Swartz, Dean of the Graduate School, and Dr Frank L. Klingberg, Professor and Advisor to the International Relations Club. Both Rotarians, these men, who were my mentors, understood the need to have rather isolated and provincial Middle Western students interact with their peers from around the world. As an active member and later president of the International Relations Club, I got to know a number of these students well and have maintained friendships with several to this day. With the encouragement of these professors and foreign friends to study abroad for an extended period of time, I applied for a Rotary Fellowship which I subsequently received.

## St Andrews

My university abroad became St Andrews but not in St Andrews. What does this mean? When the Rotary Foundation notified me of my scholarship to St Andrews University, my immediate response, given my background, was one of elation. According to my research, the university and town, the latter about the size of Carbondale, were tied closely together and figured prominently in Scottish history down to the seventeenth century. The town's place in religious history, for example, dated back to the Dark Ages when the relics of the Christian martyr St Andrew were brought to what was then known as Kilrimont (meaning 'cell of the king's mount') which promptly changed its name to St Andrews and gave Scotland her patron saint. By the tenth century the town was the seat of the Bishop of the Scots. The twelfth century saw the founding of a great cathedral which survived until its almost total destruction during the Protestant Reformation. John Knox and George Wishart were among the great religious figures of St Andrews.[1]

The town was also connected with secular history. The Scottish Parliament met in St Andrews in 1645–46, and Mary, Queen of Scots, lived there for a time, so it is believed. James Wilson, one of the Founding Fathers of the American Constitution, came from there and was apparently a university student before emigrating to America.[2]

The history of the university was also interesting to read. The oldest university in Scotland, St Andrews was started in 1410, sanctioned by King James I in 1411, and received confirmation of Pope Benedict XIII of Avignon in 1413. Benedict granted six bulls recognizing St Andrews as a 'studium generale,' a university of international scholars. It was said that the university was founded largely because Scotsmen could not attend French and English universities which supported the rival pope of the time, Martin V of Rome.[3]

In its early history, the university had three colleges: St Salvator's (1450), St Leonard's (1512), and St Mary's (1537). Several of the university's buildings which dated from the sixteenth century were still in use in the 1950s. These included the Chapel of St Leonard's and much of St Mary's, the theological college. The latter was founded by Archbishop James Beaton, a former St Andrews student, and the adjacent University Library was started by King James VI of Scotland in 1612. Always a small university, St Andrews more than doubled its enrollment to over 2,000 students between the end of World War II and the middle 1950s. Most students were housed in university residence halls, some of which had recently been built.[4]

All of this about the town and university of St Andrews – plus of course information about the Old Course of the Royal and Ancient Golf Club which the great Bobby Jones called the finest course in the world – had tremendous appeal to a history and politics student and sometime athlete who had never ventured very far out of the American Middle West before. However, to my deep disappointment, the university notified me shortly before I sailed that I would have to enroll in Queen's College, located in Dundee some thirteen miles away, because political science was not taught in the town of St Andrews. My previous information had not told me that Queen's College had become a recent addition to St Andrews University when several Dundee professional schools, loosely associated with the university, along with the old Dundee School of Economics, came together as Queen's under the university's full jurisdiction. Had I known at the time that it was possible to live in residence in St Andrews and commute by train to Dundee for classes, I might have spent my year living in the former. Instead I began to prepare myself for a stay in Dundee.

## Dundee

As I gathered information about Dundee, my disappointment became deeper still because I found little about it that compared favorably to St Andrews other than size. With a population of about 175,000 people Dundee should be able to offer things that were not available in a town of about 9,500. Although growing up in an Illinois village, I was close enough to St Louis to enjoy rather frequently some of the delights of that city: the baseball Cardinals; the Municipal Opera, Zoo, Art Gallery, and Highlands in Forest Park during the summer; the American Theatre and St Louis University Billikin basketball during the winter; various shows, including the circus, at the Arena; cruises on the Mississippi; and shopping and eating in some very fine stores and restaurants, especially those featuring German and Italian food. Obviously Dundee would not be

St Louis, but there was hope for having some interesting things to see and do in a city approaching 200,000.

On the other hand, Dundee's history suffered by comparison to St Andrews'. While Dundee's early recorded history – like that of St Andrews – seemed to be a mixture of truth and fable, it had no towering figure like a saint associated with it. Yet many believed that a person of some stature, King William the Lion (1165–1214), was the actual founder and builder of Dundee as a royal burgh shortly before 1200. A written document of the time, a charter, mentioned the creation of Dundee – spelled Dunde – a name seemingly derived from the combination of 'dun,' the Celtic name for a fort, and 'de,' probably derived from the name of a Celtic chief of old called Deaga. Apparently William's objective was to develop at various strategic points in his realm – obviously the high ground overlooking the entrance to the Firth of Tay was one of them – royal castles guarding trading centers. By the end of the twelfth century Dundee had a castle, a parish church, and a market place.[5]

As I read these brief accounts, the market place seemed to be the most important element of the three in Dundee's subsequent history. Clearly the castle had its day, especially in connection with Scottish-English affairs, and the church was the focus of attention at various times, especially during the Reformation, but the market place seemed to be the thread that tied together Dundee's history from its early days down to the twentieth century. Obviously commerce had its ups and downs but was the key factor in Dundee's continuity nevertheless.

By the sixteenth century, for example, Dundee could boast that next to Edinburgh it was the wealthiest town in Scotland, mainly due to the personal fortunes of its merchants who sold their products of foodstuffs, raw materials, wool, and hides to home and even to continental markets. Though decay and depression set in during the eighteenth century, the town's fortunes revived as a result of the spectacular development of the textile industry during the nineteenth century. At first it was flax, but by the middle of the century it was jute that brought the return of prosperity. As one commentator put it: 'Great fortunes were accumulated by the "jute lords," whose "palaces" ringed the late Victorian city; in their new mills and factories toiled an army of 40,000 workers, two-thirds of them women, a quarter of the whole population of Dundee.' Before the end of the century, the town became the jute center of Britain. These developments so impressed Queen Victoria that she granted the town a charter making it a city in 1889. By 1900 Dundee had a population of over 160,000 (up from only 26,000 in 1800), but interestingly enough only 175,000 by the middle 1950s, an increase of just 15,000 in over fifty years.[6]

Since I did not have time before sailing to acquire additional information and to reflect upon the little I had, my first sight of Dundee was a big shock. Had I seen something like Liverpool's docks, it might have been less shocking, but Dundee had not been bombed flat. Apparently only one or two bombs actually hit the city during the war, and they did little damage. As the population figures above suggest, Dundee, at least its central area where I would spend much of my time, had really not changed significantly for many years. In some Old World cities that could be very fortunate but not in Dundee's case. Perhaps because it had mushroomed as a mill town last century and because of financial and other difficulties stemming from two world wars and a major depression since, parts of central Dundee appeared to be something out of Dickens. Even the better and newer areas suggested that the city was still in fact a big old mill town rather than a modern city.

Dundee's skyline told much of the tale of its current economic base. If the skyscraper is New York City's symbol, the tall jute mill chimney, seemingly skyscraper in height, was Dundee's in the 1950s. It was said that over forty firms were engaged in spinning and weaving jute in Dundee and its immediate surrounding area at that time.[7] An interesting cultural observation I was told upon my arrival – when I was experiencing great difficulty understanding the Dundonians – was that the local accent, much harsher than those found in other Scottish cities, was mainly caused by adaptations in speaking required of many thousands of people down through the years as they tried to make themselves understood above the relentless din of the jute machinery

*Some of Dundee's jute mill chimneys and the Tay Rail Bridge across the Firth, April 1957.*

*A nineteenth-century 'palace' of a Dundee 'jute lord' just off Perth
Road near the outskirts of the city, April 1957.*

in the mills where they worked. As noted above, about two-thirds of
these workers were women, society's language teachers of the very
young.

The skyline, especially that part of it near the edges of the city, also
featured many 'palaces' of the 'jute lords.' Although the great nineteenth
century houses – some might call them monstrosities – were still there,
the 'lords' as well as most of their offspring were either gone or living
in more modest dwellings. In fact, most of the 'palaces' had been
subdivided into several flats each or had become dormitories or similar
facilities for institutions of one kind or another.

These developments were signs about the future of Dundee's jute
industry. Already sensing decline during the early 1950s as the newly
independent Commonwealth nations of India and Pakistan, the main
sources of the jute fiber, began to consider domestic manufacturing,
the Dundee industry experienced shortages and increased costs with
the closing of the Suez Canal at the time of the Crisis in late 1956.
While jute remained Dundee's major industry for some years thereafter,
today the mills are gone.

Fortunately Dundee's economic base in 1956 was broader than jute
alone, but the future of some of the other industries was no brighter.
Shipbuilding, for example, which made Dundee the leading center on
the east coast of Scotland and second only to Glasgow, was to have
its great days numbered with the increase in air travel. What Dundee

seemed to be counting on for the future was its developing American connections, one aspect of the 'special relationship.' Three large American corporations, headed by National Cash Register, had made Dundee their manufacturing headquarters in Britain. Dundee also hoped to build on its reputation as an engineering center, again second only to Glasgow in Scotland. There were other smaller industries that contributed somewhat to the economy, perhaps the best known world-wide were those making marmalade and cake.[8]

So as I reflected on my new home away from home, I was reminded of Queen Victoria's disillusionment when she wrote in her *Journal*, 'Dundee has a beautiful situation, but the town itself is not so.' Dickens came to a similar conclusion when he observed that Dundee is 'an odd place, like Wapping, with high rugged hills behind it.' Perhaps, then, on my arrival, Dundee's only apparent redeeming feature seemed to be its beautiful setting at the mouth of the Tay which so impressed Victoria and Dickens. Clearly not much had changed for the better since the nineteenth century.[9]

As I learned more about the city, I began to look for the kinds of things that I liked about St Louis. But no matter what I found – and I found *some* interesting things – one fact remained abundantly clear, however, and that was that Dundee was essentially a working-class community, a blue-collar town, if you will. Certainly most of its entertainments were aimed at that class. For example, Dundee had two major football (soccer) teams, something somewhat unusual for its size, whose games were usually well attended at their local playing fields which accommodated over 80,000 spectators total. It also had seventeen movie houses or cinemas, several of which were theaters as well, including Green's Playhouse that seated over 4,000, apparently one of the largest in Europe. It seemed that nearly two-thirds of the films presented were American productions, perhaps the most visible aspect of the 'special relationship' in Dundee. In addition there were twenty dance halls, five bingo establishments, and an ice rink seating over 3,000.[10] I was surprised to find relatively few pubs, but perhaps that statement says much more about my German background than it does about a largely Scottish-Presbyterian town.

The middle and upper classes of Dundee seemed to find their amusements in some of the above as well, especially the cinemas, but perhaps they were more inclined to seek out things connected with private or semi-private clubs. For example, many of them, both men and women, seemed to be rather avid golfers at the many clubs in the area. They also supported and some of them performed in the local dramatic societies, and they were the classes that kept financially sound the rather famed Dundee Repertory Theatre, which was the training ground for Virginia McKenna and several other stars of the British stage and screen. Their involvement in other things of a cultural nature included attending largely imported attractions from elsewhere in Britain and occasionally from abroad. The Scottish Symphony Orchestra, for instance, gave several concerts in Dundee each year.

While these classes gave some support to the local museums and art galleries, they seemed to be more inclined to be active in the Royal Tay Yacht Club or the Rotary and other clubs that brought them face-to-face with others engaged in commercial activities. As a Rotary Fellow I was destined to meet a number of these people during the ensuing year when I attended the occasional Rotary function. Of the several men I got to know well, they were clearly creatures of commercial activity but almost to a man, they had a delightful sense of humor, usually expressed in a self-deprecating manner. At their invitation I became a member of one of their organizations, the Dundee Curling Club. A few of its 140 members actually did some curling, but really the purpose of the organization was to bring like-minded men together for fellowship and good fun.

This strong commercial orientation of Dundonians spilled over into their educational institutions. Dundee had a rather large technical college and a trades college, for example. Yet, in typical Scottish fashion, educational interest extended beyond the mere material into art and teacher training. Most important of all, of course, was Queen's College which started as University College in the 1880s. Over the years degree programs were developed in medicine, science, dentistry, applied science, and law. With the absorption of the Dundee School of Economics under the University of St Andrews Act of 1953, University College became Queen's College and had the added capacity to offer degree programs in the social sciences.[11]

## Queen's College

While most of the Queen's campus was located on a 52-acre site along the Perth Road near the center of Dundee, the social science faculty was housed in Bonar House, Bell Street, a good ten minutes' walk away. Although it was difficult to know how this situation affected the faculty, the social science students felt rather isolated from campus affairs.

Certainly there were services, facilities, and activities at the main campus that were designed to help integrate the social science students into the rest of the student body. There were, for instance, library, refectory, and residence hall facilities, but unfortunately each had little power of attraction. Take the library. Like so many things I saw at Queen's, it had not had an adequate budget for years, and the building itself was almost literally falling down, the floors being supported by temporary wooden beams.

Perhaps the less said about the food in the refectory the better. It was without question the worst institutional food, including the US

*Queen's College campus in Dundee with the Library and Student Union on the left, pulled down a few years after this photograph was taken in 1957.*

Army rations I ate during basic training, I have ever had either before or since. Needless to say most students ate elsewhere if they could afford to.

The social science students I knew did not live in residence halls. Since they were from Dundee and the surrounding villages, they lived with their families at home. I therefore decided to live with a family, too, a Scottish dental surgeon and dental faculty member and his wife and young son. This family also had two daughters who were studying in St Andrews. The consequence of all of this was that I felt like only a daytime student in Bonar House rather than a 24-hour student of Queen's College.

Given this situation and the fact of Queen's own transition, I had serious doubts about just how typical of Scottish university life this experience was. Certainly Bonar House itself was different from university buildings I knew. Sandwiched between other buildings a short distance from Dundee's center, the three-storey brown stone structure had six ionic columns between the second and third floors of the facade. Hence, in appearance Bonar House looked more like a government building or perhaps even a commercial establishment rather than part of a college. The interior, which was spotless and cold in both senses, had an institutional rather than a homey collegiate feeling about it. Since the numbers of both faculty and students at that time were very small, one rarely saw or even heard other people in the building after passing the porter's lodge near the front door. The library, one large room, was usually mine alone when I used it.

I never knew exactly how many social sciences faculty members in total occupied the building. Studying only political science and history, I met all of the faculty in these two disciplines. To my surprise, there was only one political scientist, a recent MA graduate, who had little teaching experience. He once admitted to our class that he had no background in political theory and American government, two areas we studied. Of the four historians there was one with the rank of Professor and he, as well as two others, had doctorates. One of these had almost no teaching experience, however.

In terms of competency, the political scientist, as suggested above, was the least prepared to teach his subject, but he was an exceptionally friendly young man in his rather shy and diffident way. A bachelor, he gave the class a night out in a pub in an attempt to get to know us better. One of the historians, the one I came to like least of all because he was pompous and arrogant, invited our class to his home one evening for refreshments. Other than that, which may or may not have much to do with competency, they were very knowledgeable and one, the economic historian, was one of the best organized lecturers I have ever had.

My two year-long classes in political science and modern British history, a typical course load, were very small with only about a half dozen students each, about equally divided between male and female. While the one man taught political science, three of the historians handled that subject, rotating every few days to cover various aspects and periods beginning in 1485. By and large the pedagogical methods used – mainly lectures – were not substantially different from what I had experienced in America with two exceptions: the group tutorials in political science and the written essays in history.

Although the political scientist usually lectured to the entire group as we sat around a table in a seminar room, every couple of weeks we gathered in his small office, seated on chairs surrounding his desk where he sat with the texts he had recommended to us. While discussion of the texts seemed to be the general goal of the tutorial, the instructor, a graduate of one of the Oxford colleges where the tutorial system was world famous, attempted to get the students to probe below the surface of the readings to think about such things as the motivation and purpose of the text's authors. Certainly this type of questioning was not entirely new for me, but the intimate tutorial setting in the instructor's office was. Although we never went one-on-one as is the case at Oxford, I came to see the value of individualized or at least near individualized instruction.

As an American student whose previous writing experience in the social sciences had been mainly confined to answering examination questions and composing long-term papers with numerous footnotes and long bibliographies, my first encounter with historical essay writing at Queen's left me somewhat at sea. For example, when I asked the instructor about footnoting, he essentially dismissed the question by saying that footnotes could or could not be used – it was my choice in other words. My immediate reaction – to myself of course, and certainly not to the instructor – was that this attitude was hardly very scholarly. What I eventually came to realize about this and other remarks from my history instructors was that an essay at St Andrews was quite different from the typical term paper at an American university. An essay was really an individual's personal digestion and reinterpretation of the knowledge gained from others and presented in such a fashion as to be persuasive. One's new insights were more important than the repeat of others' old insights.

While the foregoing account about Dundee and Queen's College was not intended to paint a completely dismal picture of what I encountered as I settled in, I was clearly very disappointed and unhappy not being in St Andrews, the town, and not being a genuine resident of St Andrews, the university. The months ahead did not look bright. Yet before the end of the year I was feeling joyful. Why? In a word: family.

## *Family*

As mentioned before, I lived with a Scottish family and my close college friends lived at home with their families, two completely unanticipated aspects of my year's experience. Let me briefly describe my friends first.

Having small classes, I got to know all my classmates very quickly and several very well almost immediately as we ate lunch and socialized before and after class almost every day. I soon met the parents of three of these students after I was invited into their homes, first, for tea, and later for dinner. Since the four of us became close personal friends during that year and three have remained such for the following forty years, some details about each of these three are in order.

All middle-class Dundonians about twenty years of age, my friends were Ian, Tony R., and Tony L. Ever the practical and matter-of-fact fellow, Ian, a Scottish Presbyterian, was inclined to support the politics of the Liberal Party, though his interests were more in business, his father's occupation, than in politics. Ian could have been the son of any of the Rotarians I came to know well in Dundee. On the other hand, Tony R., whose father was a teacher, was quite different. A Catholic with a strong social conscience, he leaned in the direction of the Conservative Party but was an independent thinker. In later life, he would become the editor of an independent Catholic publication.

Tony L. became my best friend. Something of a romantic who insisted

*My best friend in Dundee, Tony L, standing on West Sands,*
*St Andrews, in April 1957.*

this trait came from his mother, he, a Catholic whose family ties reached back to Northern Ireland, was a staunch and very vocal Conservative, a great admirer of Winston Churchill. He felt that the socialism of the Labour Party had taken Britain down the wrong path in 1945 and looked forward to the repeal of many of their policies with the return of the Conservatives to power. Tony and I ate lunch together nearly every day we had classes and took day trips occasionally to such places as St Andrews and Glasgow. At Christmas we spent a week seeing the sights of London, thanks in part to the generous financial support of Tony's father who must be described as well.

Mr L started his professional career as a secondary school English teacher and had become a deputy headmaster of a Catholic academy in Dundee by the time we met. Head of a devout Catholic family which included three children, he had a very significant religious experience during World War II when he was given an audience with Pope Pious XII at the Vatican. Though an education officer of the RAF at the time, he was attached to an American unit in Rome, and his American commander arranged the audience. From then on, apparently, there was little Americans could do wrong in his view of most things. This same attitude became central for the entire family, and hence I, one of the few Americans they knew in 1956 and the only one on their doorstep, was welcomed to their home almost as family.

*Tony L and another good friend, Ian W, pose during a dinner conversation in the L home in Dundee, April 1957.*

While there was little in their household trappings that suggested pro-Americanism, the family watched all television shows about or by Americans whenever they were available. Since British television was still in its infancy – only one channel of the BBC was available on a limited time basis – much family entertainment consisted of a night or two a week at the cinema. For this family, American movies were always preferred and were usually judged to be far superior to British productions.

During my frequent visits in the L family home, I was struck by the almost continuous animated conversation among the family members. Not previously knowing any people of Irish background, I did not associate the two until after learning much about the American Kennedys in the early 1960s, whose dinner conversations became legendary. While a number of topics were covered in these conversations by the L family, sooner or later, they, like the Kennedys, settled on politics. I was brought into these conversations to explain various aspects of American and world politics. Reading widely in the newspapers became a must before a visit to the Ls as well as daily lunches with Tony, who might have been the best conversationalist I ever knew.

While Mr L usually dominated these family conversations, he seemed to enjoy having others take issue with his views which more often than not were anti-British and pro-American – perhaps another Irish characteristic? In any event, he was a very kind, considerate, and generous person who made me feel that my views were important to know. He was undoubtedly a great teacher and a superb father figure.

If Mr L were the most memorable figure of this family, Mrs W was such a person of the family I lived with. From the very beginning she and I seemed to be on the same wavelength about most things. In fact she had the capacity to anticipate most of my questions before I asked them. For example, during our first meeting in her home about my renting a room, she offered me without my asking a second-floor bedroom – there were five altogether – which had the best view of the Firth of Tay from her hillside house. Again and again throughout the year she demonstrated this sixth sense to do things for me that had gone no further than my thoughts. I came to refer to her as my British Mother.

Although Dr W was originally from Glasgow – as were Mr and Mrs L – Mrs W came from a local commercial family whose members had become scattered around the world. One brother had spent the war in a Japanese prison camp, for instance. She had gone to a finishing school in London during the early 1930s and returned to Dundee to

*Dr and Mrs W enjoying a favorite pastime at Kinloch Rannoch in 1957.*

marry Dr W who had a dental practice and later completed a Ph.D. at St Andrews. Their home, just off the Perth Road near the edge of Dundee, had been built in 1939, shortly after their two daughters were born. Their son was born in 1946.

Unlike the Ls, the Ws, who were Presbyterians but rarely attended church, showed little interest in politics, but like the Ls, they were Churchill Conservatives. Concerning entertainments, the Ws were avid golfers, and frequently spent their summer holidays near golf courses. In addition, they performed in and directed plays of the Dundee Dramatic Society for many years. As great lovers of the theater, they saw plays in Scotland and occasionally in London.

Upon my arrival in their house in early October, the Ws made me feel very much at home. For a mere three pounds ($8.40) a week, I was given virtually everything a family member could receive with the exception of lunches during the week. I was well fed at breakfast and dinner – Mrs W was an excellent cook – but the most enjoyable times of my stay were the teas in the late afternoons and again in the evenings between ten and eleven. While the former were less frequent than the latter, which occurred every night, these gatherings around the open fire in the lounge – there was no central heating in the house – always included Mrs W and me, usually Dr W in the evening, occasionally the young son in the afternoon, and now and then the two daughters when they were home for a short visit from St Andrews. Although there were always tea, with milk and sugar of course, and plenty of

*Dr W playing "mother" for evening tea, April 1957.*

thin sandwiches, cakes, and other interesting delights, good conversation was the real purpose – there was no television set in the house. This social interaction with 'my family' was perhaps the most rewarding experience of the entire year abroad. I learned tremendously from them and perhaps the Ws learned something as well. One thing for sure did result: friendship for a lifetime.

Since this family situation developed almost immediately after my arrival, it was not too difficult to establish a more than adequate and even a highly enjoyable daily routine. The typical day usually started between 7:30 and 8:00 a.m. with a knock on my door by Mrs W indicating that the bathroom was now clear as the son had just gone off to school. Initially Mrs W prepared the typical hearty British breakfast but I soon cut back on the amount I ate as the pounds began to pile on. With the completion of breakfast just before 9:00 a.m., Dr W and I were off in his car to his office just round the corner from Queen's where I started my ten-minute walk to Bonar House, picking up one of the quality newspapers such as the *Manchester Guardian* or *The Times* along the way. If Dr W were out of town on one of his rather frequent trips to London, I caught a bus, which had recently replaced the tram, at the foot of the Ws' driveway to the city center and walked to Bonar House.

There was usually enough time to skim through part of the paper and to chat a few minutes with classmates before the history lecture started at 10:00. An hour later, it was morning teatime with friends, plus some library reading until lunch at 1:00 p.m. in a little restaurant near the city center. More often than not only Tony L and I ate together, and sometimes our conversations there lasted an hour and one-half or even two hours if the political science class did not meet that day. In the event of class, we were back at Bonar House before 3:00 p.m. for the political science lecture.

Occasionally several of us had tea after class but usually we headed home. If the weather were nice, as it was throughout October, I walked; if not, I took the bus back from the city center. A cup of tea was usually waiting for me, and I often talked at length with Mrs W as she began dinner which was served immediately upon Dr W's return just after 6:00 p.m.

Reading or perhaps an occasional visit to the cinema filled the early evening hours until tea at 10:00 p.m. Additional study followed until 1:00 or 2:00, sometimes 3:00 a.m. if an essay were due, and then to bed.

Of course all situations have their tensions – we certainly had ours – but everything seemed to run very smoothly during the early weeks of the term as we all had much to tell one another about our respective backgrounds, customs, practices, and interests. Obviously there were many differences among us, but clearly we shared many things including basic values and outlooks. I was amazed at how well I fitted into this middle-class British culture, and hence I came to appreciate the observation of a national character scholar who argued that there are probably greater differences between the classes in one culture than there are between the same classes in different cultures. Certainly for me middle-class British and middle-class American family lives were very similar indeed.

## *The Suez Crisis*

However, our compatibility and congeniality were soon to be significantly tested. The background for this testing originated in international politics. In many respects, of course, international politics had drawn our two nations together in the recent past. While it seemed for a short time at the end of World War II that we might go our separate ways again, though certainly not to the same degree as during the interwar period, we quickly came together in a number of ways, most significantly through a military alliance, NATO, to 'fight' the Cold War. We did indeed have something like that which William James called 'the moral equivalent of war' and came close to the real thing and a variation on the real thing during encounters over Berlin and in Korea. In both instances the British were probably our most reliable ally.

By the middle 1950s, subtle evidence, though not widely reported at the time, began to mount that compatibility and congeniality at the highest levels were beginning to dissipate. A recent study by a former British diplomatic correspondent sees much of the growing problem between Britain and the United States stemming from the mutual hostility between Anthony Eden, the British Prime Minister, and John Foster Dulles, the American Secretary of State. John Dickie reports that as early as May 1952 when Eden was Foreign Secretary under Churchill he, Eden, approached Dwight Eisenhower, still Allied Supreme Commander at NATO, to make a highly unusual request of him. Knowing that Eisenhower was about to leave the US Army to become the Republican candidate for the Presidency, he urged the General to choose someone other than Dulles as his Secretary of State in the event of victory. Eden said he could not work with Dulles. The latter, of course, became Secretary of State in 1953 and Eden became Prime Minister in 1955 after Churchill retired. Dickie sees that by the middle of that period of time, April 1954, there was deep antagonism between the two.[12]

As events unfolded in the Middle East, close Anglo-American cooperation was obviously needed. While Britain's power in that region had been declining, her interests remained high, mainly because of her need for the Suez Canal and oil. On the other hand, America's power and interests there were on the increase since the end of World War II.

More than any other factor, the event that caused the most rapid political changes in the region was Colonel Gamal Nasser's seizure of power in Egypt through an army coup. Nasser led a very angry group of military men who had been humiliated at the defeat inflicted on the Arabs by the Israelis. Nasser wanted arms to rebuild Arab power but the Western powers were unwilling to supply them. Therefore, in September 1955, Egypt concluded an agreement with the Communist government of Czechoslovakia to supply tanks and artillery. The Cold War was rapidly coming to the Middle East.[13]

Nasser's game seemed to be that of attempting to play one side off against the other in order to get what he wanted. Dulles became a player when he expressed interest in providing American financial support for the planned Aswan Dam on the Nile River. Britain joined the American initiative and the two countries agreed in principle in December 1955 to help finance the project. Nasser thereupon formally requested $100 million in aid from the United States but nothing happened.

Why? Apparently because of other actions by Nasser in his political game. For example, in April 1956, he concluded a military alliance with Saudi Arabia, Syria, and Yemen with Israel as his obvious target. In May, he recognized the Communist government of China. Sensing now what Nasser was doing, Dulles bluntly declared in July that the United States would not send aid to Egypt for the Aswan project.

Within a week, Nasser nationalized the British-owned Universal Suez Canal Company. Though he promised to keep the canal open to all former users, the British and French did not believe him. Dulles tried to mediate the situation by proposing a users' association to manage the canal but neither side found this acceptable. At the end of July the British notified Dulles that they and the French would move militarily against Egypt if the crisis were not resolved quickly.

It was during the following months that communication broke down completely between Dulles and Eden. No solutions were forthcoming, and things were allowed to drift out of control. By October, with Egypt still operating the canal, the British and French secretly adopted a plan to go to war and coordinated their strategy with Israel. The United States was left out.

On October 29, the Israeli army crossed the frontier into the Sinai Desert, and the next day Britain and France announced that they would intervene 'to protect the Suez Canal' which had become closed by sunken vessels. On November 1, British and French troops occupied the area around the canal and demanded that the Egyptian and Israeli forces withdraw to a zone five miles on either side of the waterway.

This operation fooled no one. At the United Nations, the United States joined the Soviet Union in condemning Britain, France, and Israel and voted for a resolution in the General Assembly demanding a ceasefire. Other pressures were exerted by the United States and in December Britain and France announced their withdrawal from Egypt. Anglo-American relations were perhaps at their lowest level this century.

Although the British themselves were badly divided about Eden's policy, especially along political party lines, I, as an American in their midst, felt that I was in a very awkward situation because even Eden's opponents were not pleased with the United States either. Certainly his supporters were outraged. Anti-American feeling was running very high, and it was fueled further by the belief that the United States had failed to keep at least its implied promise to assist the Hungarians who were in revolt against the Soviets at that time.

One of the very interesting aspects of this feeling was that little criticism in Britain was leveled at President Eisenhower personally and virtually all of the fault was placed on Dulles. I recall giving a talk at a Rotary Club during this period about American politics, and since I was a supporter of Adlai Stevenson, the Democratic nominee against Eisenhower in the 1956 election, I did not spare any criticism of the President. When I concluded, the responder said simply, 'I still like Ike!' The reputation of one of Britain's American war heroes had not been tarnished by Suez.

In one respect had I been living in a university residence hall, this anti-Americanism would have been easier to handle. Discussions would have taken the form of the usual student bull sessions, something I was used to. But since the two families I knew best of all – and it is important to see them as families – were strong Conservatives, I was not sure how things would work out. Perhaps it was fortunate that it was Eden rather than the now retired Churchill who was at the heart of the controversy. In the eyes of my families, Eden was no Churchill, and besides he was a sick man (who would soon resign giving poor health as his reason).

In the end – to my surprise – the most difficult aspect of the situation was not anti-Americanism which was not really at the heart of the matter for my families. For them it was more of a problem of national pride. Since the fathers and mothers of these families were in their forties and fifties and had lived through two awful world wars and a major depression, they had experienced a dreadful turn of events. Within their lifetimes, they had seen Britain drop from being hailed as the most powerful nation in the world to one that could not even successfully challenge a Nasser, a rather puny dictator of a third world country. This hurt. While my families were not as discouraged as some British students I knew who concluded that Britain was 'finished,' as they put it, the Ws and Ls were greatly stunned and saddened by the rapid course of powerful events which were so difficult to accept. This very painful experience for them was something I could understand

and empathize with to a great degree. For my families, then, it was not anger at America but hurt national pride that troubled them, feelings that tended to draw us together rather than split us apart.

## The Special Relationship

This experience with the Suez Crisis forced us to take a closer look at the Anglo-American relationship both at a national and a personal level. What we all finally realized from this painful event was that Britain's great days as a major power were indeed over and that the moment of truth for her had arrived. What was her choice going to be? Did she really have a choice in fact? For my Conservative friends, the answer was not Europe or the Commonwealth but the United States – a special relationship with my country, something their great hero Winston Churchill, now retired in his old age, had been advocating since the late 1930s. But what did this mean in 1956?

One could rather easily talk about a special relationship on the more mundane and practical level of a military alliance – close cooperation among the military and intelligence services, for example – but obviously my British friends meant something more, though it was not clear how far they really and seriously wanted to go. Dr W jokingly used to talk about Britain becoming the 49th state of the United States, something that was actually rather seriously debated by some student groups. Tony L, who rarely spoke about such things in a light-hearted way, seemed to take the position expressed by Harold Macmillan, soon to become the new Prime Minister, that Britain should become Greece to America's Rome. Exactly how far Tony really wanted to go neither I nor Tony himself seemed to know at the time.

As events were unfolding before us, I did not really understand the true nature of the special relationship concept, and I still have doubts that I fully understand it today, but one thing is clear: like Macmillan, I think ordinary words are inadequate to express its meaning and metaphors are the best concepts to use.

Based on my experience, I came to believe that a general metaphor which illuminates most is the nuclear family idea and a more specific one is the female figure of such a family. Certainly many previous discussions about the basic relationship between the United States and Britain have used elements of this general metaphor. Two studies by eminent scholars of American culture and character immediately come to mind.

In his monumental study *America as a Civilization*, Max Lerner argues that to have its true and unique identity America had to 'slay' its 'European Father,' which can be read as Britain, the target of America's violent revolution. Lerner traces his metaphor to James G. Frazer's book *The Golden Bough* which uses the theme of the tribal killing of the sacrificial king or the symbolic slaying of the father. For Lerner, an adolescent, as well as a young nation like the United States, does this as part of the process of disowning a parent 'to assert himself as a person in his own right.'[14]

Margaret Mead's *And Keep Your Powder Dry*, a study of the nature of the American character, argues that essentially all Americans, no matter from whence or when they came to the United States, are 'third generation' types. Basically, she means that the rejection of the father by the son lies at the heart of the American character. Hence, the first generation immigrant, the one who leaves Europe for America, rejects his father's world, the Old World of the past for the New World of the future. The second generation man, the first generation American by birth, rejects his father because the latter is only half American. For his part, the son intends to be all American: 'he eats American, talks American, dresses American, he will be American or nothing.' This generation – American born of foreign-born parents – says Mead, sets part of the tone of the American eagerness for their children to go forward: to surpass the parents. So rejection, not of course like that of the past but rejection nevertheless, is expected and encouraged. With the third generation, then, the son is expected to do better than his father because the latter, who might have been pretty good for his day, is now out-of-date. His ways are a thing of the past and hence are to be rejected.[15]

Placed in a nuclear family context, these father-son relationship metaphors are illustrative of much that has been written about the nature of American culture and character, but there seems to be a fundamental oversight in their use: the role of the female figure, the mother, is ignored. This is surprising because the traditional nuclear family of father, mother, and son has found expression again and again in three key mythological figures that have recurred in many cultures throughout the world. For example, the father or the Hero, sometimes human, sometimes divine, and sometimes tyrannical, is found in every major human culture. Also seen in these cultures is the mother, often called Helper, who is identified through a collection of tradition female virtues, a wholly positive version of the great mother or white goddess. Found, too, is the son or Rebel, sometimes identified as the younger version of the Hero, the rebel against the gods who brings knowledge to man, using such things as guile and deceit that are the weapons of the physically weak.[16]

These three figures have been so important in human experience down through the ages that modern psychoanalysts have defined them as projections of basic human needs, from the narcissistic need of the aggressive Hero to be admired, to the nurturing affection of the Helper, and the youthlike revolt of the Rebel who displays 'protest masculinity' which involves a strong rejection of nurturing – or female behaviour.[17]

So, building on Lerner and Mead, I follow this interpretation: when America, the Rebel son, 'slew' Britain, the Hero father, he also rejected Britannia, the Helper mother, though at the time of the Revolution, he did not fully understand this or its consequences. Since he was his father's son, America retained the important and necessary masculine attributes of his father which served him well during his early development isolated from the world community and actually protected by his father's navy. But having also rejected Britannia, America lost those feminine attributes that would make him a whole and complete person in his physical maturity, a Hero in his own right. Hence, in the twentieth century as America has joined the world community, he has had great trouble in finding his proper role in the world, especially the role as a leader. Therefore, in order to become an effective leader, America must recover these lost attributes, and the best way to do so is through a special relationship. Perhaps it should be noted here that a significant insight from contemporary leadership literature is that many outstanding male leaders have been identified as 'mama's boys.'

No attempt will be made to compile a long list of these lost Helper attributes, but some of the more important ones are the following: cooperative, broadminded, understanding, nonjudgmentally loyal, accommodating, fair, honorable, kind, optimistic, and sacrifice of personal interests.[18]

That the special relationship concept should be expressed in terms of a female figure might seem surprising. Yet, is it nothing more than coincidence that the three prime ministers who were the greatest champions of this notion from the British side, the side that has been far out in front with this idea, were Margaret Thatcher, Harold Macmillan, and Winston Churchill? Nothing needs to be said about Thatcher, of course, but Macmillan and Churchill, you ask? While they had many things in common, important here is the fact that these men had American mothers. Perhaps, in the end, the concept took this form for me mainly because my year's stay in Britain enabled me to see it personified in a woman I got to know well, Mrs W.

## *Postscript*

My studies of politics and history and other experiences during my year in Dundee convinced me that a worthy goal for the years ahead was the promotion of the special relationship. The question was how to do it. Obviously my friends and I agreed on the first step: the continuation and deepening of our personal relationships. But what should be the second? Tony L and I reached the same conclusion almost immediately: Alma Mater. We would continue our own university educations leading to the doctorate, establish ourselves as professors at universities in our respective countries, and then exchange 'pulpits' regularly as well as our students through foreign study programs in Britain and America. From Tony's perspective, his first need was to study in the United States for a year or so. Together we contacted Dean Swartz at SIU, and Tony subsequently received a graduate assistantship there for 1957–58.

Although America was home base for both of us during the following years, we tended to go our separate ways, keeping in touch by letter and the occasional meeting. I spent nearly three years in military service, taught a couple of years, married, and finally returned to graduate school.

At SIU, Tony spent several years working on a graduate degree and teaching classes, during which time his parents visited Carbondale twice, the second time for a year's stay with their two daughters. Mr L taught in the SIU English Department.

After receiving his degree, Tony returned to Britain to teach for a year but came back to America in the fall of 1963 to complete a doctorate in political science at the University of Illinois. Tragically, four months later he was killed in an automobile accident on an Illinois highway.

We, family and friends alike, were devastated by his loss. Tony had so much promise, enthusiasm, and energy for the things we all believed in. Now he was gone. Clearly, he had been his family's pride and joy, and hence his parents never fully recovered from the shock of his sudden death at age twenty-seven. Unfortunately for them, tragedy struck again eleven years later when one of their daughters died just as suddenly.

Since I was still in graduate school and was soon to become a father, my work and growing responsibilities helped me come to terms with the death of someone who had almost seemed like a younger brother during my year in Britain. Although the special relationship was not forgotten, it was put on hold for a time.

## Notes

1. *St Andrews: Official Guide* (St Andrews: St Andrews Publicity and Information Association), 14.
2. Ibid.
3. Ibid., 42.
4. Ibid., 44–5.
5. *Dundee: Official Handbook* (Dundee: Corporation of Dundee), 5.
6. Ibid., 9.
7. Ibid., 46.
8. *Dundee and Round About* (Dundee: D.C. Thompson & Co. Ltd. and John Leng & Co. Ltd.), 3.
9. *Dundee: Official Handbook*, 11.

10. *Dundee and Round About*, 28.

11. Ibid., 18.

12. John Dickie, *'Special' No More: Anglo-American Relations: Rhetoric and Reality* (London: Weidenfeld and Nicolson, 1994), 87.

13. Robert D. Schulzinger, *American Diplomacy in the Twentieth Century*, 2nd ed., (New York: Oxford University Press, 1990). The discussion on Suez is based on pages 250–2 of this book.

14. Max Lerner, *America as a Civilization*, vol. 1 (New York: Simon and Schuster, 1957), 25–6.

15. Margaret Mead, 'We Are All Third Generation,' in Michael McGiffert (ed.), *The Character of Americans: A Book of Readings* (Homewood, Illinois: The Dorsey Press, 1964), 138.

16. Marvin W. Mindes with Alan C. Acock, 'Trickster, Hero, Helper: A Report on the Lawyer Image,' in John J. Bonsignore, Ethan Katsh, Peter d'Errico, Ronald M. Pipkin, Stephen Arons and Janet Rifkin, *Before the Law: An Introduction to the Legal Process*, 3rd ed., (Boston: Houghton Mifflin Company, 1984), 309.

17. Ibid.

18. Ibid., 307.

# Chapter II

# Oxford et Alibi

Hendrix College
November, 1993

Dear Hendrix Oxonian,

A handshake. It all started with a simple handshake within the precincts of St Peter's College, Oxford, on a gloriously beautiful day in June, 1979. I had come up from London on an early train out of Paddington to meet a man I had heard about during a summer program in Cambridge several years before. The short walk from the station to St Peter's was absolutely marvelous. Oxford had had a rain storm the night before, but by morning a stiff, fresh breeze out of the northwest had blown the clouds away, and the wet 'dreaming spires' were as sparkling as only they can be. Francis Warner met me at the entrance to his rooms at the top of the stairs. The chemistry was just right. By morning tea we had agreed that six Hendrix students could participate in the Oxford Overseas Study Course beginning in October, 1980. The rest, as they say, is history – your history! To this day, the parting handshake with Francis serves as the bond between Hendrix and Oxford.

Fourteen years and over one hundred Hendrix Oxonians later, it's time, ladies and gentlemen, please. Why it's time to have a reunion, of course! Since Francis and Penelope (and perhaps the children, too) are planning a trip to this country next April, we think our Oxonians and the Warners can be brought together here at Hendrix. We hope you agree ...

Sincerely,
John Ziegler

And so the invitations went out to the alumni of the Oxford Overseas Study Course, a foreign study program known as Hendrix–in–Oxford on the Hendrix campus, for the first reunion of our special relationship participants. During the reunion one lovely Saturday afternoon the following April, my attention was directed of course to the many familiar faces of past participants whom I had not seen in years. Yet, my thoughts went back instead to Tony L, dead now for over thirty years, who was my fellow planner of the special relationship project in 1957. This part of it was a long, long time in coming. Oh, how I wished Tony could have been there to share in the joy of that day! When the punch was served, I silently drank a toast to him.

Tony's death had almost ended things even before a good start had been made. During the summer of 1964, a few months after his tragic accident, my short trip to Britain produced very little other than a renewal of an old friendship. Although I did not see Tony R, I spent about a week with Ian who had married and was living in Newcastle. Since he had entered the business world, there was little common ground between us to revive special relationship plans. Word from Ian was that Tony R had entered local government, and thus little hope seemed to be there for anything to develop with him as well. Perhaps the whole idea of university exchange would have to be dropped.

Very discouraged, I returned to America with the thought of getting my own life in order first since a doctoral dissertation still had to be written and a permanent job had to be found. Nevertheless, I kept in touch with my British friends and every now and then did things that in my mind at least kept the special relationship idea alive.

One of these was to establish a connection with the project to move a gutted Christopher Wren church from London to Westminster College, Fulton, Missouri, to commemorate Churchill's 1946 'Iron Curtain' speech there. Having seen the shell of the small Church of St Mary, Aldermanbury, on several visits to London, I had lamented the fact that it would probably have to be razed, like a number of other churches, because nothing but business and government offices seemed to be destined for the rebuilt City. At least one old church would now be saved and used for a good cause on a college campus. The special relationship idea would be alive and well at Westminster in the American Middle West – that was something, however small it might be.

By the early 1970s, with doctorate in hand and now two young daughters by the hand, I took a permanent position teaching political science and history at Hendrix College, a strong, small liberal arts college in Arkansas. Knowing about its academic reputation for many years and hearing that a young, vigorous president was strengthening it while many institutions were beginning to retrench, I felt there might be some opportunities to return to the special relationship idea Tony L and I had pledged to implement.

Almost immediately after assuming my new post, there appeared reasons to believe that I had made a serious mistake about interest in international study at Hendrix. During fall discussions of a recent revision of the college committee structures, it was disclosed that the standing committee on international programs had been dropped and nothing had been put in its place. At the meetings no objections were raised and no one seemed to be concerned at all. In addition, the college was withdrawing from an overseas program connected with Vanderbilt University. Since Hendrix had no person other than the Dean of the College, who had a multitude of other things to do, in charge of overseas study, the outlook for the opportunities I had in mind looked dim.

There was one reason for hope, however. Hendrix had recently received a large grant from a major foundation to work on curriculum development. To stimulate individual initiative part of the fund was divided into smaller grants to each faculty member. I used mine to spend several weeks at Caius College, Cambridge University.

## *Cambridge*

With what appeared to be declining interest in foreign study at Hendrix, the thought of using an international education reason to justify my trip seemed to be less than wise. A better approach appeared to be something advancing political science on campus which was by far the weaker partner of the combined History and Political Science Department. Before my arrival, Hendrix did not have a 'full-blooded' political scientist but only faculty trained as historians who taught one or two political science courses each, whether they were qualified or not. With its aspirations for regional and even national recognition, the college obviously had to upgrade political science. Since little comparative politics was being offered and since my last formal instruction in that subfield occurred almost twenty years before at St Andrews, the Caius Summer Program on British Politics and Culture seemed to fit our needs.

Unfortunately, the Caius Program which was run not by the college but by a private organization renting the Caius' facilities did not meet expectations both in terms of content and as a possible special relationship connection for the future. Although some rather interesting books were recommended for class reading, little was done by the instructors, most of whom seemed to be connected with a local college, to relate their lectures, which tended to be rather superficial, to the readings. A quick glance at our class told why. Ages ranged from about twenty to seventy-five with most students being middle-aged Americans who had come more as tourists than scholars. There were only one or two other college professors like myself, and Hendrix-aged students numbered less than ten.

There were, of course, some redeeming features of the program. A few of the lectures were given by rather well-known practicing authorities and politicians, such as MPs Tam Dalyell, Peter Kirk, and Bryan Magee. These people usually gave their presentations just before lunch and then ate with us at the long dining tables in college, often staying on for an hour or so for informal conversations.

For me the best feature was living in a residential college, a missed opportunity at St Andrews University years before. Although not enough was done during the very short time we were there – about two and one-half weeks – to bring the group together, we did eat two meals a day as a group and often experienced small group excursions in and around Cambridge a few afternoons a week.

But it was the college itself in an ancient university city that was the most appealing. Caius – actually named Gonville and Caius College – was a very old Cambridge college with modern accommodations. Founded by Edmund Gonville in 1348 at another site a short distance away, Gonville Hall, as it was called originally, moved to its present location shortly thereafter and was slowly expanded during the rest of the fourteenth and fifteenth centuries with the chapel being finished in 1393.[1]

The Caius part of its name came from John Keys who Latinized his name in the typical Renaissance manner. Keys, a graduate of Gonville Hall and a Fellow of the College, also studied medicine at the famous University of Padua and later became a prominent London physician. In 1557 he emerged as his old college's chief benefactor by obtaining the charter of foundation it lacked before and doubling its endowment. For these services his name became part of the College's and he was appointed its Master two years later. Although Keys' Catholicism generated a sharp religious controversy with the Fellows which led to his resignation in 1573, one of his enduring legacies was to establish Caius as a center for medical studies rather than religion. A favorable consequence of its growing preoccupation with such studies was its avoidance of theological issues that divided a number of other colleges and presented serious political difficulties during the Civil War in the seventeenth century.[2]

Although the college declined somewhat in the eighteenth century, Caius made a strong comeback during the next century and into the twentieth century. Continuing to emphasize medical studies, it attracted students to the natural sciences generally and also to engineering by the 1950s. With about 390 undergraduates, Caius was one of the larger colleges of Cambridge University after Trinity and St John's. An interesting footnote is that its closeness to the river encouraged the development of athletics beginning in the 1840s, perhaps a major reason why the famous runner Harold Abrahams, featured as is Caius in the film *Chariots of Fire*, enrolled there.[3]

Steeped in history, this marvelous academic institution, as well as the beautiful setting generally, compensated for many shortcomings in the program, but the tourist aspect raised serious doubts about achieving the special relationship goal. As the program neared its conclusion, an informal conversation with a young woman assistant with an American accent changed my attitude. 'Why the accent?' I asked. Had she lived in America for a time? No, she was an American, a student at Stephens

College in Missouri who had just completed a year's study in Oxford where there was a companion program.

As she explained things, the current Cambridge program was really one of several programs, including summer programs in Oxford, York, and Edinburgh, a winter program in Barbados, and year-round programs in Oxford and Cambridge. Since I now had serious doubts about summer programs, I asked her to outline the year-round ones.

She handed me a brochure describing the Cambridge program, and my interest soared. Under this program American students could spend up to three terms, a whole academic year, studying under the direction of Cambridge University dons or with recognized authorities outside the university, such as playwright Edward Bond, BBC drama director Alan Shallcross, and educational consultant John Hipkin. These instructors, so it said, follow 'the customary Cambridge pattern of individual tutorials. Each student will have one hour alone with his tutor weekly and will write weekly essays for that tutor. In addition he or she will also have one tutorial every other week with another tutor in a different subject.' The list of subjects offered was rather long and seemed to cover most of the Humanities and Social Sciences but only mathematics from the Natural Sciences.[4]

The total cost of $3,000 a year was comparable to Hendrix prices and included tuition, excursions, and accommodations. The last were lodgings or furnished houses where students would have their daily meals, except lunch. Hence, the brochure emphasized that students would not be living in the colleges because they were not enrolled in Cambridge University but in a private program. All academic credit would have to be given by the students' universities and colleges at home.[5]

The young woman told me that the program in Oxford was similar and that prior approval by Stephens College had enabled her to complete her junior year's work in Britain. With great enthusiasm, she described the experience as a 'dream come true.'

Before leaving Cambridge, I had a brief conference with the program's director about some additional details. Since most things seemed positive on both sides, we agreed that I would contact him again after speaking with my dean. He invited me, at reduced cost, to attend his program in late August at the University of Edinburgh titled 'Music, Art, and Drama at the Festival.' This program, scheduled in conjunction with the Edinburgh Festival, was used as an orientation session for many students coming on the year-round program in the fall. While participation was impossible at that time, I attended a couple of years later.

Reflecting on the Cambridge Programs on my return to London, I developed a list of pros and cons. Since the latter were somewhat troublesome, I decided to investigate personally a couple of additional programs in London before returning home. Two others, one at Richmond College and another in South Kensington, had some promise, but the urban environment seemed to be less than desirable.

## *Problems, Problems*

While my enthusiasm for foreign study was very high when fall faculty conferences at Hendrix were held, my optimism was not as I contemplated the task ahead. Since I still did not know many of my colleagues very well, it soon became clear that I would have to talk to a number of people at length informally during the coming year to gauge the level of interest which at best seemed only latent. There just was little overt enthusiasm for foreign study. Fortunately, about a half dozen people – perhaps half each of senior and junior faculty and staff – were willing to pay more than mere lip service to the notion of foreign study. Together we approached the Dean, who actually had considerable interest in such things, and asked for the creation of a new International/Intercultural Studies Committee the following year. He agreed to put the request before the faculty. I took the opportunity to brief him about the Cambridge Program and the others I investigated, but he declined to take any action until the new committee was in place. The committee was voted in by the faculty the following fall.

Just as the necessary college structure was finally in place another event stopped us. Early in the academic year the President announced that the Dean was being named a Distinguished Professor of the College and would be replaced by a new Dean recruited from elsewhere in the country. A national search committee would be named immediately in order to have the new person on the job by the following September. When something like this happens at a very small college virtually everything except day-to-day routine activities come to a halt. Certainly something as 'radical' as foreign study is put on hold until the new Dean arrives. Unfortunately no faculty or staff member with a strong interest in such study was put on the search committee. Consequently, the new Dean, a relatively young physicist from Florida with a Cornell University doctorate, had almost no interest in the area.

At least he was very honest and up front about this fact. He neither played games nor paid lip service to the idea as I have found many in academic life doing in this area both before and since. He was willing to consider ideas and suggestions, but no college funds would be made available: that was his position loud and clear.

Now freed from his former duties the old Dean showed renewed interest in foreign study. Perhaps his most important contribution was the construction of a rather sophisticated opinion poll which he submitted to the student body to determine the level of interest in such study. His findings clearly showed that their interest was quite high, certainly much higher than that of the faculty and Administration. A positive consequence of this poll was that additional faculty members, like so many other would-be leaders, started running in the direction of international education in order to get ahead of the group they wished to lead.

Since some of the faculty, mainly those in the Foreign Languages Department, had developed individualized programs abroad for their students, precedent was there to strike out on my own, but my feeling was that the chances for success in the long run would be higher if the new committee gave its endorsement. The program adopted had to be seen as the college's, not just mine alone. The issue was, then, how to sell the Cambridge Program to the committee members. A glimmer of hope appeared in a letter from the director of that program who said that he planned a recruitment tour in America and would be willing to visit Hendrix. About the same time a couple of other contacts made with American-based overseas programs also expressed interest to visit. With the 1970s rolling by as quickly as the 1960s had and with still nothing in place for the special relationship plan, I urged them all to come immediately.

The visits generated substantial interest among faculty and students alike. After reviewing the presentations, the committee gave its approval to the Cambridge Program and recommended to the Dean that Hendrix should become involved for a trial period. The Dean approved and two students were selected to participate during the following year. At long last something was happening, but it turned out to be a near disaster.

About halfway through the students' year in Cambridge, the program went bankrupt and the director was incapacitated by ill health. Fortunately the tutors worked for little or nothing and the students were able to receive some academic credit for their studies at Hendrix.

## *Oxford*

To their credit the committee did not become discouraged but looked for other opportunities. It was at that time that I recalled my conversation with the student from Stephens College who had attended the Oxford Program. Since Stephens was only a few hundred miles north of Hendrix, I volunteered to visit the campus for a conference with the college's overseas program director. Actually she conveyed so much enthusiasm for the Oxford Program by telephone that the committee was satisfied to move ahead by making direct contact with Francis Warner of the Oxford Overseas Study Course.

Among other things mentioned during our telephone conversation, the Stephens director said that Warner, a Fellow and Tutor in English Literature at St Peter's College since 1965, had started his program nearly ten years ago and that Stephens had become involved almost immediately. Other member colleges were William Jewell, also in Missouri, and St Olaf in Minnesota. Since Warner limited enrollment to only thirty students a year, about ten from each college, his program had been stable and financially healthy, unlike the Cambridge Program. Also Warner's faculty status at Oxford University had guaranteed the selection of responsible, first-rate tutors. All-in-all Stephens had been well-pleased with the Oxford Program.

Initial contact was made by letter to Warner's administrative assistant.[6] She responded with a brochure, very similar to the one about Cambridge, and a long letter in which she gave additional details, many unique to Oxford. Like Cambridge, students would not be enrolled at the university but would hold membership in the famous Oxford Union Society and could join any of the numerous undergraduate clubs and societies which engaged in a variety of social, political, athletic, dramatic, religious, and other types of activities. Students would not be permitted to use the famous Bodleian Library or College Libraries but would have access to the Union, Central, Polytechnic, and College of Further Education Libraries. Some University lectures would also be open to them.

She wrote that Hendrix might want to follow the pattern of the other three colleges and give students three-course credits – two for the major and one for the minor tutorials – each term during the three-term year. To earn credits students would be required to write essays for their major tutorials weekly and for their minor tutorials fortnightly during the nine-week terms. The students and their tutors, who are assigned by Warner according to each student's interests, agree on the specific essay topics after the students have chosen their subjects.

For example, a hypothetical student who is generally interested in English literature and history but who also wants to work on his French for a trip to the continent over the spring vacation might choose his program as follows:

|  | *Major* | *Minor:* |
|---|---|---|
| *Michaelmas Term* | Nineteent-Century English Novel | Nineteenth-Century Social History |
| *Hilary Term* | Modern European History | Intermediate French |
| *Trinity Term* | English Poetry | Shakespeare |

Please note that he has taken two majors and one minor in different aspects of English literature, one major and one minor in different aspects of history, and the remaining minor in French. A student may also stay for all terms with different aspects of the same subject for his major and/or minor or arrange a wide variety of other possibilities, but no more than the two subjects can be studied at the same time.

During each term, she continued, students meet for at least an hour each week with the tutor for the major and for about an hour fortnightly with the tutor for the minor. Generally students are expected to bring completed essays to these sessions to be read aloud and discussed with the tutors. This work schedule of three papers every two weeks requires a great deal of independent direction and extensive reading by the students. Thus, they do not attend regular classes and rarely use textbooks as such but spend many hours on their own in libraries reading from a range of sources, digesting volumes of information, and writing the essence of what they have learned in well-composed prose. Personal discipline, individual initiative, self-reliance, and good analytical and writing skills are prerequisites for success in these independent study projects. The tutors give guidance, suggestions, encouragement, and, yes, criticism. At the end of each term they prepare written evaluations of student performance and suggest letter grades to Hendrix.

In addition to tuition costs, the fees, $3,300 per year, cover accommodations mainly in furnished houses with cooking facilities and a weekly food allowance returned to the students. The latter is done to ensure that students, who sometimes do not budget their funds well, do not go hungry because of the lack of pocket money. Since the houses are not normally open during the long vacation periods between terms, rooms are usually available at an extra charge for students who wish to remain in Oxford. The houses are located between one and three miles from the center of Oxford.

She closed her letter by mentioning that the program has a Social Secretary to help students 'pursue their particular recreational and sporting interests,' usually through the clubs mentioned previously and to arrange excursions to places of historical and cultural interest in England. Theatrical visits are also provided.

Remembering the outstanding features of my tutorials and essay writing at St Andrews University, I felt this individualized instruction at Oxford – the one-on-one relationship between tutor and student – had great promise for academic excellence and the realization of many aspects of the special relationship. Since one of the keys to the latter was personal contact and interaction, an ongoing process over an extended period of time, the institutional arrangements at Oxford would be in place for positive results. Of course, no one could make things happen, but the potential was there for desirable consequences to flow from the tutor-student relationship.

Since the committee and I were enthusiastic about these prospects, I was asked to visit Warner in Oxford the following summer.

## *Francis and Penelope Warner*

My first handshake with Francis Warner occurred in June 1979 at St Peter's College. Since most of my questions about his program had already been answered, we talked mainly about Hendrix College and its students, unknown subjects to Warner. We agreed that a trial period of a couple of years was in the best interests of both sides.

At that point, I asked him how his program started. He said as a young poet in the 1960s he made frequent visits to American universities and colleges to read his poetry and to teach classes. Since many of his hosts asked about sending their best students to Oxford – an impossibility in most cases because of stiff competition and other factors – he developed the idea of 'extra-mural teaching' which is at the heart of his program. He believed that it would work because many Oxford dons, who were generally poorly paid, were always in search of additional income through teaching. For American students he thought it would work well, too, because they would study within a very personal and flexible framework – rather than in highly impersonal, rigid classes – in an ancient university city which had become well known in America through such things as the Rhodes Scholarship Program, films, and television.

Although I did not broach the special relationship idea before we parted, I sensed that Warner was a kindred spirit because of his long and close association with several American colleges and universities and with the American academic community and its students generally. Having touched the lives of hundreds American students and faculty through his program, he was indeed laying the foundation for a very special relationship between Britain and the United States. Many years later he summed up his long-term purpose to me in this way: 'These times abroad as you know make all the difference to the young: they always look back on them with a glow, and as the years pass the

*Francis Warner, Lord White Fellow in English Literature, St Peter's College, Oxford; Founder and Director of the Oxford Overseas Study Course*

memory of their transatlantic and Oxford student days becomes more and more important.'[7]

Thus, in this way the Oxford-Hendrix connection was made in 1979, and it continues to this day. For me the relationship started as a mere academic association, but it has developed into something much more as a deep personal friendship with Francis and his family evolved over the years. Actually the friendship began rather slowly until both of us engaged in a number of exchange visits as the 1980s unfolded. In fact it was not so much Francis' program but his academic and creative achievements that brought him to Hendrix during the early years. These achievements, which ultimately led to his appointment as the Lord White Fellow in English Literature at St Peter's College, included several volumes of poetry and numerous plays, the latter being acclaimed by a critic of the *Sunday Times* as 'possibly the only truly unique drama of our time.'[8] A Hendrix foundation founded to promote the study of literature and language financed his visits.

A very brilliant, charismatic, and outgoing man, Francis took the Hendrix campus by storm during his visits. Students and faculty alike were drawn to his public presentations and informal conversations about a whole range of subjects. His depth of knowledge about these topics was so impressive that I, who often had the pleasant but difficult task of introducing him, usually told the audiences that I would take the easy way out by urging them to think of Francis as a true Renaissance man, one of the few among us today. The classes he taught stimulated student interest in various aspects of English literature and generated enthusiasm for the Oxford Program. Since Francis has been very generous with his invitations to me to visit and lecture at Oxford, I have come to know him rather well, too, within the context of his day-to-day work life. Not only has he had important positions of trust and responsibility within his college and university, but he is also held in very high esteem by his colleagues who know him well, some speaking of him in almost religious terms. Francis Warner is perhaps the most extraordinary man I have ever met.

During the first several years of our participation in Francis' program, a few students, especially some of the young women from rather small Arkansas towns, had difficulty in adjusting to the Oxford environment. The tutorial system was like nothing they had ever experienced before and Oxford itself seemed rather overwhelming and intimidating. That problem soon disappeared or at least was dealt with rather effectively after Francis married Penelope in the early 1980s.

Penelope is someone special as well. Having been involved with the treatment of cancer patients in a London hospital before she and Francis married, she brought to the Oxford Program as its chief administrator a sense of personal caring and concern for each student enrolled. Operating mainly from the Warner home in central Oxford, she made herself readily available to the students for consultation about a whole range of problems, both academic and personal. To most students she became much more than an administrator: a good friend and to many she was also counselor, confidant, and even 'mother.' This sense of family that Penelope brought to the program was greatly enhanced by the birth of the two Warner children.

As the children have become older, they have been accompanying their parents to Hendrix. Their presence has conveyed to the prospective Oxford students – as well as to their parents who have occasionally visited with the Warners on campus – the feeling of a family operation rather than an impersonal corporate enterprise in a foreign country many thousands of miles from Arkansas. This personal family-to-family connection has been a significant psychological factor that has helped to alleviate anxieties and concerns of students and their families.

Penelope has promoted the sense of family through group excursions to plays in Stratford and London and to historical places like Bath near her family home where her parents have entertained the groups before the return to Oxford. She has also helped our students celebrate Thanksgiving Day with family-style dinners of turkey and other appropriate foods in a private dining room of an Oxford hotel.

While most of Francis' time has been taken up with his university duties, he has been available daily at St Peter's for student conferences. Perhaps many of the students' more memorable connections with Francis have been through his plays which have been frequently presented in Oxford by dramatic societies. In fact a number of Hendrix students have played minor roles or worked back stage.

While obviously the returning Hendrix students have grown academically and in many other ways as well during their stay in Oxford, the impact of the Warner family has been apparent, too. No long list of things will be attempted but merely one generalization will be offered. To our students, Francis, who has been greatly admired and respected, has been seen as someone bigger than life, a Hero figure, if you will, and Penelope, who has been loved by all, has those many qualities of the Helper.

On the other side, the Warners have been very pleased with the Hendrix students as well and have welcomed as many applicants as possible for the spaces available. With only a few exceptions since the beginning, they have found the typical Hendrix student bright, conscientious, and respectful – excellent qualities for the Oxford experience. They have also been pleased with the large numbers of women, something Francis has had as a goal of his program from the outset because the Oxford colleges have been slow in their recruitment of promising women students. Rewarding such talent, the Warners have employed several outstanding Hendrix women to help administer the program after they completed their studies.

For me the Warners have probably come as close as anyone could on the British end to the implementation of the special relationship idea as it was forming in the minds of Tony L and me in 1957. Although we have not had British students coming to Hendrix, well over 150 Hendrix students have studied in Oxford. This of course does not mean to imply that the Oxford Program has been near perfect. Some of the major concerns of 1979 are still present today. The students, for example, continue to live mainly in American groups in houses rather than with British students in colleges or with British families, though upon occasion a few of our students have lived in a British theological college. As known to all, Americans, generally, have tended to form 'Little Americas' while living abroad and though the Oxford situation is not at that stage, it is nevertheless a little troublesome.

Another ongoing problem is the unavailability of Oxford's outstanding libraries. Since Hendrix students are not official Oxford University students, they do not have as many library privileges. While a few of our students have shown some ingenuity to gain admittance to places like the Bodleian — perhaps with the unofficial help of their tutors or British student friends — most of them have not. The lack of such privileges has caused some degree of frustration, especially among the more conscientious students, who have wanted to examine primary and other excellent sources in their areas of study. To their credit, the Warners, who are well aware of the problem, have taken steps to resolve such difficulties.

## *London*

In my desire to implement the special relationship even further, I became involved in the middle 1980s with a one-term London program initiated by two Hendrix College English professors. One, a graduate of the University of London, knew some faculty members at Birkbeck College in the heart of Bloomsbury. Several of them were interested in teaching additional students and had time to do so because of a unique characteristic of their teaching assignments: all-evening classes.

In fact, this is a principal characteristic of Birkbeck College itself, and thus something should be said about how it developed. Actually, it stems from the purpose of its founding in 1823 by a physician, Dr George Birkbeck, and others to provide a college education for people earning their living during the day. In short, this was a college for the working man. It was the first of its kind in England and clearly filled an important need. When classes began the following year, 1,300 students enrolled.

An interesting story related to its founding is that the college, first known as the London Mechanics' Institution, caused such apprehension among the upper classes that Dr Birkbeck and another colleague had to make speeches on how the education of the working classes would not subvert society! Apparently, they were very persuasive, for a wave of enthusiasm for other mechanics' institutions followed, leading to the founding of seven more in Greater London shortly thereafter.

Other landmark events in the college's history include the admission of women in 1830 and an enrollment reaching 3,000 students in 1868 after the University of London was given a new charter which allowed anyone to sit for a degree. The current name became official in 1907, and the college was designated a school of the University of London in 1920. A Royal Charter was granted six years later. Birkbeck College moved to its present location in a new building on Malet Street in 1951. Among its famous former students is Ramsay MacDonald.[9]

Several features of my colleagues' Birkbeck plan made this program an attractive undertaking. Although our students would not be officially enrolled, they would be taught by the college's excellent faculty using Birkbeck facilities which were readily available during daytime hours. Moreover, given the range of privileges Birkbeck administrators were prepared to provide, the students seemed to have nearly the equivalent of official status with the one exception of grades for their courses of study. This problem would be resolved by having the faculty pass grades to a Hendrix College professor who would accompany the students to London and who in turn would record appropriate credits at Hendrix.

While the Hendrix professor, given the title Coordinator, would have no teaching responsibilities in London, he or she would be given a vast range of other things to do as the College's on-site representative. Perhaps the most demanding would be organizing and leading a number of course-related excursions, some overnight, to various parts of Britain during the term. Since these, as well as lodging and meals generally, would be quite costly, the Coordinator would have a major job as financial officer as well.

With potential costs to Hendrix students and the College itself mounting very rapidly, my colleagues arrived at a brilliant solution: to have the program heavily subsidized by a Hendrix-related foundation created to promote the study of literature and language. Since the program was viewed as an experiment which the foundation would not have to fund permanently, its members, to our pleasant surprise, voted to approve. Their one major condition was that two of the three courses the students studied at Birkbeck had to be in the area the foundation promoted. It was agreed that one course would focus on Shakespeare's plays and the other on British novels.

The only other major problem that had to be resolved before Hendrix College officials would give their approval was housing for the students and Coordinator in London. No college dormitories were available. No other arrangements, such as the renting of a house or apartments or individual rooms, seemed feasible. However, the solution was a relatively easy one to find: a small hotel in Bloomsbury not far from Birkbeck College. Two major factors made this possible. In the first place, there would be one faculty coordinator and only twelve students with the latter willing to share rooms with one or two others. In the second place, there was an abundance of such hotels in Bloomsbury that were often half empty during the winter months – January to March – when our term was in session. One landlord was found on Gower Street who so welcomed the idea of having his hotel nearly full for the winter months that he reduced his rates for the Hendrix program.

The first Coordinator was one of the English professors who made the proposal. A well-organized, self-reliant, and innovative leader, she set an example for those of us who followed her. She led a number of her excursions outside London in a hired van, which she drove herself, to such areas as the Hardy country. When she returned to Hendrix after a very successful term in 1984, she asked me to coordinate the program the following year, mainly because she was aware that I knew London and much of Britain rather well. After a thorough briefing from her, I agreed, though I had some reservations primarily about the housing arrangements, the short length of stay, and certain aspects of the academic offerings. I also had doubts about how well the complete program would foster the special relationship.

After the students and I were settled in, several of my concerns were indeed present. As with the Oxford Program, the 'Little America' problem was immediately apparent, but unfortunately it was worse in London because of the virtual isolation of the students in their small hotel. They only got to know reasonably well the hotel owner and his wife and a few of the cleaning staff. While our students certainly had many of the privileges of the Birkbeck students, they made few friends with them because the British students were at work during the daytime and besides they tended to be much older. In short, there were few opportunities to make meaningful connections with other people.

I tried to alleviate this situation to some degree by arranging for each Hendrix student to spend a weekend with a different English family in a London suburb. The families were members of a Methodist church that had some loose ties with Hendrix, a Methodist-related college. Since the student visits occurred at the beginning of the term, some of the connections made blossomed into friendships during the following weeks. The daughter of one of these families became so attached to Hendrix students in the years that followed that she ultimately took her degree at Hendrix.

I looked for other ways to help our students become connected, and given my background in government, thought that a few such institutions might provide a means. Having close friends in the London Metropolitan Police, the House of Commons, and the Foreign and

Commonwealth Office, I prevailed upon them to give me some help. Being great and good friends, they did not let me down.

The day with the police turned out much better than anyone anticipated. Certainly the students were rather apprehensive when the police van, though it was unmarked, picked us up at the hotel. Since my friend in the police was in charge of a section of East London, an area that had improved only some degree since Jack the Ripper roamed the back streets there, the students felt attracted by the folklore but repelled by the reality. However, once they learned about the nature of the area today and the methods of community policing, they came away with not only a better understanding but also much less apprehension. They found it extraordinary that the police on the beat there did not carry guns and did not wish to carry them. Unlike America, what a civilized way to do things!

On the more entertaining side of the day's events, the students were given an excursion on the River Thames in a police boat with commentary provided by a very colorful character, a policeman soon to retire, whose knowledge of the river's history and buildings alongside, was truly remarkable. In fact, his reputation as both expert and comedian was so great that he had done tours for a range of well-known people including Prince Charles and Bob Hope. But I imagine the high point of the tour for many if not most of the students was when they were given a turn at the boat's helm.

The visit to the Houses of Parliament occurred one Monday morning before sessions of the Commons and Lords resumed after the weekend break. The students had a private tour followed by an informal luncheon in one of the dining rooms presided over by a Labour Party MP. Looking much like a character out of Dickens, he entertained the students with many political stories but also dealt with some serious policy matters. With our small group in an equally small private room, he was able to speak in a conversational style and answer student questions whenever they came up. This informal, inside look at the British legislature provided some understanding of how British political institutions operate.

Several friends at the Foreign and Commonwealth Office arranged two other excursions. One was a private briefing at the Office by a diplomat of the North American Department. Since Prime Minister Margaret Thatcher had recently returned from meetings with President Ronald Reagan in Washington, he was able to elaborate upon their understandings and differences on a range of topics. Again, the size of our small group made it possible to have a conversation around a table. With the special relationship idea such an important part of the Thatcher-Reagan association, the students gained some insights into the nature of that relationship at the highest levels. The timing of the briefing was absolutely perfect.

The other excursion involved a weekend stay at Wilton Park, Wiston House, near Steyning, Sussex. Since both Wilton Park and Wiston House are described at length elsewhere in this book, only a few points will be mentioned here. The students arrived at Wiston House early one Friday morning in time to attend the closing session of a regular conference and to have lunch with the conferees. The conference dealt with the impact of the media on public attitudes and the students were graciously invited by the participants to offer their views. The students found this session to be a very rewarding experience because, as one student put it, 'here were these government leaders from around the world taking our ideas seriously.' Perhaps nearly as rewarding was the mini-conference conducted specifically for the students in the afternoon and early evening. Many British issues, such as the situation in Northern Ireland, were discussed as well as aspects of Anglo-American relations. The special relationship was addressed directly in the marvelous Wiston House setting.

Not everything was work. Late Friday night, two of the Wilton Park staffers, one of whom lived in Wiston House much of the time, told stories about the ghosts of the old country house, part of which dated from the sixteenth century. Since the house was empty for the weekend, except for the students, they had a great time around midnight searching several wings of the mansion for signs of its ethereal residents.

Several of the other excursions outside London, which were organized in connection with the program's courses, also went well. Perhaps the group's weekend in Stratford seeing three Shakespearian plays and the local sights tied into academic material better than any other experience, though as one student said, 'That was a lot of Shakespeare to absorb in twenty-four hours.' Two other trips focused mainly on British history – the third course my group had – in northern England and Scotland and in East Anglia. The first was a four-day excursion to York and Edinburgh and the second was a day-trip to Cambridge and Ely.

Yet, one of my main regrets about this attempt – which I thought was basically a good idea – to connect classroom activities with outside experiences was that we did not go far enough, given the resources readily available in London. Had the students been given the opportunity to have an internship or something of that nature in a museum, an art gallery or even a newspaper or law office, they would have made closer connections with the British people and their institutions. My feeling was that although the students were in London, they were never really of London; they never became a part of the London experience.

When the London term ended, I concluded that the experience with twelve Hendrix students went well. There were no major problems. With the exception of one student who tended to break away from time to time, there was strong group cohesion and a minimum of personality clashes. In general, it was a very bright and serious group, seven females and five males, of whom four were pre-med and two pre-law. They attended classes regularly and participated in all excursions. When they traveled outside London, including outside Britain, on their own, they did so both before and after the term's classes. Class attention and cooperation were perfect.

Yet, despite the many positive aspects – the students' evaluations were uniformly positive as well – I came home feeling that the program did not really facilitate the making of deep connections for the students which I had hoped for. Had the living situation been different – a residential college or with British families, for example – and had the length of the stay been longer – a whole year, for instance – perhaps we could have come closer to the special relationship ideal. Certainly the opportunities for making closer connections with the British people and their institutions were much better through the Oxford Program.

Unfortunately, the London Program has not improved over the years. Nothing has happened to push it in the direction of the special relationship; on the contrary, forces have pulled it towards that of a typical tourist experience.

## *Conclusion*

The struggle to implement the special relationship ideal through the university, Alma Mater, has been very long and only partly successful. While I believe that the family institution is the best means, educational institutions, especially the university, offer the next best avenue. Yet, my experience of over forty years shows that while the promise is there, implementation is an entirely different matter. Certainly some degree of success can be rather easily achieved if the goals are essentially superficial ones. A tourist-level experience can be had in a number of ways. But a deeper experience, one approaching the level of the special relationship, is much harder to realize.

As indicated before, part of the problem lies with the difficulty of defining precisely what the term means. In the end I have been able to write mainly in metaphors only. Another aspect of the problem is that the special relationship idea is actually more of an ongoing process than a specific thing. It tends to result – it is a consequence, if you will – from people engaging in various behaviors within certain structures or under certain conditions over an extended period of time. Therefore, it is perhaps easier to say what it *was* in the past than what it *is* now or *should be* in the future. Hence, the best hope is to try to work through established institutions, such as the family and the university, which allow for and encourage face-to-face connections and which have as many or more informal connecting points as formal ones. The process of multi-dimensional living within these institutions offers the best hope for the realization of the special relationship.

My dear British friends Francis and Penelope Warner have understood this better than most. Penelope, the Helper, has been the very personification of the special relationship idea as it has unfolded through the Oxford Program. Francis, the Hero figure, has had the vision, commitment, and strength to construct a transatlantic institution through which the process has been occurring. When I think about the Warners and what they have done for the special relationship, I am reminded of words George Bernard Shaw has one of his characters say in *Man and Superman*:

> This is the true joy in life, the being used for a purpose recognized by yourself as a mighty one; the being a force of nature instead of a feverish selfish little clod of ailments and grievances complaining that the world will not devote itself to making you happy.
>
> I want to be thoroughly used up when I die, for the harder I work the more I live. I rejoice in life for its own sake. Life is no 'brief candle' for me. It is a sort of splendid torch which I have got hold of for the moment, and I want to make it burn as brightly as possible before handing it on to future generations.[10]

While success is never complete and therefore must be considered in degrees, my belief is that the Oxford-Hendrix Program has been highly successful, mainly because of the Warners. My major regret is that Tony L did not live to see and to participate in something like it. As young students, he and I were indeed developing a special relationship that had much promise for the future and hence those days of youthful idealism in Dundee will not be forgotten. We had become almost like brothers, and though a relationship like that can never be replaced, my connection with the Warners has helped to ease the pain of Tony's very early death.

## Notes

1. Bryan Little, *The Colleges of Cambridge* (New York: Arco Publishing Company, Inc., 1973), 38.
2. Ibid., 39–40.
3. Ibid., 41–2.
4. *Cambridge Courses* (Cambridge: F. & P. Piggott Ltd.), 2–3.
5. Ibid., 4–5.
6. Mrs S. Owen to John Ziegler. The discussion that follows is based on this undated letter.
7. Francis Warner to John Ziegler, 31 March 1995.

8. Quoted on the back cover of Francis Warner, *Requiem* (Gerrards Cross, England: Colin Smythe, 1980).

9. This brief history of Birkbeck College is based on 'Birkbeck College,' in *The London Encyclopaedia*, 1983.

10. This passage is quoted in Warren Bennis and Burt Nanus, *Leaders: The Strategies for Taking Charge* (New York: Harper & Row, 1985), 32.

## Chapter III

# *Pulpit Exchange*

*W*hen Tony L and I pledged to implement the 'special relationship' via the university, we thought mainly in terms of student exchange between the United States and Great Britain. But faculty participation through the 'exchange of pulpits' was another important dimension of our plan. From our perspective in 1957, we hoped these exchanges would last perhaps a year – certainly a semester – and would occur on a rather regular basis through the years after each of us became established as professors in our respective countries. After Tony's death in 1964, I nearly dropped the idea entirely but tried to keep the hope alive as best I could. Francis Warner's occasional short visits of about a week's length each to Hendrix in the 1980s and 1990s moved things forward somewhat. As a result of his generous invitations to me to lecture several times at Oxford and a couple of times at Cambridge for his summer program at Clare College during the same decades, we were able to go a little further but achieved only limited success. Yet I felt that some exchange was better than no exchange at all and that I should try to provide as much substance as possible in the few lectures I gave.

## *Isolationism*

When Francis extended his first invitation in 1983 to give a lecture at St Peter's College, I was initially undecided about a topic. What eventually came to mind was something related to the question asked me numerous times by the British over the years: Is America going isolationist again? While I never kept count of the times asked, I am sure it ranks at the top of the list, somewhat above the other popular question I considered: What is the difference between the Republican and Democratic Parties? The decision on these two questions was easy to make because the former is of course related to the 'special relationship' idea and because much of my graduate work addressed the question of American isolationism.

Since this topic is vast and complex, it was difficult to decide what to say within the time constraint of fifty minutes, followed by thirty minutes of questions. In the end I decided to focus on major explanatory theories and themes leading to my anthropomorphic approach to understand America's relationship to Britain as well as to the rest of the world. Briefly, I said the following in my lecture titled 'Some Thoughts on Trying to Understand American Isolationism.'

American isolationism should be rather easy to describe and to explain. Certainly many newspaper writers and television reporters – and even some scholars – give the impression that it is all very simple and clear. Yet a brief look at the literature of American isolationism is enough to convince most that there is very little about it that is either simple or clear. In fact, we could spend the rest of our time just debating the meaning of the term 'isolationism' itself, for the literature does make it clear that the definitions in use vary to a great degree. For example, there are some scholars, such as the so-called Nationalist historians, who have adopted, either explicitly or implicitly, such broad definitions of the term that it has become virtually meaningless. On the other hand, other writers, such as the so-called Radical historians who have followed the lead of William Appleman Williams, have adopted such narrow definitions that the term has virtually disappeared. Recognizing this problem, I shall nevertheless plunge ahead with the hope that I can shed some light on the topic.

Since we need a working definition of the term isolationism, I shall borrow the one developed by American historian Wayne S. Cole. According to him, the concept 'isolationism' is used to identify a theory concerning the role the United States should play in international affairs. It is also used to cover a major pattern of American reactions to changing world conditions. As a theory of international relations few proponents of isolationism have wished literally to isolate the United States from the rest of the world. Most of them have tended to favor foreign policies having 'unilateralism' and 'noninterventionism' as their central themes. As unilateralists they have expressed determination to maintain a maximum degree of sovereignty and freedom of action for the United States in world affairs. As noninterventionists they believed that it had been a mistake for the United States to enter World War I and that the United States could and should have stayed out of that war. They took the same attitudes toward World War II. Those who were consistent noninterventionists, and many were not, extended these attitudes to developments in Latin America, the Pacific, and the Far East as well.[1]

In trying to explain American isolationism, Cole and many other scholars have put forward a number of theories – too many to discuss all of them here. But I would like to sketch a few of the more important ones. Before I do, two important observations are in order. First, these theories have often found explanations why many Americans have embraced isolationism in conditions and developments within the United States itself rather than in international affairs. In other words, domestic rather than foreign issues and problems often seem to be controlling factors whether one is an isolationist or not. Second, most theories on the causes of American isolationism do not pretend exclusiveness. No one grand theory of isolationism has been found.

One of the oldest theories is that of geographical remoteness. It has often been used to explain isolationist attitudes found among Americans in the Middle West and Far West. Another theory can be called 'Republicanism' because empirical evidence indicates that historically Republicans tend to be more isolationist than Democrats. Why? One reason is that the Republican Party is the political party of conservative nationalism, a unilateralist party. Perhaps another reason is that that Party has frequently been in political opposition when major foreign policy issues have been considered. For example, it was the opposition party before, during and after America's involvement in the two world wars of this century.

Another theory is often called the religious roots theory because members of certain religious denominations tend to be more isolationist than the population as a whole. Examples include Quakers who favor pacifism and oppose militarism and some evangelical Protestants who reject war as an evil – something not to be accepted as part of life.

A fourth theory identifies emotional and psychological factors as causes. The so-called 'antis' are identified with this theory – that is, those people who are anti-alien, anti-foreign, anti-European, anti-isms (socialism, communism, etc.) and anti almost everything considered to be non-American or unAmerican. Put in a more positive way, these people tend to be rather extreme romantic nationalists.

Fifth, there is the ethnic roots theory. It has been found that certain so-called hyphenated-Americans tend to be more isolationist than the population as a whole. These include several groups but German and Irish-Americans in particular. German-Americans, for example, have felt very uncomfortable during the two world wars because their 'American-ness' was questioned by other Americans. The Irish-Americans, on the other hand, have been anti-British and hence have loved 'to twist the Lion's tail' whenever possible.

Another theory has stressed the ignorance of and disinterest in world affairs of many groups of Americans. More will be said about this theory later on.

A seventh theory is an agrarian one. This theory states that as American farmers encountered economic difficulties and as these difficulties surfaced in their relationships with East Coast bankers and businessmen who tended to be internationalists, the farmers became isolationists.

The last theory stresses economic factors as well. In fact there are really two theories here. One closely resembles a Marxist interpretation of causality in that capitalists are viewed as being interested in promoting foreign policies of imperialism and war, while workers are seen as favoring opposite and hence isolationist policies. The second theory is a conservative economic one. This theory states that conservative businessmen have often opposed international involvement, especially in a war, because they believed that such action would bring about national bankruptcy and the collapse of the American system of capitalism and free enterprise.

As I have studied these and other theories in detail and as I have carried out my own research in this area, I have been struck by the appearance and reappearance of a half-dozen major themes. For me these themes have been very important in my trying to gain an understanding of the nature of American isolationism. Perhaps these themes can be called the 'Six I's' and can be identified as follows: isolation, insularity, idealism, instability, ignorance and imperialism. I will give a brief sketch of each.

Isolation. During the Republic's first century as a nation-state the connection between America's physical isolation from the major power centers of the world and the country's development of isolationism as its major foreign policy is perhaps too obvious to require much comment. Yet, one should not accept this connection too readily, for history shows that America, both before and after the Revolution, did not escape involvement in the conflicts of the European powers. Perhaps the key factor in the development of this policy was the growing British-American reconciliation that began a few years after the War of 1812. Both sides began to recognize certain realities including these two: that Britain controlled the seas and that America, now a viable nation growing in strength, had in its British neighbor to the north, Canada, a potential hostage. There was, too, that 'century of world peace' down to 1914 which helped to make American isolationism appear to work very well indeed. At any rate, with their two-ocean moat Americans felt that isolationism was the right policy to follow. And besides hadn't THE Founding Father himself, George Washington, indicated as much in his famous Farewell Address?

Insularity. The temptation is indeed great to trace America's insularity to its British heritage. I remember very well an incident during the 1950s when I first arrived in Britain as a young student. Hoping to get off to a good start with my classmates, I remarked to them how happy I was to be in *Europe*. Needless to say, I was put down very quickly with the icy comment that I was not in Europe but in Great Britain. So much for the geography lessons I learned at home! Whatever the source of America's insularity, a similar attitude prevails in the United States but manifests itself in a different way. To people in my country the word 'America' can mean only one place: the United States. This narrow-minded disregard of such places as Canada and Mexico involves much more than the fact that these countries are not taken too seriously – are taken for granted. It also involves the attitude of cultural superiority, an attitude of ethnocentricism. Americans, people of the United States, are happy to educate others about the American ways of doing things, but they tend to lose patience very quickly if the superiority of these ways is not recognized and accepted. This impatience was an important factor contributing to America's return to isolationism in the 1920s.

Idealism. Of these six factors, perhaps idealism is by far the most culturally ingrained and hence the most likely to endure over time. Certainly some, including the very influential American historian Frederick Jackson Turner, have argued that Idealism and Americanism are synonymous. Included in this view are the ideas that America is something new, something unique, something quite different from the rest of the world. America is the exception. Being such, the country's mission is to make a new beginning – to develop a new person and a new society for the future which will serve as a model for other nations. To achieve this goal rejection of the rest of the world, especially the Old World Europe, might be necessary. Indeed, at least it would be necessary to tell the rest of the world that this had been done. It is certainly there for the world to see in the Declaration of Independence It is also there to see in the choice of words used to describe the nature of the violent action between America and Britain in the late eighteenth century. Many, perhaps most, British historians have called it the American War of Independence. Our historians have called it the American Revolution.

Instability. Perhaps few would argue with the contention that the United States has had difficulty in trying to follow a consistent foreign policy in the twentieth century. In fact many would say that some rather extreme swings were very much in evidence. At the beginning of the century the country seemed to embrace imperialism, followed by internationalism, than a twenty-year period of isolationism, followed by internationalism, and so on. Realists would argue that such instability stems from the fact that the people, the fickle public if you will, have too much influence in foreign affairs. A consistent, stable policy is possible, so the argument goes, only if the foreign policy elites are in control and only if those elites ignore the periodic swings of public opinion. Others might argue that the problem is much deeper: that instability stems from certain deeply ingrained cultural factors, some of which have already been mentioned: idealism and insularity, for example. Such factors pull very strongly against attempts to develop a stable foreign policy based upon an enlightened self-interest. Whatever the source of this instability, it seems to be still there, and hence real doubts are raised both at home and abroad about America's ability to be a responsible and dependable leader in the international community. Certainly the fear is there that given this tendency to swing from one extreme to another the United States might one day return to isolationism, or at least to the neo-isolationism of the 1950s.

Ignorance. Survey research polls and other indices of the level of public knowledge have demonstrated again and again the fact that Americans are not very well informed about matters outside the United States. Indeed, it has been shown many times that Americans are even woefully ignorant about their own political institutions, history and geography. So it should have come as no great surprise in the 1980s that one of President Reagan's appointees to a high position in the State Department was unable during a Senate hearing to name the prime minister of a nation very much in the news of the day. By the way, that same person eventually became Mr Reagan's National Security Advisor! One's immediate reaction to this embarrassing display of ignorance on the part of a prominent person is to exclaim, 'Such stupidity!' And perhaps it was. Yet, I don't think we are necessarily talking about stupidity – indifference is perhaps much closer to the truth. A quarter century ago, I heard in my home state of Illinois one of Britain's distinguished scholars on America, the late Denis Brogan, say that he could well understand the American indifference to foreign affairs after spending some time in America's heartland. From that location, he said, the rest of the world does indeed seem far, far away. Obviously, many factors – in addition to a geographical one – are involved here. Certainly some students of American society and culture would argue that pressures to work hard and to get ahead – 'to keep up with the Joneses' – encourage this indifference. Perhaps some others would stress the idea that many Americans feel very uncomfortable outside their own environments. As is known, there is the tendency of these Americans when abroad to seek out other Americans and to build 'Little Americas.' Even some recent political leaders – Lyndon Johnson, for one – have been 'fish out of water' in the world beyond the United States. Given the problems in understanding and in coping with the outside world, many Americans have tried to ignore it. Whatever the source, there are strong factors present in America that encourage the tendency to ignore knowledge and information about the rest of the world.

Imperialism. At first glance imperialism and isolationism would seem to be polar opposites. Yet, many American isolationists have also been at one time or another imperialists. Why? Perhaps the term 'unilateralism' which was used in the definition above is helpful here. In America, unilateralists have in the main been staunch, and perhaps even romantic, nationalists. As such, they have usually been anti-Europe and pro-Far East and the Pacific Basin. For them America's great future lay to the west in the Orient, not to the east of the Old World. Hence they favored involvement in the Orient but not in Europe. Therefore, a compelling case can be made, I believe, for the proposition that many isolationists were strong supporters of America's involvement in Viet Nam.

On the other hand, some isolationists only flirted with imperialism, probably out of ignorance or political considerations. Eventually becoming enthusiastic domestic social reformers, they completely rejected imperialism and most other forms of interventionism. In fact, many of these isolationists came to accept, though perhaps not at a completely conscious level, a Marxist interpretation of the causes of war. The famous LaFollette family of Wisconsin and their many followers in the interwar period are examples of this type.

What can be made of this discussion? Certainly the vast amount of literature about isolationism as suggested by my summary requires some simplification and generalization. There is of course the desire to find a single concept, a telling phrase, or even a key word that encompasses rather neatly the essence of isolationism. Going too far in this direction can be hazardous because too little is used to explain too much. Yet, ignoring this warning somewhat, I think it is possible to point out something of significance that seems to lie at the heart of American isolationism. That is, this traditional foreign policy, the centrepiece of America's relations with the rest of the world for a long time, is an extremely nationalistic idea positing American superiority – America first, if you will – based on the rejection of other nations deemed inferior.

Rejection is the key of course, and it started most dramatically with the violent break with Britain. As seen from the American perspective, the break was a revolution, an overturning of old institutions and the setting up of new ones. (It is interesting to note that Britain saw the war as only one of independence, something quite different.) Hence, America looked to the future and attempted to deny its past, its history. In other words, instead of being Janus-like – looking in both directions as all nations must – America tried to look forward only in an attempt to establish a new identity that had to be developed with the rejection of the old. Doing this, the young Rebel remained one dimensional in development and hence lacked the complete character and personality needed to interact with the rest of the world.

As this sentence suggests and as discussed in the Introduction and Chapter I of this book, I found the metaphor of the nuclear family with the three figures of Hero, Helper and Rebel useful in developing this analysis. This approach suggests that the Rebel not only rejected the Hero, his father, but also the Helper, his mother, and in so doing trampled underfoot her attributes and values. It seems to me that the birth of American isolationism is largely the consequence of this action. Perhaps we need to go no further than to consider the two elements in the definition of isolationism mentioned above. Think about unilateralism. Clearly it is a policy that rejects such Helper values as cooperation, accommodation and loyalty to others. And noninterventionism, which includes the idea that participation in the affairs of the world's nations should be avoided, certainly runs counter to the value of sacrificing ones personal interests for the greater good of the community.

Others may look upon isolationism in a different way, but I was interested to learn that the great international relations scholar Inis Claude, a Hendrix College graduate by the way, also takes an anthropomorphic approach in his analysis. Using baseball metaphors, he sees America as a player who does not want to be a regular on the team in the game of world politics. America wants only to be an auxiliary, a player who sits on the bench or the sidelines and only comes into the game when there is a crisis situation. In other words, America wants to play the role of the pinch hitter or the relief pitcher who comes in for one at-bat to drive the winning run home or who comes to the pitcher's mound in the last inning to save the game by getting the other side out. Claude sees America developing this limited role in the nineteenth century because of geographical and historical factors of the time. He is not sure whether this role has strong cultural roots which might serve as a major impediment to its modification. Certainly many geographical and even some historical factors can be countered without too much difficulty, but cultural values, especially core values, are something else.[2]

Thus, this is one of my major concerns: that isolationism is so rooted in the most important defining moment of America's birth – the American Revolution – and so much a part of America's formative development during the first hundred years of the new nation that it is essentially a permanent cultural element. Core cultural values – and hence isolationism if it is one of them – will change very little or not at all over a long period of time.

What can and should be done? There is both a hope and a need. The hope is that the rejected Helper values – all of those listed in Chapter I – of Britannia can be regained in full and the need is a strategy to reconnect Britain and America in a number of ways that will foster the growth and development of those values in the United States. Evidence is present in the US that the values were once there and in fact manifested themselves among the American people domestically in our history. What was lost was their application and use in America's relations with the rest of the world.

Let me conclude with another metaphor. Seeds of the Helper values were planted in America during the colonial period, and they took root. But the young plants that came up were trampled underfoot during a war of rejection. The seeds are still there and need only to be cultivated by us together.

## *The Decline Thesis*

With this concern about American isolationism, I immediately became interested in several books that appeared in the 1980s about America's declining influence in the world and its decline at home as well. Hence, taken together, these books were seen as presenting a 'decline thesis.' When Francis Warner asked me to present a lecture to his summer school class at Clare College, Cambridge, in July 1988, I agreed and titled my talk 'The Decline Thesis and the Future of American-European Relations.'

Of course, academic debates go on all the time, but I thought this topic would be of interest to Francis' students, who were Britons and Americans of all ages, because international public interest had developed after the publication of Paul Kennedy's *The Rise and Fall of the Great Powers* in early 1988. Making the rounds of the various television talk shows, Kennedy had attracted much media attention.

Actually, the academic debate had probably started in 1982 with the publication of *The Rise and Decline of Nations* by Mancur Olson. In this book, he argues that societies with entrenched interests – such as government bureaucracies, labor unions, lobbyists for special interests and the like – induce a kind of self-serving sclerosis in their economies. The debate continued with books by Walter Russell Mead and David P. Calleo. Mead's *Mortal Splendor* and Calleo's *Beyond American Hegemony* focus on the topic of America's world domination, especially in Europe, and the factors undermining it.

Taken together, Olson, Mead, Calleo and Kennedy, though representing different academic disciplines and interests, present a similar basic thesis. For them, the United States, like other great powers before it, rose to a position of global dominance largely through economic and technological achievements. Reaching its zenith just after World War II, the United States devoted increasingly large portions of its wealth to its military establishment in an effort to maintain the hegemony it had achieved. In recent decades, America has failed to strike a balance between these overseas commitments and the demands of a maturing domestic economy. Left uncorrected, this imbalance, which Kennedy calls 'imperial over-stretch,' will continue to erode the economic foundations that are the true base of America's global power. Hence, America is already in decline, a relative decline.

What really troubles these authors is not America's external but its domestic decline, two related but yet two very distinct phenomena. External decline was expected and in fact welcomed. It has come about largely through America's own efforts to build up Western Europe and Japan since the end of World War II. In the early postwar years America's share of world industrial production nearly reached 50 per cent. Prodded by the Marshall Plan and protected by institutions and alliances such as the World Bank and the North Atlantic Treaty Organization (NATO), global distribution of wealth and productivity shifted to a multipolar configuration. One result was the extraordinary growth of the European Economic Community's gross national product. The move towards 'pluralism,' while intensifying competition, also forged a mutually remunerative trading bond between America and Europe and America and Japan. While there are problems with these relationships, as are known, the good far outweighs the bad, say these authors.

On the other hand, the domestic decline of the United States is another and a much more serious matter. Beginning in the 1960s when Japan and West Germany in particular were rebuilding their heavy industries, encouraging private savings and cultivating public education around mathematics and science, America began to experience the chronic ailments of a maturing economy. A shift from manufacturing to service industries, the triumph of short-term profits over investment in infrastructure, deteriorating schools, a growing underclass, and many other factors all contributed to the shrinkage of the economic base relative to other nations. Consequently, the American domestic economy entered a period of deep trouble in the 1980s.

This in outline form is the basic thesis of the 'philosophers of decline,' as they were often called. It did not take long for highly vocal critics in America to emerge. Actually, two different factions, one from the political right, and another from the moderate left, entered the debate. The first, the conservative group, rejects the decline thesis root and branch. It contends that while twin deficits, budgetary and trade, are regrettable, the Reagan years strengthened America's hand, both at home and abroad. Far from 'over-stretch' these conservatives argue that the United States has been strengthened by its military commitments.

On the other hand, the moderates agree with almost every part of the thesis, from relative decline to overstretch. What they object to is the sense of inevitability, the ultimate decline and fall of America if you will, that is conveyed by these authors. They argue that the decline philosophers fail to appreciate the wealth of American resources, resourcefulness, and technology as well as the value of expanding links with various parts of the world.

In general, my own criticism of the decline thesis follows that of the moderates, but my concerns are somewhat different. In presenting their thesis in the manner they do, the decline philosophers are helping to develop a state of mind – or at least to reinforce an existing one – that is extremely pessimistic about America's future in general and as a world leader in particular. In other words, they are giving support and encouragement to isolationist tendencies, which were much in evidence in the 1980s in such things as the so-called Viet Nam Syndrome and opinion poll results.

For me, David Calleo's book, subtitled *The Future of the Western Alliance*, is the most troublesome in this regard. Perhaps one or two examples will illustrate my concerns. The two central themes in Calleo's book are the need for America to put its own economic house in order and to modify its relationships with European allies. The second is of course his major one and early on in his discussion of it he identifies two 'heroes' (my term, not his) of the past who in his view were on the right track about how NATO should develop, The first is the distinguished scholar-diplomat George F. Kennan, usually identified as the 'Father of Containment,' and the second is the late conservative Republican Senator from Ohio, Robert A. Taft.

Calleo's choice of Kennan as one of his heroes comes as no surprise because it was Kennan who proposed in the late 1940s when NATO was being considered by the Truman Administration that the alliance be based on the so-called 'Twin Pillars' concept. This concept is also known as the dumbbell model for transatlantic relations, with Europe at one end and America at the other. In other words, Europe and America were to be equal partners in a joint adventure that would transcend mere military considerations of an alliance.

Calleo's other hero, Senator Taft, is a big surprise to an isolationism scholar like me. Unlike the usual view of Taft, Calleo sees him as a Realist, one shrewdly anticipating the likely consequences of the military alliance system. While acknowledging that Taft was generally seen as a neo-isolationist in the early 1950s, Calleo asserts that he

> does not fit the isolationist stereotype. He was anything but a primi-
> tive provincial, ignorant or uninterested in the rest of the world. On
> the contrary, it was a substantial knowledge of history and politics
> that fed his worry about America's impulses toward moral preten-
> tiousness and economic overextension. Like Kennan, Taft was
> skeptical of how well the American political system was suited for
> an imperial role ... Taft understood the importance of maintaining
> a balance of power but was skeptical of grand ... schemes for a
> world order managed by the United States. Like Kennan, he believed
> the United States should play a selective rather than universal role
> in sustaining a world balance, one dictated by a prudent definition
> of national interest. Taft favored a maritime strategy that avoided
> continental commitments. The United States should, he believed,
> concentrate on a powerful navy and air force and eschew a large
> standing army.[3]

This view of Taft as a shrewdly perceptive international Realist is mystifying to me because my own rather extensive research into Taft's writings has led to far different conclusions. As I see Taft, he was essentially an unrealistic isolationist in the sense of my definition above. That is, he was someone who wanted America to have a free hand to act unilaterally with respect to other powers and to limit its interventions abroad as much as possible. When Taft spoke about *any type* of alliances with other nations, he frequently used the term 'reasonable' without ever defining it but clearly meaning a very limited commitment. Moreover, he seemed to be willing to make a 'reasonable alliance' with *only* three countries in the world: Britain, Australia, and Canada. Taft's isolationist stance toward Europe was well summed up in one of his own highly publicized statements in 1951: 'Our aim should be to make Europe sufficiently strong so that American troops can be withdrawn from the continent of Europe.' In fact, Taft believed that American troops should not be sent anywhere abroad during peacetime and even in time of war should not be sent to a continental area 'unless we are reasonably certain of success.'[4]

Other examples questioning Calleo's assessment of Taft could be given, but I hope my point is clear. Calleo's revisionist view of the great conservative senator from Ohio, often called 'Mr Republican' because of his influence in that party, seems designed to gain support from the political right for his version of the decline thesis and its implications for NATO. As noted above, to their credit Reagan conservatives have remained unmoved.

While I do not believe that Calleo is an isolationist himself, I think he does play on this American tendency in other ways as he promotes the decline thesis and his view that the Western Alliance needs to be changed as a result. For him, what is wrong is that NATO, instead of incorporating the 'Twin Pillars' concept, is an American military protectorate of Europe in fact. He grants that this outcome came from an American decision involving a number of factors, including military, political, ideological and economic. However, Calleo emphasizes the point that the Europeans themselves strongly favored the decision, too. The Europeans

> insisted on a hegemonic American alliance. Each country had its own particular reasons, but all sought to borrow American strength to further their individual national purposes.[5]

But above all, the Europeans craved American dominance in the late 1940s because they wanted 'to yoke America' firmly to a responsibility for continental leadership, something they had been trying without success to do since the end of World War I. Calleo concludes:

> With America's power thus domesticated, each European state could proceed to manoeuvre for its best position within the American

hegemony. European initiatives might include building a European bloc or cultivating detente with the Soviets. Neither effort, however, was so much a substitute for American hegemony as it was a strategy for increasing European leverage within it.[6]

Ah! Those Machiavellian Europeans are at it again! I must say that I find this part of Calleo's argument a rather cynical attempt to use traditional American fears and dislikes of Europe – part of the basis of isolationism – to promote his ends. My own view – and I reject his loaded 'military protectorate' term as well – is that Europeans, after two devastating world wars stemming in large part from their own historical rivalries and hatreds, agreed that they needed outside help from America – not only to deal with the Soviet threat but also with others in Europe itself. While they did not trust America all that much, they trusted one another even less.

Since much of Calleo's entire book is devoted to a detailed analysis of how the military protectorate, as he sees it, can be changed into a viable alternative, I will not attempt to provide what should be a fair and balanced summary in a few lines or paragraphs available here. I do, however, want to mention one other point which, like Calleo's use of Senator Taft, has symbolic importance. This concerns the withdrawal of American troops from Europe. Calleo's position:

> Once the pretension to run European defense is abandoned, Amer-ica's standing contribution to Europe's territorial defense can be limited to the equivalent of two or three divisions, with perhaps another division or two in the continental United States earmarked for Europe.[7]

Perhaps one can make a strong case for such reductions on military grounds, but I think it sends the wrong signals to the Europeans. By the late 1980s they, the Europeans, had become very uneasy about the nature of the American commitment to Europe. Beginning in the 1960s with the Mansfield Amendment and continuing later on with the Nunn Amendment, the United States Senate kept on its agenda proposals to reduce the number of American troops in Europe. While there were good reasons to keep pressures on the Europeans to bring about 'burden-sharing,' I question the need for a real tough stand during the present critical stage of European integration.

The most difficult problem facing the Europeans is, I believe, political integration. Clearly this problem has many dimensions, and thus we cannot go into it very far. John Palmer, a British political journalist, has identified one of the more important elements in his book *Europe Without America*? He states that European politicians on the left as well as those on the right tend, under pressure, 'to think and act in purely national rather than in "European" terms.' To some extent this simply reflects the strengths of the lobbies and pressure groups which operate at a national level. But in the final analysis it reveals that 'Europe' as an operational political concept still means little or nothing to ordinary people. This is why, if it is to survive, 'Europe must become the "citizens" Europe, the "workers" Europe,' the new Europe of all those social constituencies presently excluded from or marginalized by the existing power structures.[8]

Perhaps one way to look at the difficulties inherent in the political integration problem is to consider the American experience. It is often forgotten that the American colonial period was rather long, about 170 years, and that the thirteen colonies were essentially British in nature – that is, British in terms of culture, language, law, politics, economics, and so forth. Yet, when independence was proclaimed in 1776, not one but thirteen independent, sovereign nations were established. Even the adoption of the 1789 Constitution with a rather strong central government did not produce a single integrated nation immediately. In fact, as someone has so aptly put it, it was not until the late nineteenth century that Americans finally no longer had to say the United States *are* but could say the United States *is*. In short, political integration was very slow in coming and had to follow economic, legal and other types of integration.

So, too, it seems to me, is the case with Europe. After centuries of division and after two horrible wars in this century alone, political integration will not come about quickly. It will have to follow on the heels of other types of integration based on a functional approach, one of the promising developments of this century. As we know, other types, especially economic integration, have moved forward rather well in the past forty years. The next forty could bring about even more remarkable developments. Hence, this is not the time to signal an American withdrawal; but it is the time to show patience and to give strong encouragement to the forces for integration. Above all, America should not undercut these forces. After all, it is America's policy – it is in America's national interest – to have an integrated Europe.

## *Functionalism*

The dramatic collapse of Communism in Eastern Europe and the Soviet Union at the end of the 1980s changed the world political situation very quickly. Although I certainly welcomed the prospect of the Cold War's end, I was concerned that this event might increase the movement towards isolationism in the United States. There was ample evidence already from numerous opinion polls and other indices taken during the 1980s that isolationist attitudes were becoming stronger as the decline thesis debate intensified. My concern can be illustrated by the well-known story about some advice the late Senator Arthur Vandenburg of

Michigan gave President Harry Truman in 1947 when the latter considered asking Congress and the American people to support the Truman Doctrine. This proposal for military assistance to Greece and Turkey is often seen as one of the first steps in the Cold War. The Republican Senator, an old isolationist who had been converted to internationalism by World War II, advised the President to 'scare the hell' out of Congress and the American people to overcome post-war isolationist tendencies. Truman of course did exactly that by raising the specter of Communist world domination directed from Moscow. With that gone in the late 1980s, what would happen? Would America return to the isolationism of the interwar period? Or had America finally accepted the role of world leader?

When Francis Warner invited me back to Clare College, Cambridge, in 1989 and again to St Peter's College, Oxford, the following year, I took the opportunities to give lectures on functionalism. I did so because I believe that the seeds of functionalism are as deeply rooted and hopefully even more so than isolationism in America's culture and character. Hence, perhaps functionalism could become a substitute for isolationism. Just as William James hoped the American people could find 'the moral equivalent of war,' I hoped they could find something similar for isolationism. The titles of my two lectures were 'Beyond Containment: An American-European Functional Commonwealth?' and 'Beyond Containment: A New Agenda and How to Address It.'

The phrase 'beyond containment' came from a statement President George Bush made in May 1989, during a trip to Europe where he urged his fellow leaders to develop a new collective foreign policy to replace the successful one of the Cold War. Unfortunately, Mr Bush, who had trouble with the 'vision thing' as he called it, was unwilling and/or unable to provide any leadership for a new policy.

It seemed to me that functionalism, which attracted interest when environmental issues began being agenda items for nations, offered a way to move beyond containment. What is functionalism? Without getting too deeply involved in functional theory, I shall try to outline some basic premises which have been identified by P.G. Bock.[9] An advocate of functionalism believes that contemporary nationalism rests on factors which cut across national lines, i.e. that there is a movement away from a demand for national rights and toward a demand for services. He also believes that social and economic maladjustments are the basic causes of war and that social and economic welfare is the precondition for peace. The real task of the collective society is the conquest of poverty, ignorance, disease, environmental problems, and the like; the world's interdependence is all-pervasive and all-embracing.

The existing nation-state system, the functionalist continues, contributes to international tensions and conflicts because it is institutionally inadequate. It cannot deal with basic global problems because it arbitrarily divides global society into national units based on territory and not on the problem to be solved. International institutions based on functions to be performed rather than on territory would be appropriate for the solution of such problems. Establishing such institutions is possible because social activities can be separated into political and non-political (that is technical) ones. The particular activity or function will determine the form of the agency in any given case. Hence, the approach here is to depoliticize rather than to politicize things, the polar opposite of the totalitarian approach.

Furthermore, the experience gained in one area can be transferred to other areas so that a successful institutional device can serve as a model for devices in many different settings. Successful experience will spread and accumulate, forming part of the foundation of a functional commonwealth for an international society.

The existing state system, the functionalist believes, promotes the subjective allegiances which send people to war. International bodies that focus attention on common problems to be addressed instrumentally may, on the other hand, foster international loyalty among people at large and counteract harmful nationalistic attitudes. Similarly, the leaders of national states – politicians, diplomats, and soldiers – are blinded by their narrow view of their national interests and do not have the proper perspective to encourage international cooperation. Experts working for international organizations will develop international loyalties and will help to create a peaceful international community in the long run. The functionalist program, then, emerges quite simply and clearly from these premises, according to Bock.

Although wide interest in the functionalist approach did not manifest itself in the United States until the 1970s, a number of American scholars, such as Paul S. Reinsch and Leonard Woolf, began writing and lecturing about it at the turn of the century. Apparently, they and others took the proliferation of international organizations at that time – such as the Universal Postal Union and the International Telegraphic Union – as an indication of a growing sense of world community and as a guarantee for future international stability.

As Americans, these scholars also found functionalism appealing because it fitted into the new philosophical trend of the time. Often called Pragmatism, though I prefer the broader term Experimentalism, this new way of looking at the world was being developed by such towering figures as William James, John Dewey and Thorstein Veblen. Sometimes identified as 'The American Philosophy,' it had deep roots in America's past which James frequently pointed out.

A brief review of the basic assumptions of Experimentalism will show the nature of the fit with Functionalism.[10]

Nature of Knowledge – Knowledge is derived from interaction with the process of change. That is, the knowledges about the process –

tools and skills – are derived by facing the continuous problem-solving challenge which evolution presents. Answers to problems, literally unknown to people in advance of their inquiry into them, possess a high or low degree of probability, but never absolute certainty. Truth is incomplete – it is seen in terms of hypotheses.

Human Nature and Behaviour – coming into the world with an impulse to live, human beings have no inborn traits. As they interact with their cultures, humans are moulded by them, and in turn, remould their cultures. In other words, people are not automatons as a consequence of some form of cultural determinism. They are a product of their experiences, but they are personally capable of organizing, reorganizing, and synthesizing these experiences.

Political Authority – ideas, the fruits of creative intelligence, are the sources of power, a non-coercive power, and they are continuously tested to determine whether they are capable of solving the problems at hand. The leader-innovator, therefore, is one who actually aids in their testing and in the creation of new knowledges. Chosen because of their competence, experimental leaders develop fresh insights into older problems and explore new frontiers which enlarge the range of human choice and discretion.

Purpose of Institutions – Institutions are developed for the purpose of resolving problems. They are tools or instruments that assist people to meet the problems at hand in an ever-changing world. As such, they are servants of the people for the completion of specific tasks.

Progress – Progress is made when there is a constant recombination of ideas and tools, focused on problem-solving. When creative intelligence is liberated, there is an enlarging of human discretion and choice within the environment.

Value – that which is desirable is the creation of new knowledges that add significantly to human know-how and give people a greater freedom of choice.

As this way of thinking manifested itself in the Progressive Movement, an important social and political reform movement in early twentieth-century America, it fostered the creation of such institutions as the independent regulatory commission at national and state government levels and the city-manager form of government at local levels. These institutions emphasized decision-making and administration by professional experts, disinterested scientists, who would be guided by the evidences from inquiry and not by political considerations. In other words, there was an attempt to depoliticize things and to solve problems instrumentally.

With America mainly focused on domestic issues, especially during the Progressive Era and the New Deal of the 1930s, functionalism in both theory and practice made little progress in the United States. Renewed interest occurred during World War II after David Mitrany put forward one of the best formulations of functional theory in international organization, something of great interest for the post-war period. Published in 1943, his essay, 'A Working Peace System', summarized the main arguments of the functionalists.

However, it took twenty-five years after Mitrany's work appeared before functionalism entered the mainstream of American thought. Why? Why the delay? In the first place, at the end of World War II, most Americans got caught up in the prevailing idealism of the time which emphasized support for the United Nations and even world government. When this idealism disappeared with the advent of the Cold War, realism or state power-politics became the new spirit of the time. Being neither idealistic nor realistic but experimental, functionalism was unable to gain much support until the late 1960s when public concern began to focus on the environment. To many thinkers functionalism seemed the most promising response to a rapidly developing problem which was clearly transnational in nature and scope.

According to one historian, thinking seemed to develop along the following lines: if national governments by themselves were incapable of solving environmental problems and if world government was impossible to create, then perhaps cooperative arrangements evolving toward supranational status offered the wisest strategy. Each step would be so modest and gradual that it would arouse minimal suspicion or fear, and eventually a complex network of specialized agencies would acquire supranational authority backed by extensive popular support.[11]

This optimism was encouraged by two developments in international relations. The first was the evolution of the United Nations into a more functional type of world organization when its duties in the political realm were rigorously curtailed or abandoned altogether. The doctrine of 'collective security,' the centerpiece of the original UN Charter, was downgraded after the disaster in Korea in the early 1950s, and the concept of 'peace by force' through international organization lost much of its appeal. On the other hand, under the UN's growing experience and leadership through its specialized agencies in such areas as health and agriculture its international reputation grew as the possible foundation of a functional commonwealth.

The second involved functional development in Europe. It all began with Europeans agreeing to the basic premise of the European Economic Community (EEC) that war will be less likely if the European nations become more economically and socially interdependent. This premise is clearly stated in the treaty creating the European Coal and Steel Community, the organization that served as the catalyst for the larger EEC. The treaty expresses functional assumptions by calling on European states 'to substitute for historical rivalries a fusion of their essential interests' and 'to establish, by creating an economic community, the foundation of a wider and deeper community among peoples long divided by bloody conflicts.' By the 1970s European interdependence had grown enormously.

The impressive progress of the Europeans, as well as the growing agenda of environmental problems, encouraged leading American scholars to put forward the case for functionalism. It is interesting to note that it was none other than scholar-diplomat George F. Kennan, the Founding Father of the containment policy for the Cold War, who helped to lead the way for a functional approach. This was a very significant shift on his part because Kennan had been long associated in scholarly circles with the Realist or power-politics school of thought in foreign affairs, a school that had been highly critical of functionalism. It is also interesting to observe that another famous Realist, the late Hans Morganthau, had some kind words for functionalism at this time as well. In the Nuclear Age with a growing list of transnational problems, Realism had theoretical and practical difficulties.

Although Kennan's contribution was first, it was merely an article in *Foreign Affairs* magazine, a publication designed more for the interested layman rather than the professional scholar or diplomat. Perhaps one of the most important scholarly books which appeared in the 1970s came from Columbia University professor Zbigniew Brzezinski, who later became President Carter's National Security Adviser. In his book, titled *Between Two Ages: America's Role in the Technocratic Era*, Brzezinski argues from a basic functional premise: that the nation-state has become too small for the big problems in life and too big for the small problems. To deal with the international dimension of this situation, which is his focus, he recommends the creation of a community of developed nations that could mitigate traditional international conflicts and center the world's attention on the more basic problems of economic development. Initially, a community composed of Western Europe, North America, and Japan would be established, an association that would find institutional expression in regular meetings of political and economic leaders assisted by a permanent organization that would supervise the study of common political, economic, and technological problems. He hoped that such a community would expand and gain enough public support to become a useful instrument for addressing global issues of environmental protection, economic development and peace. He also hoped that a functional approach that emphasized ecology rather than ideology would encourage the spread of a more personalized, rational, humanist world outlook that would eventually replace the institutionalized religious, ideological and nationalistic perspectives that dominated modern history.

This book was only one of a number of such monographs scholars and theorizers produced at the time. Perhaps of more importance, practitioners became active as well and established, among other institutions, the Trilateral Commission. Such well-known individuals in international affairs as David Rockefeller and George Ball, a former high-ranking United States State Department official, led the way in creating and promoting this organization in America. It also received support in Western Europe and Japan. With assistance from major foundations in the United States, the Commission was formally founded in 1973.

Concerned that most people continued to live in a 'mental universe which no longer exists – a world of separate nations,' the Commission wished to nurture the collective management desirable and necessary for an interdependent world. In particular, it hoped that a community of democratic, economically developed nations would be created and maintained through a process of 'piecemeal functionalism.' Within a context of similar values and parallel economic and security interests, Western elites would apply their technical expertise to problems of trade, finance, communications, ecology, economic development and peace. The Commission presented no blueprint for a major international organization, but it hoped that the very process of routine consultation and cooperation would create a community of shared perspectives and a willingness to transcend the forces of narrow nationalism.[12]

The world situation of the time encouraged much optimism among both theorizers and practitioners. The war in Viet Nam was finally coming to a conclusion. Even more important was President Nixon's policy of detente with the Soviet Union and the beginning of the normalization of America's relations with China. While few believed that the Cold War was about to end, Jimmy Carter, when he became President in 1977, tried to build a new foreign policy consensus for a future post-Cold War policy that focused on such agenda items as the promotion of human rights, the scaling back of the arms race, the prevention of nuclear proliferation, the curtailment of arms sales to Third World countries, and assistance to developing nations to create a new international economic order.

Unfortunately for the development and implementation of functionalism, Cold War Reassertionism began to gain ground even before the end of Carter's one term in the White House and of course attracted great public support during the Reagan and Bush Presidencies that followed. Now that the Cold War has indeed ended, the time seems right to return to functionalism once again. The foundation has been laid and now the building should start.

Having outlined functionalism, experimentalism where its philosophical roots can be found, and its brief history, I concluded my lectures by urging those in attendance, both Americans and Britons, to explore these ideas further because much needed to be done to encourage these habits of mind for the future. Isolationism and other forms of extreme nationalism could be countered, I believed, by this way of thinking.

Therefore, I asked the students to consider taking three additional steps in their young lives. First, concerning a career choice, they should explore the possibility of joining the growing numbers of transnational and functionalist elites of business people, scholars, professionals, and public officials whose ties cut across national boundaries: the cosmopolitans of our time. A beginning could be made with a British-American connection.

Second, both on a formal and an informal level, they should make international contacts and promote networks of communication to facilitate the exchange of ideas and experiences, for it is through the development of common ideas and experiences that an international culture can slowly emerge. Again, I urged them to make a start with a British-American connection.

And finally, I asked them to become teachers – teachers in the broadest sense of that term – to help educate the vast majority of humanity who still neither shares nor supports any sense of global consciousness needed to have functionalism take root around the world. They could make a start by teaching people about the 'special relationship' between Britain and the United States, a good place to get things moving.

## *Notes*

1. Wayne S. Cole, *Senator Gerald P. Nye and American Foreign Relations* (Minneapolis: The University of Minnesota Press, 1962), 4.
2. Inis L. Claude, 'American Isolationism,' Paper presented at Hendrix College, October 30, 1997.
3. David P. Calleo, *Beyond American Hegemony: The Future of the Western Alliance* (New York: Basic Books, 1987), 37–8.
4. Robert A. Taft, *A Foreign Policy for Americans* (Garden City, New York: Doubleday & Company, 1951), 66.
5. Calleo, 34.
6. Ibid., 36.
7. Ibid., 124.
8. John Palmer, *Europe Without America? The Crisis in Atlantic Relations* (Oxford: Oxford University Press, 1987), 189.
9. P.G. Bock, 'Functionalism and Functional Integration,' in *International Encyclopedia of the Social Sciences*.
10. John A. Ziegler, *Experimentalism and Institutional Change: An Approach to the Study and Improvement of Institutions* (Lanham, Maryland: University Press of America, 1994), 6–7.
11. Wesley T. Wooley, *Alternatives to Anarchy: American Supranationalism Since World War II* (Bloomington, Indiana: Indiana University Press, 1988), 159.
12. Ibid., 175.

# Chapter IV

# Alistair Cooke and the Manchester Guardian

*G*iven my family background, perhaps the time would come when my search for the special relationship between the United States and Britain would focus on newspapers. Both parents were very much into newspapers, though in different ways. My father was an avid reader, covering everything thoroughly including the comics in the evening and Sunday papers delivered to our door. However my mother, though only inclined to skim through the papers, was the real newspaper enthusiast of the family because she spent many years reporting for a daily and a weekly. While never more than a part-time reporter, she nevertheless spent many hours most days collecting information for her 'New Athens News' columns that appeared once weekly in the daily paper of the county seat and also in the weekly paper of New Athens.

The time factor was frequently a point of dispute between my parents mainly because of the manner in which my mother collected her news. Unlike many reporters, she got most of her information by telephone calls from various sources throughout the village. As one can easily imagine some of these sources could more accurately be described as 'gossips' who very early on Monday mornings telephoned to say that Mr and Mrs X had 'company from out of town' over the weekend. My mother was a fine reporter in that she was a good listener with an ear for significant details, but her main failing was a reluctance to cut off the source after the key facts were known. Hence, conversations, usually one-sided in nature, that should have been over in ten minutes often lasted an hour. This infuriated my father because having the same telephone line into our house and his business next door, he could neither telephone out nor, perhaps more importantly, receive calls from prospective customers while these conversations ensued.

To my chagrin, since I usually felt that I had better things to do, I was frequently 'recruited' by my mother to bicycle to Mrs Y's house to pick up her news so the telephone would not be engaged. This experience, however, led to my own newspaper 'career' which, as I grew older, included interviewing people for my mother's stories, telephoning box scores of high school baseball and basketball games to the St Louis and county newspapers, and reporting for the high school paper. It was, perhaps, my nine years as a carrier of evening and Sunday newspapers, especially the St Louis papers, that got me interested in actually reading newspapers, for often there was not much to do other than read old papers as carriers waited for a bus or a truck to drop off the next delivery.

Since my parents, as well as the vast majority of the other villagers, usually voted Democratic, I easily gravitated in the direction of more liberal opinions. It shouldn't be surprising, therefore, that my favorite newspaper became the St Louis *Post-Dispatch* which was, of course, liberal editorially but which was also the area's best newspaper in terms of general quality and coverage of national and international news. While my study of politics and history at college later on greatly strengthened both my interest in newspapers and my liberal orientation, I became familiar with and began to appreciate specifically the *New York Times* and *The Times* (London) as important sources of information for academic studies. Hence, among the first things that I did upon arriving in Britain as a student in 1956 was to subscribe to the Sunday edition of the *New York Times* and to purchase a copy of *The Times* daily.

However, the more I read *The Times* the less satisfied I became with it. Certainly its stodginess had much to do with my growing dissatisfaction but actually it was its Tory politics that was clearly the problem for me. Now many things Tory I had no difficulties with – including the Scottish family I lived with and my best friend at St Andrews University – but more than anything else it was the Tory policy of Anthony Eden in the Middle East which produced the Suez Canal crisis in the fall of 1956 that was most troublesome. This policy, of course, led to a serious split between Britain and the United States, and *The Times* seemed to be incapable of dealing with this development fairly, something my Scottish family and friend had no significant difficulty with despite their strong nationalistic feelings.

I began to look for another paper to read. The British are well known, of course, as avid newspaper readers. Consequently, their papers are many and varied and range from perhaps the best or nearly so to some of the worst anywhere. Unfortunately, the local papers where I lived fit the latter category. After ruling them out, I began to focus on the national quality papers and chose the *Manchester Guardian*, known in Britain today as simply the *Guardian*.

## *The* Guardian

As well as I can recall, I had not read the *Guardian* before arriving in Britain for the first time despite the fact that the *Manchester Guardian*

*Weekly*, a newspaper designed for readers abroad, had been published since 1919. In the 1950s – just as it does today – the *Weekly* apparently not only had a large number of its worldwide subscribers in the United States but it also tended to have Americans rather than simply British expatriates as readers. In short, the newspaper had something in it that appealed to at least some Americans even at that time.

What appealed to me in 1956? Initially, of course, it was the manner in which the *Guardian* dealt with Suez both in editorial and news terms that made it attractive. In both cases, the newspaper showed a subtle understanding of the situation by carefully distinguishing three separate elements: geographical ones, ownership of the canal, and world opinion. Perhaps most important of all, it condemned early on the Anglo-French ultimatum, which eventually led to the invasion of Egypt, as 'an act of folly without justification.'[1] Virtually standing alone among the press in Britain at the outset, the *Guardian* was instrumental in winning over both press and public support to this position as time went on.

This impressive editorial stand was matched by excellent reporting led by Max Freedman, the *Guardian* Washington correspondent. As events unfolded during the crisis, it was clear that Freedman had outstanding sources of information for his reports from the United States, but it was not known until years later whom they were. According to David Ayerst, Freedman had 'ready access' to Secretary of State John Foster Dulles as well as to such leading US Senators as Lyndon Johnson and John F. Kennedy.[2]

Perhaps more should be said about Freedman because it was largely due to his writing and that of several others that I continued to read the *Guardian* long after the Suez Crisis had passed. Like so many other leading *Guardian* reporters, Freedman was more than just an experienced political journalist when he was appointed Washington correspondent in 1953 at age forty. A Canadian of Ukrainian-Jewish background, he was a well-read cosmopolitan, reported to have a personal library of 24,000 books. He had very wide interests and tastes – including the theatre, cinema, and civic institutions – and these came alive in his articles. One of his editors described him as follows: 'He was a sensitive observer, and a deeply committed man, a "keeper of the *Guardian*'s conscience."'[3]

Another *Guardian* reporter of the time also contributed outstanding articles about an equally important event. The event was the Hungarian Revolt against the Soviet Union in the fall of 1956, and the reporter was Victor Zorza. Like Freedman, Zorza was Jewish, but he had spent his early life in Poland. At the outbreak of World War II, he and his family were deported to a forced labor camp in Russia from which he escaped. For the next two years, while still a teenager, he was on the run living from hand to mouth, twice arrested, at first without a passport or identity card, then later, with a forged one. Eventually, he made contact with the Polish Air Force and served in its Intelligence Corps until the war's end. During that time and immediately after the war when he worked for the British Broadcasting Corporation, he became a self-educated man, reading widely in history and contemporary European affairs. Always an admirer of the *Guardian*, Zorza began to submit articles for publication which were rejected until subsequent events proved the accuracy of his writing. For example, he was one of the first to predict that Nikita Khrushchev would emerge as a leading political figure in the Soviet Union. From then on he became a regular Eastern European reporter for the *Guardian*.[4]

While these men and another who will be considered below were the reporters who 'sold' the *Guardian* to me, there were other things about the newspaper itself that were equally important in its appeal. One of these was its political orientation. As a liberal publication – in fact a Liberal newspaper in that it had a long association with the British Liberal Party – the *Guardian*'s editorial position by the 1950s tended to be middle-of-the-road in relation to British politics of the day. On the left was the Labour Party, a socialist party that had recently been turned out of office, and on the right was the Tory or Conservative Party, which was indeed a conservative party led by Winston Churchill until he stepped aside for Eden. To an American like myself neither of these two political parties appeared very attractive. On the one hand, the Labour Party seemed to be too strongly committed to socialist doctrine, while on the other the Conservative Party appeared as in the case of Suez to be tied too much to the old notions of empire. As I saw it, Britain needed a much more pragmatic approach both in domestic and foreign affairs, and this seemed to be the *Guardian*'s position.

Since the word 'pragmatic' is often misunderstood, some clarification is necessary. It is not used here to suggest mere expediency – that is, action devoid of principle – because one of the *Guardian*'s long-standing characteristics is that of taking stands based on principle. Rather it is used to suggest that within a rather well-defined framework of values the *Guardian* exhibits flexibility based upon the concrete facts or evidences involved. Doctrinal rigidity and an unbending commitment to the past are both rejected in favor of a practical step-by-step incrementalism based on evidential persuasion.

What are the *Guardian*'s values? In the 'Introduction' to *The Bedside Guardian* of 1985, writer George Melly provides one of the better short summaries I have seen: 'a belief, however qualified, in the power of reason, in the application of fairness, in the possibility, however frequently frustrated, of the improvement of the human condition;' and in 'moderation, social concern, compassion for the poor, for the hopeless, anger at injustice, tolerance for minorities.'[5] One can see in

Melly's statement many of the Helper values mentioned before: fairness, kindness, optimism, understanding and broadmindedness.

As novelist John Fowles points out, however, these important *Guardian* values and other features of the newspaper often present a dilemma or a contradiction. In the 'Introduction' to *The Bedside Guardian* of 1983, Fowles states: 'As liberals we may denounce unfair public privilege ... yet increasingly we dread and resist any diminution in the traditional personal perquisites of belonging to the educated cream of society.' Hence, 'juxtapositions in the *Guardian* – between, say, the committed pieces and those on good restaurants, or wines, or holiday places, or other "worlds" reserved to the fortunate minority – always disturb me.'[6]

As Fowles suggests, part of the *Guardian*'s appeal stems from the paper's 'good life' or perhaps even 'gentlemanly' features. Among these the British countryside articles became one of my favorites almost immediately. Certainly one of the reasons for this was the quality, as well as the quantity, of writing, something the *Guardian* was noted for down through the years. For example, as long ago as the 1880s, the *Guardian* gave its country-loving readership abundant pleasure with a long series of articles on 'Rare Birds of Lancashire,' the 'Past Fauna of Lancashire and Cheshire,' and 'Our Northern Birds of Prey.' Later, a shorter series followed the River Irwell downstream from its source and single articles discussed 'The Sea Birds of Walney Island' and 'A Westmoreland Haunt of Sea Birds.'[7]

This long-standing tradition of countryside writing has continued to this day. It manifests itself on a regular basis in the 'Country Diary' column, a feature of usually no more than a half-dozen column inches in length, but one that often paints very vivid word pictures of animal and plant life in rural Britain. Over the years some of the best writing has been done by Enid J. Wilson near Keswick and John T. White in Sussex and Kent.

Two other features, 'The Arts and Book Reviews,' have also been favorites of mine. As a London theatre enthusiast from my first visit there in 1956, I have always consulted the *Guardian*'s reviews of the current West End offerings before arriving in London. Generally speaking, the *Guardian*'s choices of books to review have filled gaps in my knowledge. Most of my other sources deal with academic and/or American books while the *Guardian* has reviewed more 'middle brow' British books.

These favorite features of mine certainly do not exhaust the *Guardian*'s list, but I must say that for one reason or another – usually lack of interest – such things as chess, bridge and sports have not struck my fancy. On the other hand, the newspaper's crossword puzzles have, but I have come to the agonizing conclusion that only Britons can actually hope to finish them.

Now some forty years after my introduction to the *Guardian*, I am still a regular reader, thanks to the *Manchester Guardian Weekly* to which I have subscribed since the late 1950s. However, with the addition of selections from *Le Monde* and the *Washington Post* in more recent years, the *Weekly* is not quite the genuine British newspaper of the past. Hence, while I still like the paper and would feel a real void without it, I doubt that it is now a very significant part of the special relationship between Britain and America. Perhaps in and of itself it never was of great importance despite its Helper values, but there was one personality long connected with the *Guardian* who in my view was – and still is – a very important part of that relationship. That person is Alistair Cooke.

## *Enter Alistair Cooke*

It was necessary to discuss the *Guardian* at some length before considering Alistair Cooke because most people familiar with his writing would agree, I believe, that he was indeed a '*Guardian* man.' Although Cooke worked briefly for other newspapers – *The Times* and the *Daily Herald* – he spent twenty-seven years with the *Guardian*, first as its United Nations correspondent and then as Chief American Correspondent. This long association was no accident because, as we shall see, Cooke's basic philosophy fit the *Guardian* like a hand in a glove.

Cooke was actually born in Manchester, England, in 1908 but spent much of his youth in Blackpool. After his grammar school education, he entered Jesus College, Cambridge University, from which he graduated before pursuing graduate work at Yale and Harvard in the early 1930s. Arriving in America in September 1932, with a fellowship at Yale, Cooke intended to acquire expertise in American film direction with the hope, as he has said, to return to Britain 'and revolutionize the English drama.' But an 'obligation' of the fellowship changed his rather grandiose plans.[8]

Under the fellowship's terms, Cooke was given a car during the summer vacation to tour as many states of the United States as possible. This first trip through Depression America had the immediate effect, as Cooke says, to shake 'me out of my deep ignorance of politics' and 'to make the landscape and the people of America far more dramatic than Broadway.' After returning to Britain, he 'weaned' himself away from the theatre during 'a tapering off period' as the BBC's film critic and then began to write and direct programs about American life and history. 'It was,' Cooke notes, 'only a matter of time before I returned, on an immigrant visa, and found myself – to my astonishment – launched as a second-string foreign correspondent for the London *Times* and the BBC.' He became an American citizen in 1941 and has lived in New York since.[9]

While Cooke's American experience of the 1930s was without doubt instrumental in bringing about his return, there are other factors that helped to bring him here in the first place. Like many Britons, Cooke credits American films shown in Britain during the 1910s and 1920s with stimulating his initial interest, but certainly even more important was his association with American soldiers during World War I while he was a nine-year-old in Blackpool. After America's entry, US soldiers were stationed there, and because of a shortage of accommodations seven of them were billeted with Cooke's family.

According to Cooke,

I doubt that I harbored then any preconceptions at all about Americans. Everything about them was peculiar and fascinating. They wore Boy Scout hats, an oddity that was never explained. All their ranks had identical table manners and, so far as we could tell, identical accents ... They treated my mother with a New World courtesy that kept them strangers long after their British counterparts would have been close, if off-hand, friends. But they addressed children as equals, and I was treated as a sort of regimental pet. Since my own father ... had been drafted in his fortieth year into an airplane factory in Manchester, from which he came on leave only once a month, I had the luck of having seven extra fathers, and no doubt my inclination to take to Americans was incorrigibly determined then.[10]

It seems, then, that Cooke's own special relationship with America was born within his own family home.

My introduction to Cooke actually occurred via television rather than through the newspaper. As host of the excellent 'Omnibus' series during the early 1950s his memorable comments came into our living room many Sunday afternoons. Later, I became familiar with his writing when I began to read the *Guardian* during my early months in Dundee, Scotland. While Freedman covered the Washington beat, Cooke ventured further afield and consequently reported on a broader range of American topics. Although this general news about home was always welcome, his extensive coverage of the American Presidential campaign of 1956, involving Dwight D. Eisenhower and Adlai E. Stevenson of Illinois, was especially interesting to me.

## Cooke and Stevenson

As a fellow Illinoisian who first developed a strong interest in politics in the late 1940s and early 1950s, I became a devotee of then Governor Stevenson who was elected to that office in 1948 and ran twice unsuccessfully for the Presidency in 1952 and again in 1956. While Governor, Stevenson brought about a number of political reforms in a rather corrupt state government, but more importantly he was a good friend of Southern Illinois University which was experiencing rapid growth at that time. SIU's President had great success in obtaining funds for various projects, thanks to Stevenson and the Illinois legislature which like most state legislatures of the time was still malapportioned and hence favorably disposed to downstate rural interests rather than Chicago's. Since the Chairman of the Government Department, whom I got to know well, was the university's chief lobbyist in Springfield, I heard much about Stevenson's political views and abilities.

As a result, my friends and I followed Stevenson's first run for the Presidency very closely and were deeply disappointed when he was defeated. Yet we believed like a large number of other Americans that Stevenson had conducted such an extraordinary campaign that he should be given another chance in 1956. Any reluctance on my part to go to Britain that year stemmed from the thought of missing a great Stevenson campaign.

It is difficult to summarize adequately in a few words Stevenson's great appeal both in this country and to certain segments of the British population. Perhaps political scientist James Q. Wilson has given some of the better insights about the nature of Stevenson's support in America in his book *The Amateur Democrat*. He argues that Stevenson was instrumental in bringing into American politics a special kind of political activist that appeared in rather large numbers in the 1950s. He calls this type 'the amateur' but does not mean that literally. For him the amateur is

> one who finds politics intrinsically interesting because it expresses a conception of the public interest. The amateur politician sees the political world more in terms of ideas and principles than in terms of persons. Politics is the determination of public policy, and public policy ought to be set deliberately rather than as the accidental by-product of a struggle for personal and party advantage. Issues ought to be settled on their merits.[11]

In my view Stevenson certainly approached politics in this way.

Although the appearance of this political type in large numbers was a significant development of the 1950s, Wilson believes that the amateur, per se, is not and can certainly be seen among the middle-class reformers of the early twentieth century known as Progressives. Many of these people came to politics from a conservative background while others, especially the more articulate spokesmen, were social gospel clergymen and university professors who advanced a new philosophy called Pragmatism or Experimentalism. John Dewey is often seen as the leading intellectual of this movement.[12]

In Britain, Stevenson attracted the attention of many reformers, intellectuals, and Liberals, including the Liberal newspaper the

*Guardian.* At the time of Stevenson's death in 1965, the *Weekly* had this to say about him during the 1950s:

> For these were the years in which America seemed to be choosing the soothing syrup of the Eisenhower philosophy when it was not turning to the vomit of the McCarthy outrages. In this dull and often ignorant era, the wit, the civilization, the courage of Adlai Stevenson shone like a good deed in a decidedly naughty world.[13]

The editorial concludes:

> And Stevenson was, at a time when it was easy for the censorious (not to speak of the malignant) to criticize the United States, a reminder that there had been better days in the past and would be better days in the future. He was a reminder too that it was not absurd to recall the description of the United States by the greatest of American politicians as the last best hope of earth.[14]

While the *Guardian* kept its adulation of Stevenson in 1956 to the editorial pages, Cooke's news articles, though presenting rather objectively the observations of a political reporter, seemed to carry hints of favoring Stevenson as well. It wasn't until the publication of an essay on Stevenson in Cooke's 1978 book *Six Men* that I learned the two had been good friends at the time. What did Cooke find so attractive about Stevenson personally that he broke his pledge with a fellow journalist 'to resist consorting with politicians beyond the bounds of acquaintanceship,' as he puts it?[15]

Perhaps the title of his essay provides some insight: 'The Failed Saint.' What Cooke argues is that although Stevenson failed to become a successful politician, he 'mastered the art, far more difficult and rarer than that of a successful politician, writer, musician, actor: success as a human being.'[16] So it was Stevenson's personal human qualities rather than his politics that Cooke found so appealing.

A cursory count of Cooke's comments about Stevenson in his essay reveals nearly thirty positive descriptive words concerning the man himself. A rather representative sample of these words includes the following: civilized, goodness, probity, gallant, humane, noble, extraordinary grace, moral, unfailing courtesy, high ideals, humility and loyalty. Cooke adds of course those things Stevenson was noted for in his writing and speaking: wit, humor and elegance. Cooke also notes that the only mean thing he recalls Stevenson saying about anyone was when he referred to John F. Kennedy as 'this kid.' Snideness and malice were beyond him.[17]

While putting Stevenson on a pedestal generally, Cooke does mention some shortcomings, though these tend to be related to Stevenson the politician rather than the man: naivety, sulkiness, indecisiveness ('the Hamlet legend') and blindness to cunning, bigotry and deviousness in others. Seeing Stevenson's politics as rather superficial, Cooke says that 'I have to admit that much, if not most of Stevenson's political thought adds up to a makeshift warning to avoid all quick solutions while trusting, in the meantime, to a general outbreak of courage, tolerance, compassion, and universal brotherhood.' [18] Cooke concludes that while Stevenson had strong political ambitions and worked hard to achieve them, he was too gentle and sensitive and not ruthless enough to be successful.

In the end, Cooke sees Stevenson as a would-be progressive who was actually a deeply conservative man by temperament and upbringing, a man with a strong sense of noblesse oblige to the less fortunate.

Although Cooke tells us much about Stevenson, perhaps he reveals a great deal about himself as well in this portrait. Even the dust cover of Cooke's book admits as much in stating that his essays enable us 'to begin to discover Cooke himself.' It seems to me what stands out most significantly about this portrait is Cooke's admiration of what can be called the ideal qualities of the true gentleman, a type not encountered very often in mainstream American affairs and certainly not in American politics generally. Hence, Stevenson is something of an anomaly here but perhaps is a type encountered more frequently in Britain and even in Europe generally. It was often said after Stevenson's political defeats that he ran for public office on the wrong continent. Certainly under the parliamentary systems of government used there, his political life as leader of the 'loyal opposition' would have lasted much longer, and perhaps he would have eventually emerged as Prime Minister.

## Cooke's Other Conservative Gentlemen

That these gentlemanly qualities are most important to Cooke can be seen in the essays about two other Americans (there are also three essays about Englishmen) he writes about in *Six Men*. These two are H. L. Mencken and Humphrey Bogart. Like Stevenson, they – also well known to Cooke but not as close personal friends – were, as he puts it, 'deeply conservative men who, for various psychological reasons, yearned to be recognized rather as hellions or brave progressives.' Significantly, Cooke adds that 'perhaps that is their real link' with himself. [19] Unlike Stevenson, Mencken and Bogart had vastly different public and private images, but it's the latter, a gentlemanly one, that actually makes them like Stevenson, too.

In his essay on Mencken, titled 'The Public and the Private Face,' Cooke tells what Mencken, whose reputation had already been made, was really like to him as a young English writer just getting started in America. Based on Mencken's writings and his known prejudices, Cooke had every reason to believe that he would be treated rudely the first time they met, but to Cooke's surprise the opposite happened. Cooke says this first conversation revealed Mencken's 'genial manners, his air of extreme attentiveness to even the most trivial remarks, and a habit of signifying approval of any bearable opinion by chanting, "Yeah, Yeah."' [20]

This very pleasant first encounter led to many others because Cooke was invited to visit Mencken's home whenever he was in Baltimore. Subsequent meetings tended to verify the first experience as Cooke came to know him as 'the serene little man with the pot-blue eyes and genial manners, and nothing cocky about him except the angle of his cigar.' He was always 'an affable and easy host,' even to his most outspoken critics, and admitted that his truth was not necessarily *the* truth. At heart Mencken was a conservative gentleman who 'longed for Jefferson's "aristocracy of talent and virtue."' [21]

Although Cooke's essay on Bogart is called 'Epitaph for a Tough Guy,' he could have used the Mencken title as well because the same point is made. Cooke's thesis is that while Bogart's fame with the public is based on his being an anti-hero, his private persona was far different: a gentleman of the old school. Cooke, who got to know Bogart and his wife Lauren Bacall as ardent Stevenson supporters in 1952, argues that people who knew the actor well found him 'gentle, gallant, modest, full of an indulgent or rueful humor, courteous with strangers, quietly and acutely sensitive to the plight of guests who were shy or being left out.' [22] In addition, Bogart had many other 'old-school virtues: loyalty to friends, respect for the old, a distaste for conspicuous wealth, for gossip, for boasting,' to name only a few. [23] Cooke concludes by saying that Bogart was 'a much more intelligent man than most of his trade, or several others, a touchy man who found the world more corrupt than he had hoped, a man with a tough shell hiding a fine core.' [24]

Perhaps the old saying about 'birds of a feather flocking together' summarizes in general Cooke's connections with his three American friends. Certainly Cooke himself doesn't give much help about the nature of these relationships because in categorizing these men, as well as himself, as would-be progressives but actually conservatives, he never really defines his terms. In view of the discussion so far, it seems to me, however, that his terms are being used in a social – perhaps one can even say cultural – sense rather than only a narrow political one. Clearly the old-school gentlemanly values he talks about are part of this type of broad conservatism. They also overlap with the attributes of the Helper as described before. At first glance this might seem strange; yet I think it is not because a true gentleman is a man with masculine traits that have been tempered by female attributes. This, then, is at least part of the special relationship I have found in Cooke. In what he has said and – perhaps even more importantly – how he has said it within the framework of the gentlemanly value system, Cooke has been part of the special relationship between Britain and America.

As he suggests, however, this gentlemanly type, while not absent in American culture, has difficulty occupying the mainstream. Mencken and Bogart, both highly successful in their public professions, could be gentlemen only in private. Stevenson, who tried in both public and private areas, failed in the former, perhaps because he was not macho enough for the American public. Yet, Cooke tells us in another book to which we now turn, that it is possible for an American to be a successful gentleman in both areas. The book is *Alistair Cooke's America* and the man is Robert Tyre Jones, Jr. – better known as Bobby Jones, the great golfer.

In Cooke's personal account of American history, which was also made into a television film series, it is impossible to find a more positive portrait of a significant American figure than that of Jones. Even the great Washington and Jefferson are not treated as well as this golfer. Why? In Cooke's words about Jones:

> His universal appeal was not as a golfer. What then? The word that comes to mind is an extinct word: a gentleman, a combination of goodness and grace, an unwavering courtesy, self-deprecation, and consideration for other people. This fetching combination, allied to his world supremacy in one sport, was what made him a hero in Scotland and England as much as in the Midwest and his native Georgia.[25]

After recounting how Jones conducted himself in a gentlemanly manner as a golfer and as a man paralyzed by a rare disease in his middle forties, Cooke concludes,

> So what we're talking about is not the hero as golfer but something that America hungered for and found: the best performer in the world who was also the hero as human being, the gentle, chivalrous, wholly self-sufficient male.[26]

Although Cooke is describing the America of the 1920s, I think he is providing an insight that applies generally: the loss but the longing for the Helper values of Britannia.

As Cooke indicates, a man like Jones, as well as Stevenson, is a connecting link between Britain and America. Of course the same can be said about Cooke himself, given his popularity in both countries. Before pursuing this theme further in *America*, a short digression about its use seems appropriate. Although a historian, I will not approach his book as a work of history, assessing its strengths and weaknesses as such. It should be mentioned, however, that I liked the film series well enough to use it for many years to supplement textbooks assigned in a beginning level American history course at Hendrix College. Like *Six Men*, *America* will be used only in a limited way to identify figures in American history who, because of the manner in which Cooke treats them, seem to provide insights about Cooke's would-be progressivism, the second term he uses but fails to define. As shown above, Bobby Jones, not the usual type of figure considered in American history books, tells us much about the nature of Cooke's conservatism, his first and more important term.

## Cooke's Progressivism: The Sense of 'Noblesse Oblige'

If Cooke's basic conservatism is best seen in his admiration of the ideal gentleman, the exact nature of his would-be progressivism is much more difficult to find. Of the galaxy of the usual twentieth-century American progressive heroes – people like Theodore Roosevelt, Woodrow Wilson, Franklin Roosevelt, Harry Truman, and Lyndon Johnson – only the two Roosevelts are reviewed at length in *America* with Truman and Johnson being virtually ignored altogether and Wilson considered mainly as a foreign policy leader of extreme moral earnestness.

Both Roosevelts are given mixed reviews. With regard to Theodore, Cooke argues that he had to be 'liberated' from his 'imperial instincts' before his other more 'splendid side' emerged. This happened when he became 'the first influential man of his time to see clearly that the United States was no longer a rural nation but an industrial giant run amok,' controlled by powerful private economic interests. When he became President, Roosevelt was 'determined, if not to break them, to bring them under the control of Congress.' [27]

However, Cooke sees that Roosevelt's greatest public service through-out his career was to the immigrant, for 'his bravest mission was to try and see, through social legislation and new resources of education, that the immigrants should no longer be looked on as nationally identifiable pools of cheap labor.' Roosevelt had a double aim: 'to liberate the immigrant from his daily grind in a polyglot compound, and to set him free from the hampering liabilities of his native tongue.' [28] While both of these objectives took many years after Roosevelt had left office to be realized, he moved the country in the right direction.

Cooke also sees two sides to Franklin, though he seems to take issue more with how FDR did things than with what he did. Starting with the achievements of the New Deal, Cooke compiles a long list of successes he attributes to Roosevelt's leadership and notes that 'like no President since Wilson' he used the 'Presidency as the spokesman of the people's needs.' [29] Although Roosevelt saved the capitalist system, a worthy goal and achievement according to Cooke, he did it in ways

Cooke finds less than desirable. For he was essentially a benevolent dictator, who even experimented with National Socialism during his first two years in office and who ultimately saved the system by 'deliberately forgetting to balance the books by transferring the gorgeous resources of credit from the bankers to the government.' He was 'an artful manipulator of the good, the bad, and the bewildered in between.'[30]

It is interesting to note that Cooke gives the last word on FDR to journalist Westbrook Pegler who, as Cooke concedes, 'loathed Roosevelt.' In Pegler's epitaph of FDR, which Cooke describes as the 'best' he read, Pegler argues that although the President was 'ornery, tricky, stubborn, wayward' and so on, he was probably needed because a 'complacent upper class' was not living up to its responsibilities to those unable to help themselves.[31]

What about the nature of the progressivism of the two Roosevelts that Cooke admires? What strikes me in both presentations is Cooke's emphasis on two upper-class men of an old American family who, even with their faults, had a sense of noblesse oblige. In Theodore's case, it was an obligation to assist the many millions of recent immigrants to become integrated as first-class citizens into American society, and in Franklin's case, it was an obligation to assist many more millions of ordinary Americans who could not help themselves and who were not being helped by 'a complacent upper class,' the class FDR came from. As we have seen above, Cooke's political friend Adlai Stevenson was described as well as having a strong sense of noblesse oblige to the less fortunate.

If we go back further in time to consider several other figures usually associated with progressive ideas we find some surprises in Cooke's characterizations. Consider Thomas Jefferson and Andrew Jackson, for example, two favorites among American liberals. Since Cooke treats Jackson in a cursory manner, he will be considered first. Instead of viewing Jackson as the hero of the common man in the 1830s, Cooke merely sees him as a President who pushed through Congress a bill ordering all Indian tribes to move west of the Mississippi River and who subsequently defied a Supreme Court order preventing such removal. Cooke sees this as 'surely one of the most shameless and arbitrary acts of an American President.'[32]

Cooke considers Jefferson at length but has mixed feelings about him. On the positive side, he praises Jefferson for writing the Declaration of Independence; for nagging 'every influential man he knew' for the Bill of Rights; for his political skills in acquiring the Louisiana Territory; and for his great intellect, curiosity, and inventiveness.[33]

Yet, on the other hand, Cooke sees Jefferson as essentially a romantic democrat, a utopian who seemed to retreat to the countryside from the real world of conflict. Jefferson, according to Cooke, seems to have had none of Madison's fear for the tyranny of majority opinion. Let everything come out, and the judgment of the common people will be sound. Over and over again, he writes of the essential 'goodness and wisdom' of the common people. It forces us to wonder how many common people he knew.[34]

Cooke concludes that until his old age when he sensed the coming of the Civil War, Jefferson

pictured life in America as a long pastoral symphony, a continuing Utopia of chivalrous and learned rulers walking hand in hand with good, honest farmers in – a favorite phrase – 'perfect harmony.'[35]

As perhaps suggested above, Cooke sees Madison as the most politically sensible of the Founding Fathers because he was able to strike the appropriate balance between the extreme positions at the Constitutional Convention as represented by Hamilton, 'the supreme spokesman of the aristocratic principle,' and George Mason, 'an uncompromising democrat.'[36]

But Cooke's real favorite among the Founding Fathers is Benjamin Franklin. Although praised politically as 'the Patriarch of the Revolution,' Franklin stands out as a progressive for Cooke by being 'the fine flower of that "ingenious and useful learning" that so impressed foreigners visiting the Middle Colonies.'[37] After listing many of his inventions and other achievements that assisted mankind, Cooke states that

the mold has been lost of this American eighteenth-century archetype, the domesticated and urbane Leonardo da Vinci who finds no knowledge odd, the very opposite of a highbrow or trendy intellectual, for he was a man with the widest range of interests who had no preconceived hierarchy of their relative value.[38]

Cooke concludes that

what makes him, after two centuries, not merely impressive but lovable is his absolute lack of arrogance and the steady goodness of his belief that in helping to create the American Republic he was founding a truer order of society.[39]

This 'service above self' to mankind is a theme of Cooke's progressivism that he returns to in his consideration of Thomas Edison, clearly the heir to the Franklin tradition. For Cooke Edison was a genius who put to himself 'the right question at the right time: how to make a scientific principle workable as a universal convenience.' Using this as his guide, Edison, along with his staff, produced a long list of inventions and discoveries, involving over a thousand patents, that improved the lives of countless millions at a low cost. Cooke notes that an attractive thing about him was that, 'until he was convinced of success beyond all reasonable, or unreasonable doubt, he assumed total responsibility for his inventions.' Equally attractive was that he rarely 'paused to wallow in the oceans of flattery that surrounded him.'[40]

In concluding this consideration of Cooke's progressive figures, mention will be made of two others that one would not think about in connection with progressive ideas: John D. Rockefeller and Andrew Carnegie. Usually, of course, these so-called Robber Barons are viewed as the very antithesis of all things progressive. Yet, while recognizing that side of these men, Cooke refuses to portray them in such narrow terms. These men were neither evil in general nor motivated only by extreme greed in particular. For Cooke, they, especially Carnegie, exemplify 'a truth about American money men that many earnest people fail to grasp – which is that the chase and the kill are as much fun as the prize, which you then proceed to give away.' In short, while these men were ruthless in their business dealings which enabled them to acquire great fortunes, they felt responsibility to the community and therefore gave back to society a large part of their wealth often, as in the case of Rockefeller, with very few or no strings attached.[41]

What stands out for me in these examples is Cooke's liking of noblesse oblige – defined broadly. In his doing this, I am reminded of something said by one of my British history professors at St Andrews University many years ago when he was asked to identify the historical periods of Britain's greatness. Instead of mentioning specific dates, he replied that Britain was at her best whenever the advantaged members of society understood and acted upon their obligations to the disadvantaged. In other words, she was great when the people with resources, talents, abilities, intelligence, and other assets used them for the benefit of the less fortunate in Britain. It seems to me that this is essentially the point Cooke is making about the Americans considered above: they were great progressive men – and made America great – because they acted upon their obligations.

## *Conclusion*

I have tried to identify the essence of Alistair Cooke's value system by considering his American heroes and friends – at least those people to whom he has given high praise in two of his important books. Using his terms – conservativism and progressivism – I have concluded that these broad terms can be defined in view of their use by Cooke as focusing on the qualities of the true gentleman and the notion of noblesse oblige broadly defined.

Both of these concepts – gentlemanly qualities and noblesse oblige – have been, of course, long associated with Britain and her important institutions, especially those engaged in education, such as the quality public schools and universities. For me these concepts, as well as many of these institutions, embody the Helper values mentioned previously and therefore are part of my definition of the special relationship. Hence, in emphasizing them in his writings and films, Cooke has been an important instrument in promoting the special relationship between Britain and the United States. Obviously, this is not to suggest that these are the only factors of the relationship presented in Cooke's works; on the contrary, there are many other aspects to be found in his journalism and his BBC broadcasts, but it would take a long book rather than a short chapter to do them justice. Yet, I do believe that Cooke's contribution to my search centers on these two concepts.

One last point: the fact that both of these concepts are not totally missing in American culture – recessive rather than dominant traits, so to speak – suggests to me that they were once present to a greater degree but were rejected when Britannia was in the late eighteenth century. Perhaps, therefore, the strengthening of the special relationship through contact with important British institutions, such as families and universities, will strengthen them as well.

# *Notes*

1. David Ayerst, *The Manchester Guardian: Biography of a Newspaper* (Ithaca, New York: Cornell University Press, 1971), 624–5.
2. Ibid., 621.
3. Ibid.
4. Ibid., 619.
5. George Melly, Introduction to *The Bedside Guardian 34* edited by W. L. Webb (London: Collins, 1985), 6.
6. John Fowles, Introduction to *The Bedside Guardian 32* edited by W. L. Webb (London: Collins, 1983), 7.
7. Ayerst, 207.
8. Alistair Cooke, *America* (New York: Alfred A. Knopf, 1973), 9.
9. Ibid., 9, 12.
10. Ibid., 8.
11. James Q. Wilson, *The Amateur Democrat: Club Politics in Three Cities* (Chicago: The University of Chicago Press, 1967), 3.
12. Ibid., 8.
13. 'Adlai Stevenson,' *Manchester Guardian Weekly*, 22 July 1965, 8.
14. Ibid.
15. Alistair Cooke, *Six Men* (Boston: G. K. Hall and Company, 1978), 7.
16. Ibid., 289.
17. Ibid., 253–4.
18. Ibid., 264.
19. Ibid., 12.

20. Ibid., 170–1.
21. Ibid., 165, 171, 175, 176.
22. Ibid., 384.
23. Ibid., 385–6.
24. Ibid., 391.
25. *America*, 322.
26. Ibid., 322–3.
27. Ibid., 299.
28. Ibid.
29. Ibid., 331.
30. Ibid., 331–2.
31. Ibid., 332.
32. Ibid., 170.
33. Ibid., 147.
34. Ibid., 153.
35. Ibid.
36. Ibid., 137, 140.
37. Ibid., 116–17.
38. Ibid., 120.
39. Ibid.
40. Ibid., 256.
41. Ibid., 262.

# Chapter V

# The Mother of Parliaments

When in that House M.P.'s divide,
If they've a brain and cerebellum, too,
They've got to leave that brain outside,
And vote just as their leaders tell 'em to.
But then the prospect of a lot
Of dull M.P.'s in close proximity,
All thinking for themselves, is what
No man can face with equanimity.

Private Willis while on guard
outside Parliament in Gilbert
and Sullivan's *Iolanthe*

*P*rivate Willis' song, one of my favorites, sums up very well in comic verse the essential difference between the British Parliament and the American Congress. The first four lines tell us what happens in Parliament while the last four, in describing the opposite, are suggestive of what occurs in Congress – with a nod to special interests, of course. Hence though much has been written in academic literature about Congress being an offspring of Parliament, clearly the 'son' has shown his rebelliousness vis-à-vis his 'mother.' As a political scientist, I am perhaps struck by this paradox more than most because of my exposure to the bias among many American colleagues towards the British parliamentary system as opposed to the American presidential system. Thus, while I am strongly disposed to favor the former, I hope readers of this chapter will agree at least that the latter can learn much from the former. My thesis is that although America should not adopt the British system as such, it should strengthen its very weak political parties through legislative action as Britain has done.

In my search for the special relationship in British political and governmental institutions, I am obliged, then, to concede my strong bias and to inform readers of its sources and nature. Basically my bias resulted from the manner in which I had been socialized by my mentors. While individual situations differ of course, in my own case the ideas of two leaders of the profession, one from the past and the other a contemporary, were important. They are Woodrow Wilson and James MacGregor Burns whose influential ideas must be outlined for an understanding of the bias I brought to my search.

## Woodrow Wilson

Perhaps most people think of Wilson only as President of the United States rather than as a professor at Princeton University and elsewhere – that is, a practitioner rather than a theorizer. Wilson was of course both and both roles are important because he was given an opportunity denied to most individuals: the chance to try out his own, personal ideas in practice. It should be stressed at the outset, however, that many of his ideas were really not his own but had British sources.

Thus, while Wilson made a significant mark as a scholar – he was elected by his peers President of both the American Political Science Association and the American Historical Association, for example – he was not a great original thinker but rather a forceful writer and speaker of ideas borrowed from others. It is perhaps significant to recall that Wilson started out as a lawyer with the intent of having a political career in order to implement important public policies. In other words, he did not see himself as a detached ivory tower philosopher but as a deeply involved mover of mankind. In fact he once said that he found academic research a tedious occupation.

As a great admirer of many things British, especially the ideas of political philosopher Edmund Burke and the policies of political practitioners William Gladstone and John Bright, Wilson was probably influenced most of all during the early part of his academic career by another Briton, Walter Bagehot, long-time editor of the well-known and influential magazine, *The Economist*. As Arthur Link, the leading Wilson scholar, has said, it was reading Bagehot's *English Constitution* that inspired Wilson's 'whole study' of American government which became the focus of his academic endeavors. Moreover, Wilson's first of his two most important books for me, *Congressional Government*, was 'deliberately modeled' after Bagehot's study – in fact, 'almost a replica.'

Hence, in analyzing and comparing the British and American political systems of their times, the two authors agreed that British political practice was far superior to American practice.[1]

What is Bagehot's central argument that Wilson finds so compelling? Basically, it is that the British system works so well, unlike the American government, because of a fusion rather than a separation of powers in the form of cabinet government. Thus, instead. of accepting the traditional analysis of the British system stressing that power is divided among Crown, Commons, and Lords, Bagehot draws a new dividing line between the 'dignified' element of the government (the parliamentary monarchy and its trappings) and the 'effective' element (the functioning cabinet). The first is the ceremonial side or what can be called political theater which includes not only coronations but also such things as elections and orations.[2] This is the 'glue' that helps to hold the State together.

On the other hand, the 'effective' element of the constitution is lodged in the cabinet which is, in Bagehot's famous words,

> a board of control chosen by the legislature ... to rule the nation ...,
> a combining committee – a *hyphen* which joins, a *buckle* which
> fastens, the legislative part of the State to the executive part of the
> State.[3]

Hence, it is the fusion of legislative and executive powers in this way rather than their separation that produces effective government.[4]

Moreover, the prime minister who heads the cabinet is the leader of his party, and thus he and his cabinet not only lead the House of Commons but they are also the spokesmen of the party in power. The result is effective party government and party responsibility, the desired end in a democratic society.[5]

By comparison, Bagehot finds the American system too rigid: it is cramped by federalism which creates a perennial centrifugal force and by the separation of powers at the national level which results in constant deadlock. The only merit he sees in the American system is its elective chief executive which Britain also has in its prime minister.[6]

While it is evident that Wilson accepted all of these as well as other fundamental premises of Bagehot and made them his own in *Congressional Government*, he goes beyond his mentor in advocating the adoption of cabinet government in the United States. However, according to Link, long before Wilson began to write in the post-Civil War period there had been in the public press much discussion of the decline of leadership in government and especially of the necessity for responsible party leadership. In fact, reform plans for the adoption of cabinet government in this country had been widely circulated before Wilson published his ideas.[7] So again, Wilson borrowed the thoughts of others.

Nevertheless, *Congressional Government* was a great success when it appeared in print in 1885 and helped to build Wilson's reputation as a rising American scholar. He went on to become a very prolific academic writer – he published nine volumes and thirty-five articles between 1893 and 1902, for example – though, according to Link, the more books Wilson wrote, the more his scholarship deteriorated.[8] Therefore, today, when we look back from our perspective to assess

Wilson's contributions to scholarship, we see very little in the way of original thought but are struck most of all by the evolution of Wilson's thinking from young scholar to budding presidential candidate. As Link observes, it is a futile attempt to try to find consistency in Wilson's thought over the years because there are too many incongruities and too many contradictions. Changing circumstances over time seem to be the key to his thought.[9]

What is most striking to me – and perhaps to most others significantly influenced by Wilson's scholarship – is the contrast between the ideas he presents in *Congressional Government,* his first book, and *Constitutional Government in the United States* which appears twenty-three years later in 1908 just before he embarks on his political career. What one sees is a shift from pessimism to optimism about the prospects for effective government under the current American system without the adoption of cabinet government. Why? For Wilson, it is now the man rather than the system that counts. In other words, while Wilson laments in 1885 the weakening effects on the presidency of the separation of powers, the committee system in Congress, and the nomination of presidential candidates by party convention, by 1908 he is enthusiastic about the prospects of a strong man being capable of acting as a strong President and about such an executive being not doomed to ineffectiveness by the separation of powers, other limits of the constitutional system or the political party structure.[10] No doubt recent Presidencies, but especially the one of Theodore Roosevelt, prompted Wilson's change of mind.[11]

Examples of Wilson's own words from *Constitutional Government* capture well his new optimism about the role of strong Presidents.

Some of our Presidents have deliberately held themselves off from using the full power they might legitimately have used ... They have held the strict literary theory of the Constitution, the Whig theory, the Newtonian theory ... But the makers of the Constitution were not enacting Whig theory ... They were statesmen ... and their laws are sufficient to keep us to the paths they set us upon. The President is at liberty, both in law and conscience, to be as big a man as he can. His capacity will set the limit; and if Congress be overborne by him, it will be no fault of the makers of the Constitution – it will be from no lack of constitutional powers on its part, but only because the President has the nation behind him, and Congress has not.[12]

Much of Wilson's optimism stems from his view of the President as the one true leader of the nation, especially the leader of public opinion. Elsewhere in the book he says this about the President:

His is the only national voice in affairs. Let him once win the admiration and confidence of the country, and no other single force can withstand him, no combination of forces will easily overpower him. His position takes the imagination of the country ... A President whom it trusts can not only lead it but form it to his own views.

The President may also, if he will, stand within the party counsels and use the advantage of his power and personal force to control its actual programs. He may be both the leader of his party and the leader of the nation, or he may be one or the other. If he lead the nation, his party can hardly resist him. His office is anything he has the sagacity and force to make it.[13]

Reflecting on these powerful words as well as others like them in *Constitutional Government*, James MacGregor Burns observes that 'it is given to few men to portray political roles as evocatively and to perform those roles as brilliantly as it was to Woodrow Wilson.'[14]

Thus, in putting his ideas into operation, it can be said of Wilson, as Earl Latham does, that he established the style for the modern Presidency which subsequent Presidents have regarded as the model for strong leadership. He not only continued to enact the various roles of the past – those of party leader and public opinion – but he also developed new ones for the modern world: the President as chief legislator and diplomat, the planner of the economy, and the world leader for peace.[15] While Wilson pursued these roles throughout his Presidency, his greatest successes came during his first term (1913–1917) which Presidential scholar Clinton Rossiter describes as the time when the 'American Presidency and with it our whole system of government, reached its highest peak of democracy, efficiency, and morality.'[16]

Although Wilson's successes resulted from many factors, which countless historians have documented over the years, Arthur Link gives much of the credit to Wilson's strong belief in party government which captured his enthusiasm after reading Bagehot many years before. According to Link, one of Wilson's major decisions early on was to work through and with his party in Congress, rather than to govern by a coalition of progressives across party lines. Moreover, he saw himself as the responsible leader of his party, as the only leader who could speak for it and the country. Therefore, he formulated a complete legislative program and worked closely with fellow Democratics, especially committee chairmen, in Congress to give it substance and to achieve success.[17]

For those of us desiring to enter the political science profession as students of American government but especially the Presidency, Wilson served first as model and then as mentor. As we studied our academic materials, Wilson in the White House provided the textbook example of how the modern Presidency should work. Later, as we read Wilson's own scholarly works, we found in those primary sources the theoretical grounding for his actions. It is often said that nothing succeeds quite like success, and hence young graduate students like myself became convinced – socialized, if you will – that Wilson had proven his theories in practice.

Yet history also shows that Wilson had his failures. In fact, as James MacGregor Burns observes, Wilson is remembered as much for his 'magnificent failures' as for his political feats.[18] Among them, the defeat by the Senate of the Treaty of Versailles, which included provisions for the League of Nations, was his main one. However, for me, a student trained in international relations immediately after World War II, Wilson, the pioneer in collective security, was not seen as a failure but as being right. It was the Senate which seemed to play partisan politics with world peace that failed, and it not only failed the American people but the world as well. The horrors of World War II provided ample evidence. Initially, then, Wilson's status with me was enhanced rather than diminished.

However, other scholars, especially those of the so-called Realist School of international politics, who were very critical of Wilson's handling of foreign affairs, soon educated me in their direction. About the same time, I also began to read the works of Professor James MacGregor Burns, a noted scholar at Williams College. Rather than focusing on foreign affairs, Burns wrote mainly about American politics and especially the Presidency. One of his books, *The Deadlock of Democracy*, made a lasting impression.

## *James MacGregor Burns*

Among other things, Burns discusses in this book some of Wilson's failures as President. Though mentioning the League in passing, Burns focuses on party leadership. While accepting Link's argument that Wilson's party leadership in Congress brought much success mainly during his first term, Burns sees ultimate failure in his inability to refashion state and local Democratic parties in his own national image. They remained disorganized and often corrupt organizations and even the national party was weaker in 1921 when Wilson left office than it had been in 1912 when he assumed control.[19]

Why did this happen? According to Burns, a main reason stemmed from Wilson's faulty grasp of the workings and limitations of the Democratic Party and his consequent failure to build strong party organization in Washington and in the field. While Wilson was excellent at giving party leadership at the very top in Congress, he failed to provide needed reorganization and realignment at the base because he had no idea how state and local politics and politicians operated. As Burns sees it, Wilson's blindness was rooted in his inability to rid himself of his youthful idea that political struggles in America could be made essentially a politics of clear party encounters and splendid parliamentary debates – his image of British politics. Too often he acted like a British prime minister leading a unified cabinet, in a setting of strong national parties, 'rather than in the Madisonian setting of disorganized parties, local politics, and federalized and divided government,' which characterized American government.[20] In short, he tried to impose his British ideal on American reality and hence ended in failure.

When Burns wrote these ideas in the late 1950s and early 1960s, they made much sense to a graduate student like myself. He seemed to be saying that while Wilson had been on the right track in dealing with immediate problems of the American system he failed to address the long-term ones, the crux of the matter. What appealed to me most of all about Burns's analysis – as hinted above with his reference to Madison – was his construction of three models of Presidential leadership which he discussed in *Deadlock* and a subsequent book, *Presidential Government*, to provide insight into what needed to be done.

Using the names of leading political figures at the Republic's beginning, Burns designates them the Madisonian, Jeffersonian and Hamiltonian models. He argues that the first of these models embraces the following four concepts: checks and balances; minority rights; anti-majoritarianism; and prudent, limited government. This model is named after James Madison, 'the father of the Constitution,' because he mainly established it in theory and in law, though John Adams, the second President, was the first to try it out in practice. It became, however, the model used by most Presidents last century and by some in this one with William Howard Taft both following and articulating in his well-known book, *Our Chief Magistrate and his Powers*, this so-called Whig Theory described by Wilson above. At the heart of this model is the notion of consensus, the deliberate building of broad agreement between the President and members of Congress before action is taken.[21]

On the other hand, the Jeffersonian model, which Burns clearly likes much better, embraces somewhat antithetical concepts: unified political system; collegial leadership; majority rule; and minority opposition. This one was indeed tried out by Thomas Jefferson during his two administrations when he presided over a strong national party – the early Democratic Party – and dominated a Democratic Congress. According to Burns, this model was 'almost revolutionary, implying government by majority rule, under strong presidential leadership, with a highly competitive two-party system and with a more popular, democratic, and egalitarian impetus than the Madisonian model.'[22] If consensus lies at the heart of the latter model, unified party leadership is at the center of the former.

Clearly, as Burns sees it, Woodrow Wilson attempted to implement this model in this century as Jefferson did in the nineteenth, but he had limited success because, as we have seen, he failed to rebuild his party at its base. More will be said about Burns's solution for this problem below.

Burns admits that his third model, the Hamiltonian, is much harder to define because at its core there lies a large element of opportunism and expediency. Indeed, this model can be and has been justified on the ground that it is flexible and resourceful enough to meet a variety of political situations. At its most limited, it could be described as Madisonianism plus a vigorous and versatile President; at the other extreme a Hamiltonian might use party machinery and serve as a national party leader, at least for a time, in much the same style as a Jeffersonian. Nevertheless, Burns believes that the Hamiltonian model also embraces four distinct concepts: heroic leadership; personal organization; expedient use of power; and disorganized opposition.[23]

Since many of us think that most Presidents today attempt to follow this model of leadership, more needs to be said about the four concepts. Heroic leadership, according to Burns, means that the President must be more than an administrative chief or party leader, for example. He must exert great leadership on behalf of the entire nation, and this might require him to ignore his party or even desert it. Indeed, heroic Presidents have some of the qualities of the hero in a modern setting: they cut an impressive figure – they are bigger than life, so to speak – before the people and the television cameras; they have style; they speak movingly and even passionately; they seem to establish a direct connection with the mass public. And if they do this well, they are invested by the press and the people with even magical qualities which make them seem superhuman.[24]

Since personal organization rather than party is important, the President depends less – and is committed less – to the party as a whole than to his personal organization built up over the years. This organization is far more centralized, disciplined, and efficient than the general party organization. It is bound directly to the leader by ties of intense personal loyalty and hope of reward. Its relation to the regular party is ambiguous and changeable; the personal organization is ascendant during presidential campaigns and moves into the White House with the President-elect. This organization usually has geographical and other highly personal ties with the President.[25] Hence, Kennedy had his Massachusetts 'Mafia,' Nixon his California 'Mafia,' and Clinton his Arkansas 'Mafia.'

The concept of expedient use of power is related to the President's lack of strong party connection. Not having such, the Hamiltonian president has no reservoir of power based in party from which to draw day to day. With none, he must therefore employ every weapon that he has to achieve the results he wants. These include his own personal reputation, his prestige, his patronage power, his political friendships, and any others he can find. He must constantly fill, draw on, and replenish his own store of political credits. He depends more on personal influence than on party influence in his dealings with others, including Congress.[26]

The last concept, disorganized opposition, is also related to weak presidential connections with party. The freedom of the President from party obligation and control gives him a latitude of political tactics and governmental decision-making that in turn complicates the role of the opposition. The 'out' party needs a clear target to shoot at but it sees only a constantly moving one. The President may even make off with some of the opposition's leadership and certainly its key issues. As a disunited opposition having lost its issues and perhaps some of its people to the President, the attacks on the President often become highly personal, questioning the character and personality of the President rather than his policies. Hence, policy alternatives are often not presented and debated and the main function of the 'loyal opposition' in a democracy is lost.[27]

As this discussion shows, the Hamiltonian model focuses on personal rather than on party leadership which characterizes the Jeffersonian model. It is the latter that appeals most to Burns and other political scientists like myself. Therefore, to understand fully why this is the case, more needs to be said about Burns's four Jeffersonian concepts. By unified political system Burns means that a united group of political leaders and government officials overcome the checks and balances of the system through party control of the executive and legislative branches – thus avoiding deadlock. This party control depends on the existence of a coherent and disciplined party that won office on a meaningful and principled party platform and hence can claim a popular mandate.[28]

Secondly, collegial leadership means that the party leader is President and governs through his party. His main responsibility in policy and programs is to the party and the majority that elected him. He is a 'team man' who governs with at least passive consent of his fellow party leaders. He is governed by party purpose and limited, as well as supported, by the other national party leaders.[29]

Thirdly, majority rule means that government acts on the basis of a mandate endorsed by a majority of voters, who have judged the competing platforms and candidates. Once granted such power, the party leaders govern subject to two basic limits: free criticism protected by constitutional safeguards; and free elections within a limited span of time.[30]

Fourthly, minority opposition means that an opposition party will maintain a vigorous and vocal opposition to the party in power. The opposition party is compelled to criticize the party in power responsibly, and with moderation, because as the alternative party it is always on the brink of gaining office and governing. To do otherwise, it would imperil its own tenure in office.[31]

Essentially, what Burns is describing with these concepts is something close to that which political scientists call the responsible party model. This model can be summarized best by a statement of its five major assumptions:

(1) that frequent elections of representatives will make them responsive to the interests of their constituencies;

(2) that these interests will be represented by means of an organizational structure centered on the member's political party;

(3) that the party will organize and promote a program in pursuance of generally stated party principles;

(4) that at election time, each party will have a record for the constituencies to judge;

(5) and that each incumbent seeking re-election will have taken positions, in the main, consistent with his party's position.

Perhaps for Burns and other political scientists like myself, the case for this model along with the notion of party government itself was made most persuasively by E. E. Schattschneider, a leading authority on political parties, in his book *Party Government* first published in 1942. Details aside, the first few sentences of this book give a sense of his argument:

> The rise of political parties is indubitably one of the principal distinguishing marks of modern government. The parties, in fact, have played a major role as *makers* of governments, more especially they have been the makers of democratic government. It should be stated flatly ... that this volume is devoted to the thesis that the political parties created democracy and that modern democracy is unthinkable save in terms of the parties.[32]

Looking round for evidence of the responsible party model in action, most of us, as Presidential scholar Louis Koenig has shown, have found it not in American party practices, but in Western European, especially British, parties. There, once British party candidates have taken office, they are committed as party members to transposing the promises of the campaign platforms into enacted public policies. Officials are 'disciplined' to act and vote in support of party commitments. Although they debate and wrangle in the privacy of the party caucus, characteristically they are united in public, including that all-important process of voting on measures in the legislature.[33] Obviously, such things rarely happen in America. Burns and I think they should.

The purpose, then, of this discussion about key ideas of my two professional mentors has been to provide an understanding of the nature and sources of the bias I brought along in my analysis of British political and governmental institutions. As my teachers through their writings, Wilson and Burns shaped my outlook very significantly, but while the former was clearly influenced by his pro-British attitudes, the latter seemed less so. In fact, my own bias is much less pro-British and much more pro-party government for the reasons given by Schattschneider. Like Koenig, I was drawn initially to Britain more because of that country's successful use of this type of government – as the best example, if you will – than because of Britain itself. Had France provided the best example, I am sure that I would have been drawn to that country instead. I imagine many other political scientists have the same view.

## The Decline of the Legislature

One other point for context needs to be mentioned before we take up a discussion of Parliament and Congress. This is the decline in the importance of legislatures which occurred at the time of the rise of political parties. No 'cause or effect' argument is being attempted here to establish a relationship.

In the eighteenth and early nineteenth centuries, legislatures were seen at the heart of national governments, especially those that aspired to be democratic, because 'the people' were best represented there. It was no accident that the Founding Fathers of the American Constitution placed the legislative article of that document first in 1787. Yet, one hundred years later legislatures throughout the world were in rather rapid decline, though Congress's started somewhat after that time.

What were the reasons for this worldwide development? Dell Hitchner and William Harbold cite two major problems leading to legislative decline: the problem of legislative power and the problem of legislative efficiency. The first of these involves the decline of legislative power itself with the increase of executive power in modern times, a well-documented development in the United States as well as in most other countries. The hugh expansion of governmental activities, both domestic and foreign, produced an inevitable extension of executive powers most often at the expense of legislative powers.[34]

In addition, legislative power and influence have also dissipated as fragmented modern legislatures, reflective of fragmented modern societies, have been unable to arrive at a consensus upon national goals and policies. Hence many issues go unresolved, or if they are it is often because they have been taken up by other branches and institutions of government such as executives and judiciaries. Moreover, if the legislature does finally act, it often does so as a result of decisions by external 'blue ribbon' commissions, committees, or other groups that recommend solutions. Hence, questions are raised about the real value of legislatures.

Further, legislative power depends as well on strong parliamentary traditions and spirit, something frequently absent in newly emerging nation-states. Thus, new legislatures often try to operate under rather chaotic internal conditions and are unable to do sp very well.

This brings us to the second major problem, that of legislative efficiency – or perhaps the lack thereof – which can and often does hamper the operation of both new and old legislatures. Many times the efficiency problem centers on the problem of adequate leadership which in the end means attaining a delicate balance between having too much – namely, a dictatorship – and having too little – namely a political vacuum. Few legislatures have been able to achieve an ideal middle ground between these extremes.

Also the efficiency problem concerns the inability of legislatures to deal effectively with the volume and complexity of today's legislation before them. Legislative procedures are commonly described as slow, cumbersome, and anachronistic, and using them legislators are asked to make decisions involving matters of utmost technicality and complexity. Clearly the results of the legislative process have often been very disappointing.

Legislative inefficiency is also seen in the general inability of legislatures to exercise well one of their auxiliary functions: the supervision of executive authority. Too often petty partisan politics rather than responsible oversight results, as many public congressional committee hearings illustrate.

And finally, there are many other aspects of legislatures that not only affect their efficiency but also their prestige – which is generally low – in the eyes of their electorates: their frequent unrepresentative characters; their solicitude for narrow, selfish interests; their unseemly propensity for maneuvering and bickering over trifles – among other factors. So the end result has been the decline worldwide of the importance of legislatures in the governing process.

## *Parliament and the Rise of Political Parties in Britain*

What strikes me most about these developments in the areas of political parties and legislatures is that the British 'Mother' of parliaments has adapted to them rather well while the American 'Son' has not. That is, as the world situation changed so dramatically between the eighteenth and twentieth centuries the British Parliament displayed many of the Helper values which enabled it to help pave the way – rather than to resist – the development of modern political parties. In particular such values as accommodation, cooperation, broadmindedness, and understanding characterized Parliament's response to the rise of political parties. On the other hand, few of these are in evidence in the Congress's or the Rebel's history during the same period.

Let's consider Parliament first. The ending of the seventeenth-century battles between the Crown and Parliament with the Glorious Revolution of 1688 established a constitutional monarchy as defined in the British Bill of Rights and the Act of Settlement. In short, Parliament rather than the Crown won the war for supremacy. As some would have it, the will of the people, as expressed through Parliament, henceforth reigned supreme.

The problem with this last statement is that at the beginning of the eighteenth century the word 'people' really meant a rather small number of Britons. While in theory Parliament represented the whole nation, in practice it actually represented few beyond a small section of the nation, namely, the landowners.[35]

Various kinds of practices, some centuries old, tended to maintain this situation even though conditions and circumstances had greatly changed. For example, county representation dating from the thirteenth century continued to require the sending to Parliament of two knights from each shire and two burgesses from each of the most prominent boroughs, no matter what the sizes of the counties or the boroughs. Worse still was the unchanged county franchise rule that permitted only every freeholder of land worth forty shillings to vote but excluded copyholders and leaseholders, no matter how valuable the copyhold or leasehold might be.[36]

Perhaps the most notorious problems occurred in many boroughs which became infamous as so-called 'Rotten Boroughs' and 'Pocket Boroughs.' Concerning the former, for example, by the beginning of the nineteenth century Old Sarum in Wiltshire had no houses and most of Old Nunwich was under the sea but yet each was still represented by two Members of Parliament who were elected by the owners of the same land holding as had always conferred the franchise upon their owners.[37]

'Pocket Boroughs' were represented by Members of Parliament nominated by the local landlord, and hence were 'in his pocket.' This was the exact reverse of an acceptable representation system because the basis for such was that a large number of persons elected one individual to represent them, but in a 'pocket borough' one man chose two to represent himself. In many cases, he was already a member of the House of Lords.[38]

At the other end of the scale, things were equally deplorable. The rapidly growing industrial towns often had little or no representation whatsoever. For example, while Manchester and Birmingham in the Midlands were computed to have about 133,000 and 85,000 inhabitants respectively, neither of them was represented directly in the House of Commons.[39]

With such conditions as these it is not surprising that pressure for change had been building for years. Yet, nothing of significance happened until the 1830s. Why? At least two factors delayed reform. First, until the late eighteenth century, land had been the chief source of national wealth and hence landowners could give a rather compelling argument that they, having the greatest stake in the nation's welfare, should control its destinies. When industrialization brought on by the Industrial Revolution changed the nature of wealth, this argument lost its persuasive power.[40]

Second, while movement for reform was in the air during the latter part of the eighteenth century, it was checked by the excesses of the French Revolution and the subsequent instability in Europe. Since conditions did not return to 'normal' there until well into the nineteenth century, gradual, systematic reform in Britain had to wait, too.[41]

Since institutions tend to resist change if such is seen as a significant loss of their power and prestige, it is rather extraordinary that Parliament's own decline as a legislature started from within that body itself with the passage of a series of Reform Acts, the first in 1832, though perhaps, as suggested below, the reformers did not intend this originally.

While the great political struggle to secure the passage of the first Reform Bill makes fascinating reading, we shall be concerned here only with its key provisions and its impact on the political system. Basically, the Bill's major clauses provided for two things: first, a redistribution of the seats in the House of Commons, and, second, a broadening of the franchise. Concerning seats, the old boroughs had to surrender 143 to the new industrial towns and to the populous counties. The change in franchise qualifications was more complex with a distinction being made between boroughs and counties. In the former a vote was given to all occupants of property worth at least ten pounds a year. In the latter it was extended now to copyholders, to leaseholders, and to other occupants of lands of at least fifty pounds annual value.[42]

While these reforms seem rather modest, their consequences, especially for the long term, were quite extraordinary. According to historian Brett, the ultimate results of the 1832 Act were 'vast beyond the calculations of anyone who witnessed its passage.' In general two things happened: the former 'aristocratic monopoly' of political power was broken permanently and the commercial elements in the towns whose new power impacted on the borough members of Parliament produced a growing appreciation for the problems and needs of the new towns.

The result was the enactment by Parliament in the years that followed of a vast amount of social and political reform legislation in such areas as education, the regulation of working conditions, and the abolition of slavery – just to name a few.[43]

But perhaps the most significant consequence for the political system, according to Hanson and Walles, was the laying of the foundation for the modern British political party organization. Prior to 1832, there existed no countrywide organization of parties or even parliamentary party organizations as known today. Up to that time parties in Parliament were essentially informal groups of like-minded men, coalitions that were constantly forming, breaking, and reforming as various issues came along. Outside Parliament candidates ran for office as individuals, not as party members.[44]

Specifically, what the 1832 Act did was to lead to the founding of registration societies or associations which were concerned with the goal of registering all potential supporters in a constituency so that they would be eligible to vote in elections. As early as 1838, Sir Robert Peel, who had recently served as a Conservative Party Prime Minister, clearly recognized from the top what was needed below when he wrote that:

> there is a perfectly new element of political power – namely the registration of votes ... That party is the strongest in point of fact which has the existing registration in its favour ... The registration will govern the disposal of offices, and determine the policy of party attacks.[45]

These registration societies were the forerunners of modern constituency party organizations which of course took many years to evolve as a result of further legislation and practice.

Yet, before the end of the nineteenth century, all the ingredients of the modern British political party system were in place: representative constituency associations with a national organization; an annual conference; a party headquarters which would become more and more powerful; an acceptance of the need for party election manifestos; and a recognition of the special role to be played by the leader of the party.[46]

As suggested above, Parliament itself continued to play a very important role in the development of Britain's political party system both before and after the turn of the twentieth century. In the spirit of the 1832 Act, additional Reform Acts – those of 1867, 1884, 1885, 1918, and 1928 – made further redistributions of seats in the House of Commons and extended step-by-step the franchise until every adult person, both male and female, could vote by the late 1920s.[47]

Each successive act, especially the earlier ones, continued to foster the creation of additional party organizational structures by the leaders in Parliament so that as the two leading parties of the nineteenth century – Liberal and Conservative – emerged they were developed from the top down in order to aid their leaders in Parliament.[48] As a former and future Prime Minister's comment, Peel's statement quoted above is indicative of this top-down approach to party organization.

On the other hand, the Labour Party, whose birth date is usually given as 1900 and which eventually replaced the Liberal Party in Britain's two-party system, grew from below after new groups of voters, mainly the working classes, were enfranchised by the later Reform Acts.[49] Hence, while the path was different for Labour, once again actions in Parliament paved the way for party development.

Perhaps one could argue that these consequences of the Reform Acts – the emergence and development of modern political parties – were really unintended results of actions taken by groups in Parliament that were merely trying to make that body more representative of the whole nation and nothing more. That is, in broadening the base of representation through legislation Parliamentary groups still intended Parliament to remain supreme no matter what new institutions should happen to emerge. Yet, as Peel's statement indicates leaders early on knew that significant political changes were occurring but still passed many more reform acts to continue the process. Whatever the case, Parliament itself was transformed into a very different institution: it ceased to be a legislature in all but a technical sense of that term.

As Hanson and Walles argue, Parliament no longer legislates but merely legitimizes party decisions taken elsewhere, that is, in the Cabinet. Hence, the primary task of the House of Commons is now generally seen to be that of maintaining the Government, composed of leading members of the majority party, in power. In commenting on the tasks of Parliament over one hundred years ago, Walter Bagehot facetiously but perhaps rather accurately suggested a possible reply a cabinet minister might give to a question concerning the chief function of Parliament: 'Parliament has maintained ME, and that was its chief duty.'[50] Maybe Gilbert and Sullivan were not too far off the mark after all in Private Willis' song!

Certainly one does not want to exaggerate what has happened, for Parliament is not merely a 'rubber stamp' as legislatures tend to be in certain non-democratic countries. For example, proposed legislation is closely examined and often hotly debated during the law-making process in Parliament. Yet the British have seemed to take rather seriously John Stuart Mill's dictum in *Representative Government* that 'a numerous assembly is as little fitted for the direct business of legislation as for that of administration.'[51]

## Congress's Failure to Develop
## America's Political Parties

On the other hand, the American Congress has clearly rejected Mill's statement. Why? What is behind Congress's reluctance to follow Parliament's path? In trying to get at the crux of the difference between British and American attitudes towards political parties and legislatures, E. E. Schattschneider focuses on the constitutions of the two countries and how they have been interpreted since their beginnings. As he sees it, the central issue in both countries has been between those who wanted to establish and perpetuate a *'lawyers' constitution'* and those who wanted to create a *'politicians' constitution'* – to use his terms. In Britain, lawyers established their constitution at the end of the Glorious Revolution, only to have a rising class of politicians assume control of government and substitute political responsibility for legal responsibility and cabinet government for a separation of powers, which gave Britain 'what is justly known as the world's foremost example of party government.'[52]

In America, on the other hand, lawyers, having copied the British model of 1688 at the Philadelphia Constitutional Convention of 1787, took control of the new government and have held it since.[53] The result has been a rigid legalistic rather than a more flexible pragmatic interpretation of the Constitution over the years, and hence little accommodation and adaptation to changing circumstances have occurred with the rise of political parties and the decline of legislatures. Certainly Congress, unlike Parliament, has shown very limited interest in trying to pave the way for political party development and has held rather tenaciously to its legislative role, though like other legislatures it has declined as well for the reasons discussed above.

Perhaps this lack of interest in Congress stems in large part from the overpowering influence of the Founding Fathers, especially George Washington and James Madison who strongly condemned the political 'factions' of their day. Living before the emergence of modern, responsible, and well-organized political parties, these men tended to view all political groupings negatively. Their attitudes, as well as their decisions at Philadelphia, have been very difficult to overcome ever since.

Since Madison gave the most powerful argument against factions, some of his ideas are worth consideration. In Number Ten of the *Federalist Papers*, Madison makes his case for the separation of powers principle in the Constitution. He justifies the use of this principle on the grounds of the supposed tendency of majorities to become tyrannical. In his argument, he outlines the origins of factions and the economic basis of politics and then contends that the rise of factions in a free system of politics is inevitable. He then demonstrates that factions are inherently oppressive and must be frustrated through a system of separation of powers if liberty is not to become self-destructive.[54]

Madison makes a second argument against factions, this time focusing on his celebrated defense of 'large republics' or the principle of federalism. Beginning with the assumption of the existence of numerous interests in a large nation-state, he posits the view that no one of them is likely to be a majority. Hence the advantage of a federal republic is that this diversity of interests in a large community – being much greater than it is in a small community – reduces the chances that a tyrannical majority, composed of a single interest or faction, will be able to oppress the whole community.[55]

Such arguments which were no doubt expressed just as forcefully at the Philadelphia Convention led to the exclusion of any specific mention of political parties in the Constitution. Nevertheless, as Schattschneider says, the Convention produced a Constitution with a 'dual attitude': it was pro-party in one sense and anti-party in another. Hence, the Founding Fathers and the authors of the Bill of Rights refused to suppress parties by destroying the fundamental liberties in which parties originate. The guarantees of civil rights established a system of party tolerance: the right to agitate and to organize.[56]

On the other hand, the Fathers also established an elaborate division and balance of powers within an intricate governmental structure designed to make parties ineffective. Clearly they hoped that the parties would lose and exhaust themselves in futile attempts to fight their way through the governmental complex that had been erected.[57]

Despite these institutional and attitudinal difficulties, political parties began to develop almost immediately after the adoption of the Constitution, and they were soon so strong that the Jeffersonian model was put into practice less than fifteen years later when Thomas Jefferson became the third President of the United States.

Yet, as we have seen, the use of this model became the exception rather than the rule as the Madisonian model was followed instead well into the twentieth century. What this suggests is that while political parties continued to be present they never became institutions of governmental importance in the British sense. Unlike British parties, America's remained weak and decentralized at the state level, having little in the way of strong organization nationally. As Karl Lamb has well said, the chief cost of American federalism is found in our party system which is actually composed of 102 parties: two permanent Democratic and Republican party organizations in each state and two such temporary party organizations at the national level. Or to put the American situation a different way: America's political parties have existed more psychologically than organizationally.[58]

Clearly any significant changes in this system would require some action by government, especially by Congress. So far little has come, though many suggestions have been offered over the years by political scientists and other scholars. In concluding *The Deadlock of Democracy* in 1963, James MacGregor Burns makes a number of proposals to bring about the use of the Jeffersonian model. In so doing he is essentially trying to strengthen the party system. His first proposal is that Congress must enable the national government to control national elections. In his reluctance to advocate major constitutional changes in part because they are so difficult to achieve, he vaguely suggests that the aim of this proposal 'could probably be realized by stringent congressional regulation of national elections administered by the states.'[59] My reaction to this is discussed below.

His other five proposals are even less far-reaching in requiring only party and minor governmental reform. They include: the need for national parties to build grass-roots memberships; the organizational merger of presidential and congressional parties; stronger party leadership in Congress; the financing of parties and their candidates on a mass, popular, and systematic basis; and the need for a clearer voice and a better organized party in opposition.[60]

Recognizing that these rather modest reforms are probably not enough to achieve his goals, Burns ultimately considers three constitutional amendments which would have to start – as most have in the past – in Congress. These are: four-year terms for Representatives in Congress to coincide with presidential terms; the repeal of the 22nd Amendment which limits Presidents to two terms; and a change in the Electoral College which would at a minimum eliminate the electors as such but retain the total number of electoral votes.[61]

Burns also mentions in passing some of the other minor suggestions that were being circulated at the time he wrote to try to solve executive-legislative deadlock and friction: question time for Cabinet members in Congress like that in Parliament; joint cabinets or councils composed of the Cabinet and Congressional leaders; and various mechanical changes in Congressional operations. In dismissing but not strongly opposing these as having little bearing on the real problems of the President and Congress, Burns ends his discussion in the same place Wilson did in 1908: the need for strong Presidential leadership.[62]

Since 1963, as we know, Congress, as well as other institutions, has failed to enact virtually all of these suggestions. Where it has tried to act, Congress has often found itself deadlocked; or even when it has succeeded, its policies have failed or only partly succeeded. One example of the latter will be briefly discussed to illustrate the nature of what I believe is the central problem that must ultimately be addressed by Congress: the failure of the Founding Fathers to give political parties a clear, specific basis in the Constitution.

Of all the proposals for reform, Congress has perhaps given most of its attention to the area of finance. One of its major laws is the Federal Election Campaign Act of 1971. Certain provisions of this far-reaching measure, along with amendments of 1974, and relevant provisions of the Revenue Act of 1971, as amended as well in 1974, were challenged in court in the now famous case *Buckley* v. *Valeo* (1976). No attempt will be made to analyze the very complicated holdings of the Supreme Court other than to note that certain First Amendment challenges in the area of expenditure limits were sustained. Some have argued that the Court has equated spending with free speech in its decision. In any event, Congress lost.

My point here is that perhaps the Supreme Court would have been more deferential to Congress's actions in this matter had there been clear authority in the Constitution for Congressional regulation and control of political parties and elections. Such specific provisions might have outweighed those of the First Amendment in the minds of a majority of justices. This can be illustrated by a parallel situation that already exists in the Constitution: the potential for conflict between the First Amendment provision for free press and the Sixth Amendment requirement for a fair trial. As we know, the Court has had to deal with cases in this area, and the specific provisions are usually seen as being of equal importance. Hence, sometimes in the interest of having a fair trial, a gag order on the press is sustained; at other times in the interest of a free press, such things are not required. In short, two sets of specific provisions produce a balancing approach on the part of the Court which might very well be absent when only one set is there.

Moreover, Congress itself should show much more interest in considering other reforms if it has clear authority in the Constitution to act. Therefore, the Constitution should be amended to give it such authority. In 1963, I was in complete agreement with the more limited approach Burns advocated, but the situation is now far different and far more critical. The major problem is of course that our political party system is now much weaker and could perhaps all but disappear in the future.

This is not just my view. In their book *American Parties in Decline*, Crotty and Jacobson, two known authorities, conclude their analysis of the American system on a very somber note. Quoting the same opening lines from Schattschneider that 'the political parties created democracy and ... modern democracy is unthinkable save in terms of parties,' they say:

> maybe so ... The contemporary era may be forced to adjust to a democratic system in which political parties no longer play a dominant role. The transformation is in progress ... A partyless era, with implications still uncertain, may be settling on us.[63]

A 'partyless era' could bring on great crises in American democracy that have been only hinted at so far. A good example is Watergate. This major problem of the 1970s can be seen as one of the negative consequences of the Hamiltonian model, which as I mentioned above has become the one used most by today's Presidents. In Watergate a President and his 'Mafia' got out of control, something that probably would not have happened with the Jeffersonian model in use. This and other developments in the 1960s and 1970s prompted historian Arthur Schlesinger to write the popular book *The Imperial Presidency* whose title says enough about the author's concerns.

Even these high profile events have not, however, been enough to stem the tide, for problems – some might call them scandals – in the Reagan and Clinton Administrations clearly demonstrate that the Hamiltonian model continues to be less than desirable in a democratic system. I continue to believe that the best alternative in the interests of democracy is the Jeffersonian model, but now we obviously have a much longer way to go to implement it than we had in 1963.

## The Special Relationship

The great political wit and sometime presidential candidate Adlai Stevenson is reported to have said that all he ever knew he learned at his mother's knee and lower joints! Applying this to Congress, it can be said that the 'son' learned too much at lower joints and too little at his mother's (Parliament's) knee. The time has come, therefore, for the Rebel to return to the Helper for another lesson in values. If any institutions in America need a strong helping hand today, our political parties stand at the top of the list, and Congress more than any other institution is situated to offer assistance. Parliament has shown the way, but certainly one is not requesting the impossible or even perhaps the undesirable from Congress: amending the Constitution to establish the parliamentary system or a modified version of a cabinet governmental system. Since last century there have been numerous suggestions of this type. Even the Committee on Political Parties of the American Political Science Association developed an ingenious plan in 1950 for adapting the British party system to the circumstances of America. All of these suggestions have been and continue to be merely academic exercises rather than realistic proposals.

Given the nature of the American system – that is, its incrementalism – little can be expected in the way of far-reaching change in the short run. We need to think in terms of what is possible during the next fifty years. Hence, we should start with something very basic and simple: a short and clear statement in the Constitution that political parties are governmental institutions that Congress has authority to control. After the adoption of this change, which I know will not be easy to achieve, it would be up to Congress to exercise that authority over many, many years in a step-by-step fashion, as Parliament did, to pave the way for stronger political parties. Thus, Congress would retain the power to back off in the event the parties were deemed to have acquired too much power at the expense of Congress or any other institution.

Such a constitutional statement would not be necessary if Americans were more politically pragmatic and less rigidly legalistic like the British. Unlike the British, Americans have a written constitution and debate on virtually every subject raised in public is ultimately defined in phrases of the Constitution. Since Tocqueville saw this practice in the 1830s, it is unlikely that it will change in the 1990s. Though the task to secure this consitutional change will be long and difficult, now is the time for a grass-roots movement to begin.

In the meantime other lessons can be learned from parliamentary practice in Britain and applied in this country without a constitutional amendment. Noted presidential scholar Louis Koenig mentions several for immediate consideration. First, Congress should institute a practice followed rather widely in all of Western Europe: free air time for presidential candidates and perhaps congressional candidates as well to assure that rivals for office enjoy a fair opportunity to be heard without the necessity of huge media expenditures where the great costs of campaigning lie today.[64]

Second, both political parties in the United States should adopt the British practice of annual conferences. Precedent was established here in 1974 when the Democratic Party began holding a 'national issues convention' midway in the presidential term.[65]

Last, and more broadly, much can be learned from a thorough study of British methods of parliamentary candidate selection and platform development, two areas of major weakness in the American political party system.[66]

Clearly it's time for the 'son' to reconnect with his 'mother.'

## Notes

1. Arthur S. Link, *Wilson: The Road to the White House* (Princeton, New Jersey: Princeton University Press, 1947), 16.

2. Max Lerner, 'Walter Bagehot,' in *International Encyclopedia of the Social Sciences*.

3. Ibid.

4. Ibid.

5. Link, 16.

6. Lerner.

7. Link, 17–18.

8. Ibid., 29–30.

9. Ibid., 31.

10. Earl Latham, 'Woodrow Wilson,' in *International Encyclopedia of the Social Sciences.*

11. Arthur S. Link, *Woodrow Wilson and the Progressive Era: 1910–1917* (New York: Harper & Row, 1954), 34.

12. Woodrow Wilson, 'Constitutional Government in the United States (1908)' in Andrew M. Scott, *Political Thought in America* (New York: Holt, Rinehart and Winston, 1959), 409.

13. Ibid., 408.

14. James MacGregor Burns, *The Deadlock of Democracy: Four Party Politics in America* (Englewood Cliffs, New Jersey: Prentice-Hall, Inc., 1963), 143.

15. Latham.

16. Clinton Rossiter, *The American Presidency* (New York: The New American Library, 1956), 77.

17. Link, *Woodrow Wilson and the Progressive Era*, 34–5.

18. Burns, 143.

19. Ibid., 143–4.

20. Ibid., 146–7.

21. James MacGregor Burns, 'Three Approaches to Presidential Leadership,' in Harry A. Bailey, Jr. (ed.), *Classics of the American Presidency* (Oak Park, Illinois: Moore Publishing Company, Inc., 1980), 66–7.

22. Ibid., 65.

23. Ibid., 68–9.

24. Ibid.

25. Ibid.

26. Ibid.

27. Ibid.

28. Ibid., 67.

29. Ibid.

30. Ibid.

31. Ibid., 68.

32. E. E. Schattschneider, .*Party Government* (New York: Rinehart & Company, Inc., 1942), 1.

33. Louis W. Koenig, *The Chief Executive*, 6th ed., (New York: Harcourt Brace, 1996), 117.

34. The discussion that follows is based on Dell G. Hitchner and William H. Harbold, *Modern Government: A Survey of Political Science* (New York: Dodd, Mead, & Company, 1963), 423–6.

35. Reed Brett, *British History 1815–1936* (London: John Murray, 1933), 22.

36. Ibid., 12.

37. Ibid., 23.

38. Ibid.

39. Ibid.

40. Ibid., 24.

41. Ibid.

42. Ibid., 27.

43. Ibid., 29.

44. A. H. Hanson and Malcolm Walles, *Governing Britain* (London: Wm. Collins Sons & Co. Ltd., 1970), 44.

45. Ibid.

46. Ibid., 46.

47. Brett, 33–5.

48. Hanson, 47.

49. Ibid., 46–47.

50. Ibid., 68.

51. Ibid.

52. Schattschneider, 10–11.

53. Ibid., 11.

54. *The Federalist* (New York: The Modern Library), 54–6.

55. Ibid., 58–60.

56. Schattschneider, 7.

57. Ibid.

58. Karl A. Lamb, *The People, Maybe*, 2nd ed., (Belmont, California: Duxbury Press, 1974), 81.

59. Burns, *Deadlock*, 330.

60. Ibid., 328–30.

61. Ibid., 330–2.

62. Ibid., 333, 337.

63. William J. Crotty and Gary C. Jacobson, *American Parties in Decline* (Boston: Little, Brown and Company, 1980), 255.

64. Koenig, 65.

65. Ibid., 145.

66. Ibid., 409.

# Chapter VI

# Family Roots in Tudor England's Kent

*Y*oung Thomas Warren of Ripple, England, stepped on American soil for the first time in 1640. Only fifteen years of age then, he was accompanied to the New World by a cousin, Captain Daniel Gookin, who had come to Virginia to help establish a commercial enterprise in the Jamestown area. Two other Warrens from Ripple, John and Edward, Thomas's uncles, also settled in Virginia at the time.

In colonial America, Thomas Warren prospered, married, and served in the Virginia House of Burgesses before his short life by our standards ended in 1669 or 1670. By that time, however, he had built what became known as the Warren House, a rather substantial structure for the early colonial period, just across the river from Jamestown. More important still, he had also started the American branch of the Thomas Warren family which eventually spread westward to Illinois where my maternal grandmother, Caroline Warren, was born over 200 years later in 1881.

Hence, for me personally, the search for the 'special relationship' with Britain had to include excursions into Kent where my ancestor Thomas Warren was born in the small village of Ripple, near Deal, in January 1625. Since I found in my search that the Warren family had been in Ripple for only a couple of generations when Thomas was born, I had to extend my inquiry beyond that place. Fortunately, one noted historian of the period gave some guidance in this quest for family roots. According to Edward Hasted, the Warrens had originally settled 'at Dover in the latter end of Henry VII's reign, where they remained till the latter end of Queen Elizabeth's reign when they removed to Ripple.'[1] As this statement, as well as previous comments, suggests, the Warrens were a family of some means and prominence in Tudor England long before Thomas and Captain Gookin sailed for Virginia to seek their fortunes in the New World.

Apparently, the first Warren of any prominence was William, Thomas's great-great-great-grandfather, whose date and place of birth during the fifteenth century are unknown but whose death at Sandwich, England, occurred in 1506. Actually, as the chart on page 120 shows, it was Dover rather than Sandwich that was important in William's life, and therefore he was buried in the Lady Chapel of St Peter's Church on the central Market Square of the former, a structure demolished centuries ago.

The chart also indicates what made William – as well as his son John and his grandson Thomas – a prominent resident of Dover and beyond. As Mayors, Deputy Mayors, Jurats, Cinque Port Brotherhood Deputies, and Members of Parliament, these three Warrens were active public officials from 1485 to perhaps 1582, a period the beginning of which started with the reign of Henry VII and extended into the reign of Elizabeth I. In other words, they were public servants during the reigns of all the Tudor kings and queens. As such, written records are much more readily available for historical study.

## *Public Offices*

Since much of what is known about these Warrens stems from their occupation of the public offices they held, something should be said about the nature of these offices in the fifteenth and sixteenth centuries. What was in place by the Tudor Period were certain government institutions that originally had grown out of customs and usages since at least Saxon times. Among them were the offices of Mayor and Jurat which had evolved over time from the Saxon Reeve, the presiding official of the old Saxon Hundred Court, and twelve of his fellow burgesses whom he had selected to assist him in administering justice. These officials became known as the Order of Magistrates. Although the Chief Magistrate of this group had his title changed several times through the years, it is recorded that the word Mayor was first used in 1257, the same year, so it is thought that the practice of his annual election by the burgesses of Dover began.[2] The fact that the offices of Mayor and Jurat evolved from judicial roots is important to keep in mind.

About one hundred years later, the Customal of Dover was drawn up to officially record for the first time these customs and usages of the town. The Customal indicated that after the new Mayor had taken his oath of office, he selected from the burgesses the twelve men to be known as Jurats to assist him in office. As years passed, it became the custom for the twelve existing Jurats to be resworn, thus giving permanence to the judicial bench. This movement to strengthen the position of the Jurats continued into the Tudor Period when the practice developed that the Mayor should always be chosen from the Bench of Jurats. As a judicial group, the Mayor and Jurats held their Court once a week on Fridays except during the month of harvest when the Court met on Sundays.[3]

| The Warrens of Dover | Years as Mayor of Dover & Deputy of Brotherhood | Years as Deputy Mayor & Deputy of Brotherhood | Years as Jurat & Deputy of Brotherhood | Years Elected Member of Parliament |
|---|---|---|---|---|
| William Warren (14??–1506) | (1493) | 1489 | 1485–1492* | 1489/1490 |
| Wife: Joane | 1494 | 1490 | 1500–1505 | |
| Child: John | | | | |
| Buried: Lady Chapel of St Peter's Church | | | | |
| John Warren (1484?–1546) | (1525) | 1528 | 1509–1521 | (1529) |
| Wife: Jane Moninges | 1526 | 1533 | 1527 | (1536) |
| Children: John, | 1536 | | 1529–1532 | (1541) |
| Elizabeth, Thomas | 1537 | | 1534 | |
| Buried: Lady Chapel | (1540) | | 1538 | |
| of St Peter's Church | | | 1540 | |
| | 1541 | | 1541–1545 | |
| Thomas Warren (1510–1591) | (1548) | 1560 | 1553 | (1555) |
| Wife: Maria Christian | 1549 | 1570 | 1555 | (1559) |
| Close of Calais | 1550 | 1571 | 1560 | (1563) |
| Child: John | (1557) | | 1562–1564 | |
| Buried: St Mary the | 1558 | | 1566–1569 | |
| Virgin Church, Ripple | (1574) | | 1572–1574 | |
| | 1575 | | 1577 | |
| | (1582) | | | |

Source: Felix Hull (ed.) *A Calendar of the White and Black Books of the Cinque Ports, 1432–1955*

Years in ( ) come from other sources but mainly: J. Bavington Jones, *Annals of Dover*

*It is assumed that William was a Jurat at this time, though the title does not begin to appear in the records until 1505.

As the years passed into the Tudor Period, the range of the Mayor's duties developed from the judicial to the executive and to the ceremonial. For example, in the Criminal Courts, he had to pass sentences, sometimes the sentence of death; and in the Hundred Court he had to adjudicate civil suits. The Mayor was also the Coroner and the Clerk of the Market, the latter office requiring him to set the prices of provisions sold. He was the Guardian of all Dover orphans, and he administered the estates of all burgesses who died intestate. The Mayor was invariably one of the Barons of the Cinque Ports who attended the Coronations of the Kings and Queens in London and down to the close of the Tudor Period he was frequently one of the Members of Parliament from Dover. Finally, if the Mayor died during his year in office, he had a public funeral, and one of the canopy cloths that had been used at the Coronation was used as a pall to cover his coffin. The dead Mayor's authority was sustained by the 'most ancient Jurat' who acted as his deputy, and he gave the charge to the new Mayor, who was elected in the church immediately after the funeral.[4]

With regard to the general business of Dover, it was transacted in Common Assembly where all Freemen had a voice. This method continued in use until October 9, 1556, when it was decided that thirty-seven Freemen should be elected from the community to form what was called the Common Council. This Council, together with the Mayor and Jurats, was authorized to transact all the business of Dover, a practice that became very controversial, as we shall see. It was also agreed that the Common Assemblies would be called to elect the Mayor annually, the Members of Parliament, the Bailiff for the Yarmouth Fishery (see below), and other officers of the Dover Corporation.[5]

For the Warrens, however, perhaps the most significant experiences they had – from an historical perspective at any rate – occurred while they were Members of Parliament from Dover. It is important to recall that Parliament evolved into a vastly different institution during the sixteenth century. According to Professor Michael A. R. Graves, Parliament was transformed from a medieval into an essentially modern institution during the Tudor Period. It was used to legitimize Tudor rule, to reject the authority of the Pope and establish the Anglican Church, and to effect a massive transfer of property from Church to Crown with substantial amounts ending up in private hands. In the process Parliament – Crown, Lords, and Commons collectively – became the sovereign authority of England, and Acts of Parliament became the supreme form of law of the land. The Commons, where the Warrens served, also achieved parity with the Lords.[6] As we shall see both John and Thomas Warren participated in some of the most important sessions of Parliament during the reigns of Henry VIII and Elizabeth I.

Actually, much of what is known about the Warrens stems from their roles as Deputies of the Cinque Ports. Historically, the name of Cinque Ports was given to a group of towns on the south-east coast of England that were associated to provide an annual service of their ships to the Crown before there was a Royal Navy. The original five towns were Hastings, Romney, Hythe, Dover and Sandwich, but more than thirty other places along the coast became joined to one or the other of these five at various times. The larger purpose of the organization was to provide defense of the coast and cross-Channel passage, but it had also a local function to maintain the common privileges and the direction of the common economic interests of the Ports. With regard to the latter, the Cinque Port organization was often seen as an experiment in regional government.[7]

While historians still disagree as to whether the Cinque Port confederation was founded before or after the Norman Conquest in 1066, there is consensus about its sudden prominence in the thirteenth century, perhaps largely because of the appearance in 1278 of its general charter from the Crown. However, the great days of the Ports lasted only into the fourteenth century, and hence the confederation was in decline during the fifteenth and sixteenth centuries when the Warrens were Deputies.[8]

Nevertheless, the organization continued to function down through the centuries. While doing so, it produced the so-called great *White* and *Black Books* of the Cinque Ports, a complete history of the meetings of the confederation from the fifteenth century onward. It is *The White Book*, 1432–1571, that provides most of the information about the Warrens.

Known collectively as the Brotherhood – apparently stemming from 'Brodhull,' an ancient popular court – the Deputies from the various ports were meeting regularly at Romney twice a year by 1432. Following a parliamentary pattern, their meetings were presided over by a Speaker, and they enjoyed a freedom from arrest not unlike that of members of Parliament. Although at no time were any of the Ports' powers formally delegated to the Brotherhood, the Deputies nevertheless spoke for the Ports as no less representative body could have done. Apparently most of the legislative powers developed by the Brotherhood were done so out of the desire of the Ports to present a common front in Parliament when issues affecting them were considered.[9]

To a great degree, however, much of the activity of the Brotherhood by the late fifteenth century centered on dispute resolution among portsmen of the towns and the towns themselves. Hence, the Brotherhood seemed to function more as a judicial court rather than as a legislature during the time the Warrens participated in its activities. Thus, like the offices of Mayor and Jurats, the judicial root is very important.

While many different disputes were recorded in *The White Book* between 1432 and 1571, no other matters were so consistently before the Brotherhood as Yarmouth affairs. Historically, the portsmen, as fishermen, were concerned with the herring and its movements. Sailing many of their boats along the Norfolk coast of eastern England, they began to claim fishing rights on the banks at the mouth of the Yar River, which later became Yarmouth. These claims eventually clashed with those of others and necessitated royal intervention. As a result of royal action, the Ports were authorized to send bailiffs to Yarmouth to administer justice in cooperation with the bailiffs of Yarmouth during the time of the Herring Fair each autumn. For the Brotherhood, the election of these bailiffs and the hearing of their reports formed a great part of the routine business of most meetings.[10]

Two other points about the minutes of these meetings should be mentioned. While the average attendance of Deputies at meetings in the late fifteenth century was about thirty-five, as many as fifty-two came to a meeting half a century later. Finding the latter figure too high, the Brotherhood limited attendance to seven persons from each town in 1572.[11]

Although originally the minutes merely recorded the names of Deputies from each Port and nothing more, by the early years of the sixteenth century their titles as municipal officers began to appear as well. Hence, William Warren of Dover is identified as a Jurat at the April 1505 meeting of the Brotherhood.[12]

## Law and The Chain of Being: Context for the Warrens' Lives

Even before closely considering these three generations of Warrens, one is immediately struck by two facts. The first, as suggested above, is the almost unbroken continuity – over ninety years – of their involvement in public affairs at the local, regional and national levels. From our American perspective in the late twentieth century, such continuity of generational participation in public service seems very extraordinary indeed. The second fact is the obvious commitment of these Warrens to the notion of the rule of law as the source of community order. Since this was apparently a major issue of the time, a brief consideration of this common Tudor concern should provide some additional insights for our analysis of the Warrens.

One of the important studies of the nature of the Tudor Period is the brilliant little book titled *The Elizabethan World Picture* by the late E. M. W. Tillyard. In it Tillyard argues that the world view of the late sixteenth-century English 'was ruled by a general conception of order.' While accepting Shakespeare's version of order as being representative of the age, he chooses instead another writer of the time, Richard Hooker, to help define the essence of this term's meaning for the Elizabethans. According to Tillyard, when Hooker speaks of order in his *Laws of Ecclesiastical Polity*, he is really talking about law – that is, 'law in its general sense' – which produces harmony in the world. Without engaging in a long discussion here, perhaps Hooker's own summary of his first book illustrates how he relates these concepts. It is important to note that Hooker personifies law as a woman in this passage:

Wherefore that here we may briefly end: of law there can be no less acknowledged than that her seat is the bosom of God, her voice the harmony of the world: all things in heaven and earth do her homage, the very least as feeling her care and the greatest not exempted from her power; both angels and men and creatures of what condition soever, though each in differing sort and manner yet all with uniform consent, admiring her as the mother of their peace and joy.[13]

With this emphasis on law, order and harmony by Hooker and other Elizabethans, Tillyard sees in their writings a traditional way of describing the world order. It is hinted at by Shakespeare in Ulysses' speech when he calls 'degree' the 'ladder to all high designs,' and it is named by Pope in his *Essay On Man* as 'the vast chain of being.' According to Tillyard,

This metaphor served to express the unimaginable plenitude of God's creation, its unfaltering order, and its ultimate unity. The chain stretched from the foot of God's throne to the meanest of inanimate objects. Every speck of creation was a link in the chain, and every link except those at the two extremities was simultaneously bigger and smaller than another: there could be no gap.[14]

Although this metaphor was very important to the Elizabethans, its origin was quite old, and its use extended beyond their time. Having its beginning with Plato, the metaphor was developed by Aristotle, was spread by the Neo-Platonists, and from the Middle Ages to the eighteenth century was an accepted commonplace when finally deemed unacceptable during the 1700s and beyond by many.[15] Yet the idea of connecting links between people – as well as things – in space and over time was not lost and has been found since in such writers as Edmund Burke, Alexis de Tocqueville, and some modern conservatives.

The metaphor is also seen in American law today. A leading American professor of law has done much to revive its use in his field. In a talk titled 'The New Great Chain of Being in the Law,' Professor Stephen B. Presser argues that growing evidence indicates that a new model for American law is emerging. Unlike the old 'economic legal man' model with its preoccupation with the individual and his confrontational controversies with others, the new 'philosophic legal man and woman model' is concerned with seeking broad community consensus based on moral or even religious values and with working out solutions that lead legal actors to reach accommodation in the interests of all. Among the many hopeful signs of the movement towards this 'organic model' or 'New Great Chain of Legal Being' is, Presser believes, the increasing numbers of women in the legal profession who bring 'a more feminine non-aggressive style of lawyering' which stresses accommodation and not confrontation.[16] Presser's emphasis on the law as an instrument of accommodation in the interests of community order, harmony and unity certainly harks back to the Elizabethan world picture. In stressing accommodation, he also sees law as embodying many of the Helper values discussed in Chapter I.

Perhaps this brief sketch down to our times – also a period of rapid and pervasive change – indicates something about the nature of the appeal of law and the chain of being metaphor to the Tudors. For in a period of great religious upheaval, Copernican astronomy, and rising commercialism – among other factors – the old medieval world of the recent past was breaking down. But according to Tillyard, the general medieval world picture survived in outline form into the Elizabethan Age, and the greatness of the Age was that it was able to accommodate 'much of the new without bursting the noble form of the old order' as manifested in the importance of law and the chain of being.[17]

Much of the following discussion, then, will attempt to show that the Warrens were very representative of the Tudor Age both in their rise to new middle-class status as commercialism became important and in their commitment to the old notions of law as the chain of being that holds the community together.

## *William Warren*

Here lyeth buried the body of Thomas Warren sonne of John Warren Esquire, who was sonne of William Warren Esquire sometymes chief customer of Sandwich Dover & the members therof said Thomas died ye XXIIIIth day of April AD 1591 being then of LXXX years.[18]

This inscription on a brass plate, now mounted on a wooden plaque and hanging on the south wall of the Church of St Mary the Virgin, in Ripple, England, is indicative of how little is known even by his grandson's family of William Warren's background. The brass, which was apparently moved to the wall from Thomas's tomb beneath the nave aisle of the church in 1861, was probably inscribed during the latter part of the sixteenth or the early part of the seventeenth centuries. However, even Thomas himself, when asked in the 1570s to provide information about his grandfather for *The Visitation of Kent*, said merely, 'William Warren of Dover.'[19]

Other sources from the period reflect the problem. For example, William Lambarde, in his now famous work of 1570, was unable to say more than to record Thomas's name from the *Visitation*.[20] And Jones in his *Annals of Dover* based on that town's records says only that Mayor William Warren of 1493 'is not otherwise mentioned.'[21]

Therefore, one can do little more than speculate about William's background. What seems most likely to have occurred is that he started at the bottom of customs and worked his way up to the level of Chief Customs Officer of Sandwich and Dover, an important position of the Cinque Ports. Having done so, he was then chosen for the local, regional and national offices described above during the latter part of his life. During his lifetime, then, he laid the foundation for the rise of the Warren family to prominence in Dover and Ripple.

There are, however, a few additional pieces of evidence to suggest that William was indeed a man of some means in his later life. It is recorded that William, who was buried in the Chapel of St Peter's Church 'near the image of the Virgin Mary,' gave 'twenty pounds towards repairing the lead on the roof' of the church.[22] At the turn of the sixteenth century such a sum of money was a rather substantial amount to give.

William is also mentioned by Charles Haines in his book on Dover Priory as having given a copy of a valuable book, *Glose super Psalterio*, 'by Richard Rolle or Hampole, the Yorkshire hermit and saint,' to the Dover library after 1493. The book eventually became the property of Corpus Christi Library in Cambridge.[23]

But perhaps the most important evidence comes from William Warren's will. According to one source, he

> left all of his 'houses and lands as well within the Towne, Port, & Libertie of Dover as within the Shyre of Kent, and alsoe ... lying in the Lordship of Marke & within the Marches of Calaye, to his wife, Joane, for life; with reversion to his son, John, in tail general.'[24]

As indicated above, William's name appears initially in the records of the Cinque Ports in 1485, the first year of Henry VII's reign which ended the so-called 'Wars of the Roses' (1455–1485). Although historians, such as Brett, see this protracted conflict as being 'only a family rivalry' with little impact on the general population of England, Henry felt it was necessary to institute a period of law and order after so many years of instability at the top. According to Brett, the people strongly agreed because although they had formerly looked 'to the barons to secure justice against a tyrannical king,' they now 'looked for a king to secure peace against disorderly barons' who had been largely responsible for the war. What this meant was that the power of the Crown was increased at the expense of Parliament where the barons were represented.[25]

Therefore, when William Warren entered the House of Commons in the early 1490s, Parliament was quite weak. Henry VII felt compelled to call only a few Parliaments – merely seven – and they enacted only 192 laws during his entire reign from 1485 to 1509.[26] In addition few of these laws can be considered as being landmark or even important in nature historically. By and large they were concerned with a wide range of minor commercial matters leading Graves to conclude that 'every aspect of England's economy was grist to the parliamentary mills', and therefore the catalogue of acts was 'seemingly endless.'[27] On the other hand, perhaps for members of the rising middle class like William Warren these matters were of considerable interest.

Moreover, this relatively inactive Parliament – its last session occurred in 1504, five years before the end of the reign – presented little opportunity for William and others in the Commons to strengthen it at the expense of the Lords, something that occurred later. At the end of the fifteenth century differences in representation were not as yet important. For although the Commons was much larger – about 300 to 90 – and chosen differently than the Lords, the two houses did not as yet express the different and even competing interests of two separate social groups but rather common concerns and priorities of the peerage and the greater gentry. However, clearly the Commons was seen at the time as the inferior body, for the Lords met in the Palace of Westminster while the Commons had to conduct their sessions outside the palace, using the chapter house or the refectory of Westminster Abbey. In addition, unlike the Lords, the proceedings of the Commons in these places were not strictly proceedings in Parliament. The Commons appeared only at the opening ceremony to hear the business of the Parliament explained by the Chancellor, to present their Speaker – their channel of communication with the King – and, at the close, to announce the decisions they had made.[28] So, no doubt William Warren's brief experience in Parliament was rather unsatisfactory – certainly far less exciting than his son and grandson would know years later – but clearly he paved the way for their service during the following century.

With Henry VII's interest in law and order and the consolidation of his power, the monarch apparently devoted little attention to the Cinque Ports in general and Dover in particular. According to Jones, Henry had little to do with Dover beyond giving a modest sum of money to encourage the building of a new harbor.[29] Of course like previous monarchs since the thirteenth century, Henry was bound by the provisions of the general charter of 1278 with all the Ports. While such charters containing privileges were common among many towns of England, this charter with the Ports had three unique clauses, two of which have been alluded to before. One clause noted that the liberties granted to the Ports were in recognition of past service and in view of a definite quota of ships and sailors provided for the King's use annually. A second clause dealt with the Ports rights at Yarmouth. And the last clause confirmed the grant of 'honours at court' which referred to the right of the Barons of the Ports to carry a canopy over the King at his Coronation.[30]

While nothing in the minutes of the Brotherhood meetings indicates the names of the 'Barons' who served at Henry VII's Coronation in London, it is assumed that William Warren, as one just becoming known and active in Dover in 1485, was not one of them. This is important to note because as we shall see both John, William's son, and Thomas, his grandson, carried the canopies for Henry VIII, Henry VII's son, and Elizabeth I, his granddaughter, respectively.

If William Warren, unlike his son and grandson, never accompanied English royalty through the streets of London at Coronation time, perhaps his royal connection was somewhat different in nature. As an important customs official of two Cinque Ports, William undoubtedly had frequent contact with the Wardens of those Ports who had royal ties. Since the Warden was still a rather important official of the Ports at the turn of the sixteenth century, something must be said about the nature of this office.

By the end of the fourteenth century, the Warden had become the chief officer of the Ports. His office was designed to satisfy the needs of both King and Portsmen. For the Crown, the Warden was a channel of communication with the Ports and a means to integrate them into the nation as a whole. For the Portsmen, he made possible the joint administration of the Ports and served as a symbol of unity among them. Although the Warden received his commission from the King, he took his oath of office before representatives of the Ports to uphold their liberties for them.[31]

As the Cinque Ports declined in importance over the years, a curious thing happened to the office of Warden: its prestige was enhanced by the appointment of some noteworthy figures, usually from the aristocracy, such as the Earls of Arundel and Warwick. Apparently the Portsmen approved of this because they felt that the prestige of their officers might secure them the privileges they desired from the Crown and elsewhere. So they undoubtedly rejoiced in 1493 when Henry VII appointed his son, Prince Henry, Duke of York and later to become Henry VIII, Warden of the Cinque Ports.[32]

Of course one of the amusing aspects of this appointment is that little Prince Henry, at two years of age, was barely out of his infancy! However, apparently most of the duties of Warden were fulfilled by Sir Edward Poynings, as Deputy Warden, who in turn delegated affairs to his own deputy, Sir Edward Guldeford. Yet, like previous Wardens, Prince Henry also assumed the title of Constable of Dover Castle, the ancient fortress overlooking the town of Dover. Always deemed royal, the Castle had apartments for royalty when they desired to stay there. Therefore, it can be assumed that Prince Henry at least visited there before – as he was to do on many occasions after – he became King in 1509. In fact Jones asserts that 'Prince Henry appears to have given his personal service at Dover for some time after taking up the office' of Warden.[33] Thus, it seems likely that William Warren as one of the leading officials of the Cinque Ports in Dover had some contact with the Prince in his capacities as Warden and Constable. However, the most intriguing question is whether William's son John met the Prince during their adolescence, for as we shall see John and Henry crossed paths on a number of occasions during their adulthoods. Again, William Warren might have paved the way for his son's career.

On the other hand, with the Brotherhood's records available, less speculation is required in discussing William's activities with the Cinque Ports. For example, at the July 24, 1487, meeting of the Brotherhood, William was appointed to serve as a Bailiff in Yarmouth the following autumn during the four-week Herring Fair. Three years later, as a burgess of one of the Cinque Ports elected to Parliament, he was authorized along with the other Port MPs to 'labour with the Lord Treasurer and barons of the Exchequer regarding the advocants.' According to Hull, advocants were freemen of the Ports living outside the liberties but contributing to the Ports' charges.[34]

It seems that much of William's personal service to the Ports centered on advocant affairs. Perhaps the most noteworthy entry in this regard is the following from the July 22, 1494 meeting:

Copy of Exchequer Memorandum, Easter Term 6 Henry VII, roll 12 of King's Remembrancer: recites that John Earl of Winchelsea and William Waren (sic) of Dover came before the barons of the Exechequer on 7 May 1491, and presented letters of attorney of 12 April 1491, in the name of all the Ports ..., appointing them representatives of the Ports and there and then entered into a bond in 1,000 li and agreed to limit claims to 500 li for all residents and advocants.[35]

For these – and perhaps other – services William received for a number of years an annual payment of usually twenty shillings. These payments continued until 1505, the year before he died.[36]

One final entry from the minutes involving William is of interest because it concerns one of the rather common legal practices of the Ports. At the April 8, 1494 meeting, the Brotherhood decided that

because William Waren (sic), Edward Hexstall, and Henry Balgey of Dover made default in a suit at Lydd against Thomas Robyns, the withernam awarded them at Dover against Lydd is annulled.[37]

According to Hull, withernam was a Common Law debt-collecting process involving a debtor who lived in a different town from his creditor and who had failed to pay through customary procedures. Apparently, the use of this process was expanded by the Port Confederation to levy and collect fines through the courts for various kinds of infractions of the law. Interestingly, William who is identified in the minutes of the April 8 meeting as the mayor of Dover, did not attend the meeting but was represented by Henry Balgey.[38]

William Warren's death in 1506 ended twenty years of service to the Brotherhood, but again he paved the way for an even longer period of service by his son John who three years later made his first appearance as a Deputy.

## *John Warren*

John Warren's public service coincided almost perfectly with the thirty-eight year reign of Henry VIII, 1509–1547. Making his debut as a Deputy of the Brotherhood in 1509, John was chosen immediately to carry the royal canopy in Henry's Coronation procession through the streets of London. John Bowle, a biographer of Henry, describes in part the nature of the spectacle:

> On the eve of their midsummer Coronation, Henry and Catherine rode through London to Westminster. The city was hung with arras and festooned with decorations, the goldsmiths stalls in Old Change resplendent with girls in white, waving branches of white may. The young king's amiable and princely bearing was much admired: he wore crimson velvet furred with ermine, and shone with rubies and emeralds, diamonds and great pearls; he rode a charger with trappings of damask gold under a canopy borne by the Barons of the Cinque Ports.[39]

With this splendid ceremony, then, both young men – Henry was only eighteen and John was about twenty-five – began their respective careers in governmental affairs side-by-side so to speak, perhaps little knowing that they would be brought together again and again in the years ahead. But for the moment, they went their separate ways after the Coronation. Incidentally, John was reimbursed ten shillings by the Brotherhood for his canopy-bearing in London.[40]

At the outset of his career, John Warren became very active in the affairs of Dover and the Cinque Ports. Given the circumstances of the time, however, he and his fellow Jurats faced rather formidable tasks in town. According to Ivan Green, among other historians, Dover was in 'a very poor condition' at this time. The old harbor had silted up rather badly, restricting trading and fishing, two activities very important to Dover's economy. In fact, it was very difficult to get any ships into the sea because they had to be launched from the open beach, something that was possible only under the best of weather conditions. Moreover, demand for fish was dropping off as well, as many of the old religious institutions – always good customers – were in decline, too.[41]

Dover Priory, for example, once a great institution, was now practically insolvent. There were too few members even to say the important masses regularly; the two or three novices were receiving no instruction; and the buildings were in a state of decay. Other religious institutions in the town faced similar circumstances.[42]

With the other Cinque Ports no better off – Sandwich's harbor had similar problems, for example – not much help would be forthcoming from the Confederation. Hence, the governing officials of Dover decided to appeal directly to the Crown.[43]

John Warren's role in Dover's appeals to Henry VIII is not known, but clearly he was recognized by his fellow Deputies of the Cinque Ports as a man to approach the King in such matters. For as early as 1513, John, along with a fellow jurat from Hastings, was authorized by the Brotherhood to petition the King, apparently in person in London, against the imposition 'of the subsidy within the Ports.' To use the language of the time, they were to 'pursue to the Kinges grace and his Councell for reformacion' of any subsidy commission against the Ports.[44]

Over the years John continued to play other roles in the Ports' dealing with Henry VIII and the London government. In April 1514, John, along with another jurat from Winchelsea, was entrusted by the Brotherhood with 'money granted by the Five Ports to the King' to be delivered at London. For this service the two men were 'to have their costs and charges' paid by the Ports. They were authorized to receive forty shillings immediately.[45]

The following year John and the same jurat were instructed to – in the language of the time – '"do ther dylygence to sue unto my lorde of York" for reformation of the privy seal to the Barons of the Exechequer for discharging the subsidy from the Ports.' They were 'to report on their mission at the next Brotherhood,' and they were to receive 'their costs.'[46]

The next year John and his fellow jurat reported at the Brotherhood's April meeting that they had done 'their trewe diligence and labour for dischargying of the seid subsidie.' They each received '3li. for their labour and 5li. 4s. 4d. costs.'[47]

In addition, John Warren was entrusted alone by the Brotherhood to deliver payments to the Queen in 1517. He was given money 'due to the Queen called *Aurum Regine*' as spelled in the minutes. According to Hull, quoting from Jacob's *New Law Dictionary* of 1757, *Aurum Regin* was a royal duty 'being one tenth above the entire Fines or Pardons, Contracts or Agreements, which becomes a real Debt to the Queen.'[48]

Perhaps John's most interesting task for the Brotherhood was one connected with an important historical event involving Henry VIII. This was Henry's state visit to France, via Dover and Calais, called the Field of Cloth of Gold. According to Brett, King Francis I of France

> did his utmost to impress Henry by entertaining him in 1520 with magnificent splendour at a camp near Calais known, from the apparel of those taking part and from the adornments of the tents,

as the 'Field of Cloth of Gold.' Henry appeared to be deeply impressed.[49]

On the other hand, the Brotherhood was less so because its Deputies apparently believed that they would have to press the King for payment of services rendered to him along his route of travel. Therefore, John Warren, along with three other Deputies, was instructed, first, to contact the Warden of the Ports 'to know his pleasure touching the late service done for the King "with ther shyppes for hys vyagge to Callys and furthermore"' and if he agreed, they were to pursue the matter in London. And second, in any case, John and two of these Deputies were ordered to 'ride to London regarding the King's service.' John's costs were to be paid by Dover.[50] The minutes of subsequent Brotherhood meetings do not make clear whether Henry paid his debts to the Ports.

It is not known whether John, because of these connections with Henry and his government over the years, was among the Dover officials who first approached the King about the town's harbor problems, but it is known, as we shall see, that John was subsequently involved when a crisis developed.

One can never really know, of course, why Henry responded favorably to Dover's requests for financial assistance. Taking a rather Realpolitik view, one can certainly argue that Henry, unlike his more isolationist father, was determined to involve himself in European politics and therefore recognized the strategic and defensive importance of Dover at the narrows of the English Channel. Known as 'the father of the English navy,' Henry could certainly see Dover as being one of his key ports.

On the other hand, the King also had some sentimental attachments to Dover. Having been appointed Constable of Dover Castle, as well as Warden of the Cinque Ports, at a very young age, he probably developed a genuine attachment to the town. It has been recorded many times that he was a frequent visitor over the years. How often John Warren was involved in any of these visits is not known, but it would seem very likely that he at least welcomed the King during his stay in 1537 when John was Mayor.

In any event, Henry VIII, perhaps also remembering that his father had made a modest commitment for harbor improvements late in his reign, extended his patronage for what was known as the Western Harbour Works near Archcliffe Point. Extensive work started in 1532 and included among other projects the building of the 'Mighty Pier' which Henry believed would be 'the salvation of Dover Harbour' as Jones puts it. Extending about 1,400 feet in an easterly direction, this 'stone mole' was designed to shelter the road and harbor mouth.[51]

Unfortunately, according to Jones, this project ended in 'dramatic' failure, for the King had scarcely got the project started when one of those devastating southwest gales ... brought the shingle round Archcliffe Point, and the great unfinished mole, then rising out of the sea at low tides, acted as a trap to catch the beach, which not only choked the new harbour mouth, but quickly formed a bench of beach fronting the town, barring the mouth of the River Dour.[52]

Henry, now 'lukewarm' about Dover's problems, was only willing to refer the matter to a specially appointed local group for investigation. Known as 'A Commission of Enquiry about a Mole or Harbour for Shipping at Dover, 7th May, 1540,' it was composed of six Commissioners, including John Warren, who were directed to carry out an extensive study of virtually all aspects of the problem, among which were a listing of the occupations of the people of Dover, the reasons for the decay of the fishing industry, and whether construction of a new quay or lock would improve the economy.[53]

According to Jones, John Warren and his fellow Commissioners sent

a very dutiful reply, with profuse thanks, to the King for his benevolence to Dover, but they avoided giving any opinion as to the proposed quay and lock into the town, because, presumably, they still hoped that the King could be induced to spend further sums in finishing the great pier ... which had only been brought up to sea level.[54]

Although Henry seemed to be willing to give at least moral support for the building of the quay and lock, he would go no further and therefore, according to Jones, 'took the opportunity of abandoning Dover Harbour entirely.'[55] Forty years would pass before another Tudor monarch, Elizabeth, undertook harbor works in 1582.

If John Warren and his Dover colleagues were not very successful with Henry's harbor projects, they had better results getting his fortifications built. Having become involved in European politics, the King felt the need to improve his defenses along England's south-eastern coast, especially in view of the growing use of artillery in warfare. With a strong but ancient castle at Dover, he had the basis for adapting and expanding his fortifications. Thus, he erected new forts at the castle and along the coast on both sides as adjuncts to it. These additions included Mote Bulwark under the Castle Cliff, Archcliffe Fort, Sandgate Castle, Sandown Castle, Walmer Castle and Deal Castle, the last several located some miles from Dover itself.[56]

With such major developments, it might be thought that Dover, in addition to receiving benefits from a modern defense system, would enjoy significant economic advances as a result of so much building activity. But apparently, as Jones suggests, the economic benefits were not as large as anticipated because Henry confiscated considerable local revenue for his projects by taking possession of the Dover Constable's lands.[57] Thus, John Warren and his colleagues obviously received a lesson in how Henry could give and take away at the same time.

But perhaps John Warren's most significant experience with Henry's brand of transactional politics came about during his years as a Member of Parliament for Dover. Although only a member of the House of Commons – one among over 300 other MPs – John had the unique experience of serving in the great Reformation Parliament of 1529–36, one of the landmark parliaments of English history. Holding seven different sessions, this Parliament, according to Professor Graves, secured the annulment of Henry's first marriage, the settlement of the succession through the heirs of his second, and – most important of all – 'a revolution in Church, State, and Church-State relations.'[58] Among the major laws passed by Parliament were the following: the Act in Restraint of Annates and the Submission of the Clergy in 1532; the Act in Restraint of Appeals to Rome the next year; and in 1534 a series of Acts which severed all remaining links with the Pope and transferred his powers to the King. In other words, Parliamentary statutes were used to create the structure of the new national Church and to acknowledge Henry as its rightful head with supreme temporal and jurisdictional authority. Parliament also equipped the King to punish those who opposed the new order.[59]

Although many other acts – both important and less so – were passed by the Reformation Parliament, one other needs to be mentioned because it apparently formed part of the basis for Henry's transactional politics with John Warren and others like him. Enacted in early 1536, this law provided for the dissolution of the smaller monasteries, those whose annual revenues were less than 200 pounds. Of the 376 involved, each lost its property to the King and had its monks sent to larger monasteries or provided pensions. However, the larger ones also experienced the same fate during the following years, and by the end of 1540 the process of dissolution was complete.[60]

With such far-reaching changes as these, one might have expected to have had a rebellious Parliament. Yet most historians seem to agree that for various reasons the members of the Reformation Parliament and Henry's subsequent Parliaments were very compliant. Brett briefly summarizes his explanation as follows:

> Henry VIII's Parliaments came as near to servility as Parliament has ever come, yet though frequently changing measures were the reflection of the frequently changing policy of Henry, those measures did in the main represent the national will: the ecclesiastical measures were the execution of the long-standing desire for freedom from a foreign Pope, and the Succession Acts were attempts to deal with a problem whose settlement was essential to the peace of the country.[61]

Yet, being the excellent politician that he was Henry knew that continued support in the country – and therefore in Parliament – depended upon the receipt of some tangible benefits by his supporters. Looking round, he saw the former monastic land he had seized as a source of these benefits. Hence, he either gave much of the land or sold it at cheap rates to courtiers or Members of Parliament.[62]

Brett sees two important consequences of this – what he terms as 'the most far-reaching of all the results of the dissolution of the monasteries':

> First, the men who thus acquired property founded new landed families. Second, every man who possessed former monastic lands became at once, if he was not already, a staunch opponent of Roman Catholicism.[63]

It seems that John Warren was one of Henry's beneficiaries. For in 1538, John acquired lands, known as Palmers and Greuawaye, in the parish of Ripple, Kent.[64] Apparently these lands had been part of the ancient possession of the abbot and convent of St Augustine which Henry had seized. No doubt John and others at the time were also interested in acquiring the principal manor of the parish, Ripple Court, which had been seized as well, but Henry decided to keep this prize for himself and his family. Elizabeth finally returned it to private hands during her reign.[65]

Incidentally, while the Warrens themselves never acquired Ripple Court, it eventually ended up 'in the family' so to speak. For the second holder of the property after Elizabeth's action was the Gookin family. In 1619 Catharine Gookin, daughter of Thomas Gookin of Ripple Court, married John Warren's great-grandson, William Warren (1597–1631). William and Catharine became the parents of Thomas Warren in 1625, and Thomas, as we have seen, went to America with his cousin Daniel Gookin in 1640.

After acquiring his lands in Ripple in 1538, John Warren, unlike many other MPs, decided not to found a landed family at that time. Instead, both he and his son Thomas, who was now twenty-eight years of age, remained in Dover where John carried on his public service as before. Now past fifty, John had only eight more years to live. When he died, he was buried with his father William in the Lady Chapel of St Peter's Church, now the church of the Corporation of Dover, in 1546. Henry VIII died the following year.

## *Thomas Warren*

It was left to Thomas Warren to found the landed family of Warren in Ripple, but he decided not to do so until his old age. Like his father and grandfather before him, Thomas was committed first to public service in Dover, the Cinque Ports, and Parliament.

Only two or three years after his father's death, Thomas Warren was elected Mayor of Dover for the first time, an office he would hold for at least three or four other terms. He would serve as Deputy Mayor on three occasions as well. Of course such service also meant that he was a Jurat for many years, too.

At this time Dover was still a rather small town. According to Haines, there were 358 houses in town, twenty ships and crayers, 120 vessels of about four tons each, and 130 people employed in trade or shipping. However, these would have been men in positions of authority because ships' crews, fishermen, craftsmen and shore workers would not have been included.[66]

Even though Dover and its activities were rather small, Thomas Warren found himself as one of its leaders living in very troubled times. According to Jones, royal neglect of Dover's harbor problems continued from Henry VIII's later years through Edward VI's reign. This inaction

> plunged the town into poverty, which so lowered the standard of independence and love of order amongst the Freemen that the Common Assemblies became disorderly gatherings.[67]

Exacerbated by religious persecutions, the situation became worse during Mary's reign. Apparently using widespread disorderliness as an 'excuse' to establish the Common Council, mentioned above, which excluded the main body of the Freemen from direct political participation, the 'inner circle of rulers,' as Jones calls them, did not help matters. After reviewing the minutes of Corporation meetings during the period, Jones concludes that it appears

> that disorder and uncharitableness amongst the leading members of the Corporation prevailed, being apparently a continuation of strife from the reigns of Edward VI and Queen Mary, when there had been bitter feelings between the Catholics and the Protestants.[68]

These local disorders continued and became so intense during Elizabeth's reign that she sent a Commission to Dover to establish peace. However, the peace that was made in the presence of the Queen's Commission in April 1559, was soon broken. After more disturbances, law and order finally prevailed, perhaps helped by Elizabeth's financial assistance to Dover's harbor improvements in 1582.[69]

It is evident from some of the records of the period that Thomas Warren was often deeply involved in Dover's local controversies. While it is impossible to get a clear picture of the issues and the sides taken by Thomas with respect to them, perhaps it can be said, as one researcher has, that he certainly favored a law and order approach to problems. According to the Chamberlain's accounts, for example, during Thomas's first year as Mayor, various sums of money were spent in mending the ducking stool, putting a new lock on the stocks, and setting up a new gallows! [70]

But perhaps Thomas Warren's clashes with another mayor while he was a Jurat were more representative. In July 1559, for example, Thomas and John Robbynes, another Jurat, were fined four pounds each – 'to be levy'd of theyer goods and cattels,' as the language of the Corporation minutes indicates – for 'theyer mysbehavior and dishobedience' contrary to Mayor Thomas Collye's commandment. Apparently this infraction, which was not explained, was relatively minor for the time because during the following month the Town Clerk, one Roger Wood, was arrested for falsifying accounts but escaped and 'was heard of no more.' [71]

Thomas Warren had had an earlier clash with Mayor Collye, for a previous entry in the minutes reports that the Mayor contended that he

dyd nott comand the said Thomas Warren to bryng or cause one James Broker to be brought to the p'sone one the Wall but to the Hall'

to appear before Collye and several Jurats.[72]

When Thomas Pepper became Mayor in late 1559, a serious attempt was made to improve the disorderly situation of the previous years by establishing a close association among Pepper and the Jurats 'to promote harmony and prosperity.' In a rather quaintly worded resolution, which mentions Pepper, Thomas Warren, and several other Jurats by name, it was agreed

that from this day forth all manner of old griefs and slanderous words that have moved and stirred between the Mayor and Jurats be clearly forgotten and forgiven, and never to be remembered or spoken of again, but to be lovers and friends, knit in one unity forever, whereby justice may be better administered for the better government of the Town. And he or they that from henceforth do infringe this present act be clearly dismissed from the Juratship, never to be of the fellowship again.[73]

While Thomas Warren may have had some serious disagreements with a Mayor and other Jurats, he nevertheless had enough local support to be elected, along with John Robbynes, a canopy bearer for Queen Elizabeth's Coronation and a Member of Parliament. It is very interesting to note that years later Thomas mentioned with some obvious irritation in his will that his wages for service in Parliament had not been paid and that he had to pay his own expenses at the Coronation.[74] Perhaps he was aware that his father had faired better some fifty years before.

Thomas Warren's encounter with disorder was probably even greater in Parliament – at least in the first Parliament he attended in 1555. This was Queen Mary's fourth Parliament in which long and bitter debates continued from her previous Parliaments. The chief legislative struggle of Mary's reign centered on the question of her marriage to Philip II of Spain and its implications. This question was considered of course in a larger context: Mary's Catholicism and her attempt to restore England not merely to the Catholicism of her father but to a thoroughgoing Roman Catholicism. According to Brett, Mary had as her mission as Queen the 'Romanizing' of the English people.[75]

Mary's first Parliament in 1553 started off well enough. It confirmed the ecclesiastical changes the Queen had already made, repealed the ecclesiastical acts of Edward VI's reign, and restored the religious settlement as it stood in Henry VIII's last year. However, Parliament also petitioned Mary to marry an Englishman. Unfortunately, she was willing neither to do this nor to stop with merely the reinstatement of Henry's brand of Catholicism. Instead she was determined to have a marriage/alliance with Philip and with Spain, the leading Roman Catholic state in Europe, both of which would ensure, she believed, the success of her religious aims.[76]

The next Parliaments tended to capitulate to many of Mary's requests. In April 1554, for example, Parliament was induced to consent to her marriage to Philip and to a treaty which laid down the conditions on which it was to be allowed.[77]

Mary's third Parliament, which met in November 1554, approved a petition to the Church asking for its forgiveness of England for breaking with Rome and for restoring full communion with the Holy See. Parliament insisted, however, that the former Church lands should remain in the possession of their existing owners. It also passed two other statutes: an act repealing the ecclesiastical laws of Henry VIII's reign; and an act reinstating laws passed at the beginning of the fifteenth century for the persecution of the Lollards.[78]

This last measure, of course, provided Mary with a weapon for her extensive religious persecutions that began in early 1555 and reached high levels just before the latter part of that year when her fourth Parliament, the one Thomas Warren attended, met. Obviously, the setting for this Parliament was not good because many people – nearly 300 men and women altogether – were killed, usually by being burned at the stake, for their faith.[79]

Clearly, Thomas Warren and his fellow Members of Parliament were shocked by what had been happening the previous months when their session began in late October. According to Keir, the mood of this Parliament was one of repentance for the previous Parliament's role in making possible the recent persecutions. But having armed the Church with its ancient authority under a Queen anxious to support Church actions by secular power, Parliament remained virtually a helpless spectator. With the authority to lead vested in the Crown, Parliament could play a different role only when the Queen reversed her policy, something Mary was unwilling to do.[80]

Although persecution was stayed during the Parliament's session – something of a concession to its mood, perhaps – Thomas Warren and his colleagues were only able to manifest their attitude towards the Church and Queen by rejecting a measure to penalize religious exiles and denying to the government the authority it sought for restoring first-fruits and tenths to Rome. With regard to the latter, when the Queen's bill finally passed, it did so by a vote of only 193 to 126.[81] Given the actions of previous Parliaments, this resistence was something of a rebellion.

Though Parliament's attempts to reverse policy were weak at best, it did deliver a message to the Queen that her legislature had had enough. Hence, after she dissolved it in December 1555, she did not call another, her last, until January 1558, and this one, according to Keir, had two 'brief and barren sessions.'[82]

As Mary's unhappy reign was coming to an end – she died in November 1558 – an event, seen by most of the nation as a disgrace, occurred which might have brought about some personal losses for Thomas Warren and his family. This was the fall of Calais, the last English outpost in France. While in hindsight its loss is usually interpreted less negatively, its surrender to the French at the time was deemed a disaster because of its sentimental value. Even for Mary, it was said she believed that 'Calais' would be found written on her heart at death.[83]

For the Warrens, as we have seen, William Warren's will mentioned the existence of personal property in Calais which he passed on to his wife and in turn to his son John. But more important still is the likelihood that Thomas Warren's wife, who is identified by him in *The Visitation of Kent* as 'Christian, daughter of Close of Callys,' had connections there at the time of its loss. While the date of their marriage is not known, it seems likely that it occurred rather late in Thomas's life because the only child ever mentioned in the records is a son John, who was born in 1561, three years after Calais' fall.[84]

Having been one of the MPs who helped to stem the tide of Mary's policies, Thomas Warren must have accepted with some pleasure his election to Elizabeth I's first Parliament in 1559. When he arrived in London in January for the opening session, Thomas found his colleagues eager to tackle the problem of the ecclesiastical settlement. Parliament soon passed the second Act of Supremacy which declared the Queen to be the 'Supreme Governor of the realm in all causes ecclesiastical as well as civil' and authorized the imposition of an Oath of Supremacy upon all those who held office in Church and State.[85]

Parliament's second important law was a third Act of Uniformity. At the heart of this statute was an order to use in church a slightly modified version of the Second Prayer Book of Edward VI.[86]

Although Thomas Warren was also a member of Elizabeth's second Parliament (1563–67) which considered but failed to pass a bill to compel all clergymen to agree to the Thirty-Nine Articles, he was no longer an MP when a similar measure finally passed in 1571. Nevertheless, Thomas was involved with all three of the most important measures comprehending Elizabeth's general policy concerning religion. In short, these acts established a national church that was moderately Protestant and that attempted to embrace all but the extremists among believers. Although Elizabeth's hope of eventually bringing the whole nation within her church was never fulfilled, she was, according to Brett, rather successful by the end of her reign in getting the mass of the English people to conform to her moderate Protestantism through a national church.[87]

Perhaps Thomas Warren's struggles with the major disorders of his day were not as intense within the Brotherhood of the Cinque Ports, but clearly his expertise in the law and his trustworthiness were valued – as had been his father's and grandfather's before him – in dispute resolution at this regional level. Although the minutes indicate that he was present at many Brotherhood meetings during most years from 1549 to 1577, his activities seemed to be much more limited than those of his father. In the main the Brotherhood appeared to value his service in the roles of solicitor and auditor, especially from 1570 onward.[88]

With respect to the former role, Hull states that the nature of the problems facing the Ports at that time frequently required litigation or at least legal advice, and hence the practice developed of appointing senior members of the Brotherhood 'to solicit' a case with the Warden or in one of the Royal Courts on behalf of the Ports. Solicitors were appointed for a wide variety of duties.[89]

In 1570, for example, Thomas, along with others from the several Ports, was appointed to represent and to be paid by Dover

> for the cause of the charter touching the impost of wine which shall be drawn up by learned counsel and exhibited to the Queen and her Privy Council at the common charge.[90]

Apparently this was a petition that was to be delivered by the solicitors in London.

Thomas and his fellow solicitors were assigned other duties as well by the Brotherhood. They were requested to 'petition the Lord Warden in all matters in dispute between him and the Ports.' Moreover, they were requested to 'prosecute the cause of the *certiorari* as set down at Tenterden with the Lord Warden and also any *sub pena* and cause of conscience.'[91]

In addition, they were told 'to refer to the serjeants' the dispute between Rye and the Ports and the 'entreats directed from the Exechequer to Winchelsea.' And finally in the case of one Thomas Lake of Fairlight near Hastings

> touching advocants the solicitors shall sue to the Lord Warden for punishment of those concerned and shall refer the cause to the serjeants the charges of Thomas Lake being borne by the whole Ports.[92]

When Thomas became a solicitor, he was also appointed, as were others, an auditor 'for the east Ports', 'to determine charges touching causes of the charter.' He was reappointed to this post in 1571, 1572 and 1574. According to Hull, auditors were appointed whenever considerable or exceptional expenses had been incurred. Collectively, they formed what was virtually an ad hoc finance committee of strictly limited powers and life for the Brotherhood.[93]

Although Jones lists Thomas as Mayor of Dover in 1582, the Cinque Port records suggest that his public service career probably ended sometime near the close of the previous decade when he was in his middle sixties.[94] Therefore, perhaps it was quite fitting that one of the last positions he filled for the Brotherhood was that of Speaker.

Apparently, the office of Speaker began sometime in the fifteenth century. It moved from Port to Port in geographical order from west to east, changing on May 21 of each year. What the Speakership entailed were the right and duty to summon meetings and to establish agendas for them. Basically the first task of the Speaker in this regard was to have letters delivered to the several Ports announcing the next meeting. Although the Warden was not involved in the work of the Brotherhood's meetings, he could advise the Speaker about calling meetings. In fact this was done in 1575 when he advised Thomas Warren, who served as Speaker that year, to call a meeting at Dover for the purpose of conferring with London Commissioners about a dispute concerning the use of withernam.[95]

As Speaker, Thomas presided over what must have been a very long and rather complex legal discussion on April 6, 1575. A dozen separate items are recorded in the minutes, but perhaps the following entry citing the documents used to justify the Ports' position in the dispute is the most interesting. 'Serjeant Lovelace' of the Ports showed the Commissioners

> confirmation of liberties from Magna Carta, viz. 'An ancyent roulle in parchment for Winchelsey. An ancient rolle from Heyth contayninge carta Magna. A custome of Sandwich in Latten. An olde booke in French of Dovor. An olde custom of Hastinge in French and

Latten. An Ancient custom in Inglysh for Romeney. An ancient book of French for Tenterden.' [96]

Apparently the dispute was ultimately resolved.

Having been active in public service to what must have been an advanced age for the time, Thomas Warren retired by the early 1580s. Then he, along with his wife and son John (1561–1613) established their landed family in Ripple where Thomas died in 1591 at age eighty. Later in the same year John married Anne Crafford, and they eventually had twelve children, five of whom were boys. At least three of these sons – John (1609–1674), Edward (1612–1676) and William (1597–1631) – survived into adulthood with the first two emigrating to Virginia. Remaining in Ripple, William and his wife, Catharine Gookin, became, as indicated before, the parents of Thomas who in turn emigrated with his cousin Daniel Gookin to Virginia in 1640.

## The Special Relationship with Britain

Even though this family history is not recent but goes back 400 to 500 years, it is very difficult not to feel a special relationship with Britain through the Warrens. Obviously the existence of rather detailed records, something quite rare, is partly responsible for this feeling. Many fore-bearers of only a few generations back seem much more distant than do the Warrens because so little is known about them by comparison. Familiarity with family history is clearly an important factor in reinforc-ing connections already there. Yet, there is much more involved here than that.

The fact that my mother's family is the focal point is important as well. Again, even though generations from centuries ago are involved, I have some understanding of the feelings Winston Churchill and Harold Macmillan must have had stemming from their having Ameri-can mothers. The nurturing role of the mother, the Helper, fosters certain values and attitudes which relate one to family and other institutions of the past. Our mothers are our first history teachers, the ones who pick and choose the important and necessary elements of the past and enculturate us with those ideas. In my own experience, much was done to connect with my mother's family, little with my father's.

Since the Thomas Warren Family of southern Illinois is large and has long been concentrated in the villages and towns in the St Louis metropolitan area, we interacted frequently with one another for many years on a weekly – sometimes even on a daily – basis. Visits with aunts, uncles, and cousins occurred regularly in New Athens and nearby communities even during World War II when gasoline was rationed. Before Grandmother Caroline's death in the early 1940s, my mother, sister, and I frequently visited her in St Louis and enjoyed the many delights of that city, previously mentioned.

But perhaps even more memorable about family connections was the often annual 'gathering of the clan,' the Warren Family Reunion in a park, occasionally on a farm, where countless relatives met for a huge meal, games – such as horseshoes, softball, and cards – and, of course, family gossip. The meal was always the high point of the day because each woman brought at least one 'covered dish' of her own specialty. Since my mother's reputation as a cook in the family was built on her extremely light and very high angel food cakes, more often than not she took one of those. When the day was over, most people returned home with full stomachs and empty dishes.

In recent years the reunions have occurred about every five years as the family has become even larger but much more scattered throughout the United States. However, perhaps one of the most significant developments, especially among cousins my age, is a growing interest in genealogy. Several of us have done considerable research in family history and have exchanged our findings among ourselves and with other Thomas Warren descendants from other lines. The Internet is fast becoming an important link in Warren connections today.

With these strong connections with the Thomas Warren Family leading back to Britain, it took only a little imagination on my part to think in like terms about my Dundee 'family,' the Ws, while a student at St Andrews University. They made this easy for me to do because they treated me like a member of their family, as described in Chapter I. Hence, in my own mind, I felt as though I was actually living with relatives – the Warrens of Britain – while in Dundee during 1956–7.

While the family element is very strong indeed, I found other things in the lives of the Dover Warrens of the sixteenth century that connected us. Having studied law, including English common law, and taught it – as well as other public service related courses such as public administration and executives – for a lifetime, I easily concluded that these Warrens were my type of people. Hence, I felt an equally strong affinity to them as professional people. As the review of their lives shows, they had lifelong commitments to public service at all levels and to the rule of law. The stage for their lives was the public forum, and their vehicle was the law: legislating, administering and adjudicating it for their communities. It is difficult for me to find a higher calling in life. My admiration of them in their professional lives is complete.

But what is also admirable and very attractive about them is their apparent commitment to the law beyond the mundane level and to that of world view, even cosmology. Since their individual working commitments were lifelong – or nearly so as in Thomas's case – at three different levels of government, it seems to me that the law was more than just a profession but also a way of life for them. An important point in this regard is the continuing service to the law of John and Thomas after Henry VIII made it possible for the Warren family to become landed gentry – gentlemen farmers, if you will – in Ripple during the 1530s. Instead of doing so, as we have seen, the family stayed in Dover until Thomas retired some fifty years later.

Hence, I see the Warrens as genuine Elizabethans in their apparent belief in the Chain of Being. As such their general goals included the achievement of harmony, order, unity and peace. In particular, as shown in the discussion above, Thomas Warren spent much of his public life trying to reach these goals through the instrument of the law during the very chaotic times of the last half of the sixteenth century. In so doing, he clearly exhibited the use of cooperation, accommodation, fairness, and other Helper values. It was not by chance or the accident of history that he was chosen for positions of judicial trust and responsibility by the Dover and Cinque Port communities during those troubled times; he was chosen because he represented the communities' values during the Elizabethan Age.

If, then, the Warrens, especially Thomas, can be seen as practitioners of the Elizabethan world view, it is likely that they also believed in the theorizers' conceptions of that view. Whether any of the Warrens were actually familiar with Shakespeare's plays or Richard Hooker's legal writings is, of course, not known, but they seemed to be in tune with many of the central ideas in them. In the end, therefore, Hooker's view of the law as a Helper-type of woman which the Warrens apparently had as well returns us to the Special Relationship concept. For me, then, the Warrens are a very important part of that relationship.

# *Notes*

1. Edward Hasted, *Kent: The History and Topographical Survey of the County*, Vol. IX, (Canterbury, England: W. Bristow, 1799), 570.

2. John Bavington Jones, *Annals of Dover*, 2nd ed., (Dover, England: Dover Express Works, 1938), 250.

3. Ibid., 252.

4. Ibid., 252–3.

5. Ibid., 252.

6. Michael A. R. Graves, *The Tudor Parliaments: Crown, Lords, and Commons, 1485–1603* (London: Longman, 1985), back cover. See also G. R. Elton, *The Parliament of England, 1559–1581* (Cambridge: Cambridge University Press, 1986).

7. K. M. E. Murray, *The Constitutional History of the Cinque Ports* (Manchester, England: Manchester University Press, 1935), 1.

8. Ibid., 9.

9. Felix Hull (ed.), *A Calendar of the White and Black Books of the*

*Cinque Ports, 1432–1955* (London: Her Majesty's Stationery Office, 1966), XII-XIII, XXX.

10. Ibid., XI.
11. Ibid., XIII-XIV.
12. Ibid., 132.
13. E. M. W. Tillyard, *The Elizabethan World Picture* (London: Penguin Books, 1943), 17, 22.
14. Ibid., 33–4.
15. Ibid., 34.
16. Stephen B. Presser, 'The New Great Chain of Being in the Law,' Paper presented at Hendrix College, Conway, Arkansas, 17 February 1983.
17. Tillyard, 16.
18. Laurence A. Davey, Churchwarden, Ripple Parochial Church Council, Ripple, England, to John Ziegler, 15 February 1997.
19. W. Bruce Bannerman (ed.), *The Visitation of Kent, 1574 and 1592* (London: John Whitehead & Son, 1924), 45.
20. William Lambarde, *A Perambulation of Kent* (Bath, England: Adams & Dart, 1970), 63.
21. Jones, 317. Among Warren researchers, much speculation abounds about William's forebears, but I have seen no convincing evidence as yet.
22. John Lyons, *History of the Town and Port of Dover* (1813), 131.
23. Charles Reginald Haines, *Dover Priory: A History of the Priory of St. Mary the Virgin, and St Martin of the New Work* (Cambridge: Cambridge University Press, 1930), 369, 398. I have seen this beautiful book, and William's name is still inscribed in it.
24. Boddie, *Virginia Historical Genealogies*, 238.
25. S. Reed Brett, *British History, 1485–1688* (London: John Murray, 1933), 4–5.
26. Graves, 52.
27. Ibid., 53.
28. Ibid., 48–9. David Lindsay Keir, *The Constitutional History of Modern Britain, 1485–1951* (London: Adam and Charles Black, 1953), 40.
29. Jones, 264.
30. Murray, 6–7.
31. Ibid., 77.
32. Ibid, 89.
33. Jones, 62–3.
34. Hull, 98, 105, XXVI.
35. Ibid., 117.
36. Ibid., 132.
37. Ibid., 116.
38. Ibid., XXVII, 115.

39. John Bowle, *Henry VIII: A Biography* (New York: Dorset Press, 1964), 39.

40. Hull, 145–6.

41. Ivan Green, *Dover: A Pictorial History* (Chichester, England: Phillimore & Co., 1987), no page number.

42. Ibid.

43. Jones, 91.

44. Hull, 150–1.

45. Ibid., 155.

46. Ibid., 158.

47. Ibid., 161.

48. Ibid., 165.

49. Brett, 40.

50. Hull, 180.

51. Jones, 92, 94.

52. Ibid., 95.

53. Ibid.

54. Ibid.

55. Ibid., 96.

56. Ibid., 20.

57. Ibid.

58. Graves, 65.

59. Ibid., 77.

60. Brett, 63, 65.

61. Ibid., 172.

62. Ibid., 66.

63. Ibid.

64. Boddie, 238.

65. Hasted, 565–6. See also Charles Igglesden, *A Saunter Through Kent with Pen and Pencil*, Vol. XX (Ashford, England: Kentish Express Office, 1927), 72.

66. Quoted in Green, no page number.

67. Jones, 264.

68. Ibid., 265.

69. Ibid.

70. Pamela R. Barratt, Secretary, Dover History Society, to John Ziegler, 23 August 1996. See also Jones, 320.

71. Edward Knocker, *A Lecture on the Archives of Dover* (Dover, England: 1878), 34. Jones, 265.

72. Knocker, 30.

73. Ibid., 35. Jones, 265–6, 322.

74. Knocker, 32. Jones, 405.

75. Brett, 91.
76. Ibid., 92–3.
77. Ibid., 95.
78. Ibid., 96.
79. Ibid., 97.
80. Keir, 76–7.
81. Ibid., 77; Graves, 112.
82. Keir, 77.
83. Brett, 101–2.
84. Bannerman, 45.
85. Brett, 109.
86. Ibid., 110.
87. Ibid., 110–11.
88. Hull, 281.
89. Ibid., XX.
90. Ibid., 282.
91. Ibid.
92. Ibid., 283.
93. Ibid., 286–7, 290, 296, XXII.
94. Jones, 324.
95. Murray, 165–6.
96. Hull, 300.

# Chapter VII

# Wilton Park

lthough my search for the special relationship began many years ago, it did not focus on a British governmental agency until the late 1970s. There were good reasons for this because, historically, the special relationship between Britain and the United States had taken a rather definite form in that area, which easily excluded me. The personal relationships at the highest levels between Churchill and Roosevelt first and Macmillan and Kennedy later on, for example, were, of course, very exclusive. And the interactive relationships between the military and intelligence services of the two nations were off-limits to a civilian. No, not being a government person, either high or low, I saw no possibilities for a long time.

However, through a former colleague in the California State University system, I found an agency in 1979. Its name is Wilton Park, which in its current form is not what the words suggest. In this peculiar sense it is indeed a very typical British institution! What, then, is Wilton Park? Often described as Britain's unique contribution to international relations, it is in one sense a permanent, ongoing international conference whose topics and major participants change every few weeks but whose organizers provide continuity which keeps the dialogue going unbroken, so to speak. More accurately, Wilton Park is today a series of four-day conferences – now about thirty-five yearly on average – focusing on current topics of interest to the international community. The participants – who can be rather generally described as theorizers of, participants in, and observers of international affairs – come from around the world, though mainly from Europe and North America. They are diplomats and civil servants, politicians and professors, electronic and print journalists, lawyers and business people – among others. What unites them is their interest in current issues, and they are united in Wiston House, a massive old country house located just below the South Downs and near the charming Sussex village of Steyning, about ten miles from the English Channel.

This splendid setting helps to explain in part both the appeal and the general success of the conferences over the years. The relative isolation from London and other cities and the rural beauty of historic Sussex keep most participants 'down on the farm,' but in my experience few participants have expressed any regrets.

## *Wiston House*

My first sight of Wiston House occurred in September 1979, after a short taxi ride from the railroad station at Shoreham-by-Sea through the Sussex villages of Upper Beeding, Bramber and Steyning itself. I shared the cab with a friendly middle-aged resident of Steyning who was returning home from London. Since I had never been that way before, I peppered him with questions about the area but especially about the Wiston House Conference Centre and the work of Wilton Park there which were virtually unknown to me at that time. To my surprise my companion related that the 'mysterious work at Wiston House' – as he put it – was also little known in Steyning as well. Needless to say, as he left the cab, I really wondered what the conference during the week ahead would be like.

As the taxi turned off the principal road from Steyning and entered the main gate to the farmlands of Wiston Park, as the old manor is called, the house could not be seen. The thick foliage of trees and bushes near the lane produced an almost impenetrable darkness that intensified the growing mystery of it all. However, after a short ride, the foliage quickly parted like a stage curtain on opening night, and straight ahead in sunlight on a low, flat hill that was almost barren of trees was the massive pile, Wiston House. What a magnificent entrance! What a magnificent setting! The latter was further enhanced by the tree-covered South Downs that served as a backdrop behind the house. The autumn colors – reds, yellows, browns, and fading greens – added to the splendor of the view. And almost like a crown on it all, the famous area landmark of trees, the Chanctonbury Ring, could be seen off to the right on top of the Downs.

As the taxi sped southwards to Wiston House, sheep and a few horses grazing in the nearby pastures raised their heads for a quick look, but their indifference showed that they were obviously used to much noisy travel on the lane. Other vehicles, including a large bus, could now be seen at or near the house as other participants were beginning to arrive as well. An old parish church, among other buildings near the house, also came into view as the taxi veered to the left for the stop at the main entrance at the east end of the house.

As I was to learn later on, there is another – and a much shorter – road from Steyning to the east front of Wiston House. Under two miles in length, Mouse Lane is well named because in appearance it reminds visitors of a somewhat enlarged rodent hole as it descends the hill from the house to Steyning – like something out of *Alice in Wonderland!* Its very narrow one-car width lane seems to disappear beneath a dense overhang of trees and rising walls of ground on both sides of the road. One supposes that use and grading over many centuries have burrowed the lane deeper and deeper into the surrounding terrain. As I was to discover several nights later, a stroll down Mouse Lane about midnight can cause the mind to imagine all kinds of things.

When the taxi stopped at the door, a couple of Wilton Park staffers with broad smiles and outstretched hands burst through the opening. Picking up my luggage, they escorted me into the house for my room assignment and keys, and then led me up two flights of stairs to my room facing the South Downs.

## Wiston House's Past

The first order of informal business was a tour of the house on one's own, aided by a brochure titled 'A Brief History of Wiston House.' This indicated that the Manor of Wiston appeared in the *Doomsday Book*, the register of all English possessions of William the Conqueror after 1066. It was then in the possession of William de Braose who, as one of William's most trusted followers, had received large areas of the county of Sussex as a reward for his service to the King. Most surprising was the fact that since the Conquest only six families have owned and lived on the Wiston Estate. The current owners, the Goring family who acquired it in the eighteenth century, occupied the house until 1926 when it was first leased out. Wilton Park's lease began in 1951.[1]

Although a manor house had existed on the estate for a long time, the original Wiston House was started in the middle 1500s and some interiors were complete by 1576. This house was much larger than the present one. There was, for example, a three-storied wing, now completely vanished, which ran parallel to the present west terrace, while the east courtyard, outside the present main door, was enclosed by a range of buildings which have also disappeared. The house was built around this paved court and behind the gables lay some magnificent rooms: a splendid Great Hall with a double hammerbeam roof, a great chamber, a panelled parlour, a chapel and gallery 90 feet long, to name a few.

It was the Goring family that began in the 1740s to alter the original house by reducing it in size. Fortunately, they decided to retain the Elizabethan hammerbeam roof and the windows of the Great Hall, apparently something that was not done in many other reconstructions of English country houses in the eighteenth century.

The nineteenth century was another period of enthusiasm for reconstructing historic houses. Wiston House was again remodelled in the 1840s by a then fashionable architect, Edward Blore (1797–1879). Fortunately, his principal recommendation was not followed, for he proposed to demolish the entire Tudor structure, leaving the Great Hall as a picturesque ruin in the Park and building an entirely new house on another site! Blore had to be content with merely altering and largely rebuilding the south wing of the house.

Since the departure of the Goring family in the 1920s, Wiston House has been altered only slightly to accommodate the needs of its tenants, which have included the headquarters unit of the Canadian Army in England during World War II, a girls' finishing school immediately after the war, and Wilton Park since 1951.

## *Wiston House Today*

Today, Wiston House has four major and three minor public rooms, all located on the ground floor. The splendid Tudor room with its hammer-beam roof, the Great Hall, serves as the dining room where participants and staff eat at tables seating six to eight persons each. The Conference Room seats forty people at a large rectangular table arrangement or sixty people with the use of seating away from tables. The Library seats thirty participants around a long table, or alternatively about twenty on couches and easy chairs for informal group discussions. The Common Room has lounge seating for twenty persons for seminars or discussion groups. It is also used for receptions and other social occasions.[2]

Opening from the Common Room are two of the minor rooms: the Yellow Room and the Bar. The former, which is the television room,

*South wing of Wiston House, facing the South Downs.*

is also used for group discussions of up to twenty people. And the Bar is often the most lively discussion room in the house!

Though actually a long corridor rather than a room leading from the main staircase to the Conference Room, the French Gallery, so named because of its beautiful eighteenth-century French carved wood panelling, is also occasionally used for small group discussions.

Most of the participants' rooms are located upstairs as well as in cottages and other buildings on the grounds surrounding Wiston House. These vary from some rather grand double rooms to smaller single rooms on the top floor where servants lived many years ago. Altogether there are thirty-three rooms, of which half are double. While the outbuilding rooms, complete with bathrooms, are the most modern, the buildings themselves may in fact be the oldest on the manor. According to Janet Pennington, some authorities believe that these buildings were constructed in 1576, while others claim that they are much older and are even of monastic origin. This theory is based on the shape and quality of the building stone.[3]

Of the remaining outbuildings, such as the stables and church, only the latter deserves some comment. Standing merely yards away from Wiston House, this parish church is also mentioned in the *Domesday Book*, though nothing is left of the Norman building. Having, like the main house, undergone alteration in the nineteenth century, little is left of the previous structure. What, then, is important about this church? Since it has always been the burial place of various people living at Wiston, it does convey a sense of the family history of the manor. There are, for example, John de Braose's brass, dated 1426, and the remains of what must have been a substantial sculpture commemorating Sir Richard Sherley who died in 1546.

At this point in the discussion, perhaps a fair question to ask is: what, then, is Wiston House today? Obviously, it began as a rather grand private manor house in the sixteenth century, but it has certainly evolved into something very different near the end of the twentieth century. What is it, really? Merely calling it a conference center does not suffice, for it does not 'feel' like one. Most conference centers, at least those I know in the United States, are rather cold and perhaps even antiseptic, like many other public buildings such as hospitals. This 'institutional' feeling is largely absent at Wiston House. On the contrary, it maintains something of the sense of a country house but certainly different from those open to the public which I have visited. Yet it is not a living museum either; rather it is a large old home – not a hotel or dormitory – well-worn, yes, but as warm and comfortable as an old jacket and a favorite pair of shoes. As the above suggests, I am unable to name something that I have experienced which would describe perfectly the feel of Wiston House. However, the closest comparable institution I can think of is the English residential college like St Peter's at Oxford and Caius at Cambridge. In point of fact this was the intention of the founder and first director or Warden as he was called of Wilton Park, Heinz Koeppler, to whom we turn our attention.

## *Sir Heinz Koeppler*

Those who accept the proposition that an institution is the extended shadow of its leader would no doubt find its validation in Wilton Park and Heinz Koeppler. Certainly it is difficult to separate the two from the time of the institution's inception just after World War II until Koeppler's retirement in September 1977 and his death two years later. Hence, any history of Wilton Park, no matter how brief, must start with Koeppler. At the beginning of each conference, a sketch not unlike the following one is made available to the participants.

Perhaps the most startling fact about the founder and Warden of this most English of institutions is that he was German by birth. Born June 30, 1912, at Wollstein in a corner of Prussia returned to Poland by the Treaty of Versailles, he grew up in Berlin where his well-to-do father, an expert on the potato, resettled his family. A brilliant student, Heinz went to the Friedrich Wilhelm University first, then to Heidelberg, and finally to Christian Albert House at Kiel University. It is thought that his experience at this last place was one of the threads which went into the creation of Wilton Park. The House, founded by a wealthy Swede named Bergmann, was a small elite residence hall where one third of the students had to be from abroad and all had to have the potential of becoming professors. Heinz was elected student president of the House.[4]

However, Koeppler's most important experience began in 1933. Earning a scholarship at Oxford University, he entered Magdalen College and graduated three years later with his Doctorate of Philosophy in Medieval History. His brilliance and fitness for the Oxford way of life led to his appointment as Lecturer in Modern History and Senior Demy of Magdalen College. Hence, Koeppler, a Jew, decided to remain in Britain where he became a naturalized British citizen just before World War II.[5]

After the war started, Koeppler joined the Political Intelligence Department of the Foreign Office, and three years later he became Assistant Regional Director in the Political Warfare Executive. Responding to Prime Minister Winston Churchill's request for creative ideas to assure a peaceful post-war Germany, Koeppler suggested establishing a learning center, modelled after the English residential college, where Germans in public life could meet for an extended period of time. The main idea was to have them discuss mutual problems in an intellectually invigorating environment which Koeppler himself had found at

Magdalen so conducive to respect for freedom and the democratic process. Since most Germans, as Koeppler knew personally, had never experienced or practiced democracy, the hope was that they would learn by seeing and hearing the British doing precisely that and would join in. Hence, among other exercises, everyone no matter what rank would be concerned about every issue; experts would be challenged by laymen; and specialists would be required to think more generally. To Koeppler, what was most important was to have the Germans experience a particular kind of educational process, a dialectical one, in which they would be active and not merely passive participants. They would learn by doing.

Personally inclined towards action rather than contemplation, Koeppler apparently had no systematic theory upon which he based this proposal. Instead, his thinking seemed to be informed by both his experiences in university residence at Kiel and Oxford – absorbing the collegiate ideal, if you will – and in personal study of the Renaissance. Concerning the latter's impact on Koeppler, one former colleague who knew him well in the 1960s and 1970s saw him as the 'reincarnation of the Renaissance humanist.' His ideal was the liberally educated generalist – the liberal arts graduate, perhaps – as opposed to the narrow specialist. Koeppler conceded that the latter's technical skills are needed in modern society, but the former is much better prepared to understand the inter-relationships of such things as culture and politics in daily life. Hence, he did not envision bringing together narrow elites for the exchange of technical ideas but in creating a forum for a wide range of people, a forum for – in a favorite term of his – the 'amateur éclairé'. He wanted to help all people to see things as a whole.[6]

Perhaps some additional insight about the source of Koeppler's ideas can be gained from a little-known biographical fact. It has been reported that he thought one of his most important formative experiences came from researching a scholarly article he wrote in 1939 titled 'Frederick Barbarossa and the Schools of Bologna.' In it, he concludes that the Renaissance had dawned in this region of Italy because its political rulers were for the most part enlightened and pragmatic. These men were such because they understood the interconnections between all branches of learning, sectors of society, and aspects of life where government, culture and a fast expanding knowledge intermingled. There is no doubt that these conclusions informed the purpose and mission of Wilton Park.[7]

## Wilton Park, Beaconsfield

Koeppler was soon given the opportunity to test his ideas on some Germans living in England but not the ones he originally had in mind.

On January 12, 1946, his first conference, composed entirely of 300 German prisoners of war, assembled at Wilton Park, Beaconsfield in Buckinghamshire. During the next two years, some 4,500 German POWs participated in this venture before they were returned home to help rebuild a devastated homeland.[8]

How did this peculiar institution operate? The student-prisoners lived together in Nissen huts, standard units of emergency housing clustered around the manor house of Wilton Park which doubled as faculty quarters and as a post of command. Although there was barbed wire around the camp, there were no guards. Within the enclosure, the creature comforts were no greater than those at other prison camps and the working day was lengthy – usually from 8:30 in the morning to 10:00 at night.

If the outward appearance seemed restrictive, the inward reality where intellectual freedom prevailed was far different. The students were given the opportunity for study and discussion of difficult problems in an atmosphere of honest give and take. Broadly speaking, the major themes of the curriculum stressed German history of the past one hundred years, current British political and social institutions, and international relations. Most of the teaching was done by fifteen tutors, all British citizens with a knowledge of German, each of whom worked with a group of twenty-five to thirty students. In working through the curriculum, the tutors had the help of special lecturers. Some were professionals who lectured several times a week, with consecutive interpretation, English to German or in reverse, as required for the lecture and the subsequent questions from the students. Other lecturers, who usually came in the evening, covered a broader range of topics related to their special areas of knowledge and experience. Among the more noted speakers were diplomat Harold Nicholson, historian Arnold J. Toynbee, and philosopher Bertrand Russell.

When the evening lectures were given by politicians, care was taken to have a balanced representation along the British political spectrum. Conservative, Labour and Liberal Members of Parliament all made presentations, and in the process reinforced the idea that Wilton Park stood for democratic variety and not narrow doctrine.

Beginning in 1947, fifty German civilians, representing a broad range of occupations and professions in Germany itself, joined the POW sessions. The coming of these civilians had the major effect of making it possible to continue Wilton Park when all of the POWs returned home in mid-June 1948. In other words, it provided a bridge for continuing Wilton Park as an all-civilian enterprise.

With this change in the student body, it was also found necessary to move the operations from the rather primitive Nissen huts to more comfortable and more permanent structures on the Wilton Park manor grounds and to reduce the length of the regular sessions from six to four weeks and to even shorter sessions for German VIPs. Another change was soon instituted with the addition of small groups of Swiss, Dutch, Norwegians, French and other Western Europeans to the sessions. While the Germans remained the largest group, this development signaled the gradual shift away from primary emphasis on Anglo-German relations towards European and international relations broadly conceived.

Finally, the last important change during the first decade of Wilton Park's existence came in January 1951, when the center moved its operations from Beaconsfield to Wiston House in Sussex. Since Wilton Park had become the internationally-known name of the center, it moved to Sussex as well.

## Wilton Park, Wiston House

The end of the first decade nearly saw the end of Wilton Park itself. Facing a deep economic crisis, the British Foreign Office, the governmental agency that administered the center, announced in July 1956, that Wilton Park would be dismantled at the end of the following year. To people in Britain and Western Europe who were then or who had been associated with Wilton Park, this was a shocking development which they were unwilling to accept without a fight. One of the first groups to react was the Wilton Park Academic Council, a body of illustrious British scholars and public figures created in 1949 as an advisory group to look after Wilton Park's interests and to convince governmental authorities of its value. Addressing a letter of concern to the Prime Minister, the Council not only pointed out the great success of Wilton Park in helping to improve Anglo-German relations in the past, but also the need to expand its operations to do the same among the countries of the North Atlantic Treaty Organization (NATO) in the future. In other words, the Council's letter, while recognizing the achievement of Wilton Park in helping to bring about reconciliation with Germany, advocated a new role for the organization in the emerging Cold War with the Soviet Union.

Other groups, both in Britain and Western Europe, also took up the cause. For the staff at Wilton Park, perhaps the most gratifying support came from Germany where many groups were determined to keep the center alive, if necessary, by raising money to help finance its operations.

In the end the Foreign Office reversed its decision, but several changes were made in Wilton Park. First, it was decided that the preponderantly German participation would give way to a much broader international participation. Membership in the Organization for European Economic Cooperation (OEEC), which had been formed in 1948, was to be made the basis for issuing invitations to Wilton Park conferences. This meant that future participants would come from seventeen Western European nations as well as from the United States and Canada which were closely associated with OEEC. The effect of this decision was to put Wilton Park's future operations in an economic rather than the military context suggested by the Academic Council, though the East-West division was still clearly apparent. In 1960, the OEEC evolved into the Organization for Economic Cooperation and Development (OECD), within which the United States and Canada had full membership. Since that time, other countries from throughout the world have also joined OECD, removing from that institution any aura of the Cold War.

Although Heinz Koeppler proposed to have eight conferences of three weeks each every year under the new format, the length of the conferences was reduced to two weeks, with ten conferences annually. It was also decided that each conference would have a specific theme or topic, though participants were free to move off in whatever directions they wished.

To cope as well as possible with the language problems introduced by the new range of participants, equipment for simultaneous interpretation into German, French, and English was installed at the general conference sessions. The conference programs, as well as the semi-annual *Wilton Park Journal*, were also printed in three languages.

And finally, perhaps one of the most significant changes, was the creation of a new body, the International Advisory Council, to be composed of the Ambassadors in London of the participating OECD countries. Along with the Academic Council, this new body was to help maintain Wilton Park's academic independence as well as to inform their home governments of the center's work and development and to offer advice on the institution's future.

## *American Participation*

Even though these far-reaching changes in the nature of Wilton Park occurred in the late 1950s, the Germans continued to provide the largest contingent of conference participants in the 1960s and 1970s. As I was told by one staffer upon my arrival in 1979, the Germans still saw Wilton Park as *their* conference center. However, although late starters – only two participated in 1958, one in 1959, and three in 1960 – Americans, with 610, easily ranked second only to the Germans in total number of participants by the early 1970s. This seems an extraordinary development when one considers that the 'home country,' the United Kingdom, had provided only 462 and such nearby European countries as France and Italy only about 300 each.[9]

Reflection on this brief history of Wilton Park might suggest that a case is being made about the special relationship between Britain and Germany rather than the United States. But perhaps the last part of the previous paragraph indicates something of the explosive nature of American interest, which burst into being to such a degree that by the late 1970s Americans, too, were looking upon Wilton Park as *their* conference center as well.

How did this happen? One of the most interesting facts about this development is that it happened mainly on a private, voluntary basis. Unlike most of the other OECD countries, the United States did not establish governmental or semi-governmental machinery to recruit Wilton Park participants. On the contrary, American nominations for participation were provided by other American individuals who had participated previously – so-called 'Old Wiltonians.' Organizationally, the principal means by which this was done was through the American Friends of Wilton Park. While many other OECD countries had similar organizations of Old Wiltonians, none had the elaborate machinery of the American Friends. In addition to a national board of directors and the usual offices of president, vice-president, and secretary-treasurer, the American Friends had other vice-presidents for membership, financial grants, and five geographical regions: East, Washington D.C., South, Midwest, and West. There was further elaboration of this nationwide network down to the grass roots, so to speak, through many of these vice-presidents who held other posts. For example, the membership vice-president was connected with the American Association for Higher Education in Washington and the West regional vice-president was an officer in the Los Angeles World Affairs Council.[10]

Several of these officers were associated with American universities, perhaps one of the most significant factors for ongoing recruitment. Often sending participants yearly, such universities and university systems as the University of Missouri, the University of Iowa, Baylor University, and the California State Universities and Colleges, among others, kept a steady stream of professors and administrators moving back and forth across the Atlantic. Because there were so many Americans, but especially American academics, who wanted to attend a Wilton Park conference, I had to wait until late September 1979, after most were back home at work, before a place was available for me.[11]

## The Conference of September 1979

The previous discussion provides an explanation of how it happened that many Americans went to Wilton Park, but it does not say much about why it happened. What caused Americans to go by the hundreds to the conferences? Why did Old Wiltonians strongly encourage friends, colleagues, and even strangers to attend a conference?

To answer these questions something needs to be said about the nature of the conference experience itself. As indicated above, I arrived at Wiston House on a sunny day in early autumn. It was a Sunday afternoon, the first day of a week-long conference titled 'Communism in Europe and Detente.' By this time, most of the conferences – and there were seventeen that year – were of that length.

Before, during and after dinner that Sunday evening in the Great Hall, the Common Room, and the Bar, much was done by the Wilton Park staff to 'break the ice' among the three dozen participants from most of the Western European countries, the United States and Canada. Care had been taken to assure broad representation. There were one or two participants from elsewhere, such as the Australian Ambassador to the Soviet Union, but it soon became clear that the three languages of the conference would be adequate. In fact, most participants seemed to feel rather comfortable using only English – at least socially. Before the evening was over, most of us were already on a first-name basis with several participants, and I had had a rather lengthy conversation with a man I would come to know quite well in the conference days

*Participants in the September 1979 Wilton Park Conference at Wiston House. The Wilton Park shield, designed by Heinz Koeppler, features a Magdalen College, Oxford, lily and a bridge and is coloured blue, red and gold-yellow, representing the British Conservative, Labour and Liberal Parties, respectively. The author is in the fourth row, second from the right, standing in front and to the left of the gentleman with glasses and walrus moustache.*

ahead: a member of the Greek Communist Party who was a physician from Athens and who had a son studying medicine in London.

At the opening session on Monday morning, Director Tim Slack, who had been Koeppler's deputy before the latter retired, discussed at some length conference procedures and topics as outlined in the program booklet we had received the day before. Basically, he said that with the exception of Wednesday, there would be four sessions each day – named Morning I and II, Late Afternoon, and After Dinner – during which several types of activities would be alternated: plenary discussions, small group discussions and open discussions.

Plenary discussions, which involved the whole group in the Conference Room, would begin with a short (no more than thirty minutes in length) presentation by an outside speaker – a professor or government minister, for example – designed to stimulate thought and provoke reaction among participants. This interactive discussion would continue for another hour and one-half, and, like the presentation itself, would be interpreted by the staff into the conference's working languages. The small group discussions, in each of the three conference languages and led by a staff member, would be designed to explore in greater depth

*The Chanctonbury Ring on the South Downs above Wiston House in 1988, showing storm damage from the year before.*

issues raised in the plenary discussions. The least formal of all, the open discussions, which might be held in any of the large rooms, would bring together all participants who wanted to continue discussions on any topic.

The topics to be addressed by the outside speakers included the following: The Nature of Eurocommunism; Social and Political Change in the Soviet System; Security and Detente; An American View on Detente; Change Within Europe – A Labour View; Change Within Europe – A Conservative View; The Aims for a Marxist Society; and East-West Relations and Detente – A Finnish Point of View.

Of course, the participants would also come together for meals in the Great Hall, for morning and afternoon tea in the Common Room, and for drinks in the Bar before dinner and after the last session of the day. During free time, other opportunities for informal interaction included walking or jogging together down Mouse Lane to Steyning, or up the pathways to the Chanctonbury Ring on the Downs; playing tennis and croquet nearby; and strolling along the many garden paths and country lanes on the Wiston House estate.

In conferences lasting one week, Wednesday afternoons and evenings were usually set aside for what were called Extra-Mural Visits. For our group this meant a bus ride together to the British Army Staff College at Camberley, Surrey, where we would be given a briefing on how the Army perceived the military threat from the Warsaw Pact nations of Eastern Europe. Dinner would be taken with several of our briefing officers in a Camberley restaurant before the return trip to Wiston House.

Before concluding his opening remarks, Tim Slack mentioned a number of brief points, the importance and significance of which would not be fully understood and appreciated until after the conference had ended. First, he said that this was the participants' and not Wilton Park's conference. Hence, its success depended on the active involvement of all participants. Second, the method of the conference was discussion, not instruction. Therefore the academic staff should be viewed as facilitators, not teachers. Their role was to assist the participants in their discussions with one another.

Third, it was important to keep in mind one of Wilton Park's key objectives: to avoid narrow specialization. Since most participants were specialists of one kind or another, this objective might be something that many would have to work at. Fourth, with the conference only one rather than two weeks in length, a great deal had to be accomplished in a very short time. Again, it was very important for all participants to be actively involved as much as possible both in formal and informal activities.

And fifth, everything said during the conference was 'off-the-record.' No statements would be made to the press, and no published reports of the conference would be forthcoming. Hence, participants should express themselves freely and honestly as individuals rather than as national representatives in the give and take of discussion. And it was not necessary to be excessively polite to one another!

For the next five days, this intensive interaction and total immersion – as Americans would call it – with three dozen participants from fifteen countries and five academic staff members in Wiston House produced an unforgettable experience and a desire for more such experiences among most of the participants. (Since 1979, I have returned to Wiston House for nine complete conferences, sessions of two others, and one weekend student conference involving Hendrix College students. I attended my last conference in October 1998.)

## The Appeal of Wilton Park

Why? What is the essence of the drawing power of Wilton Park? While obviously a number of factors are involved, perhaps the most important one is the educational process used during the conference, as suggested above. Before discussing that process further, however, it should be made absolutely clear that Wilton Park, though administered by a British governmental agency, is indeed an academically independent educational institution – not unlike America's independent colleges and universities. The two Councils mentioned above guarantee both independence and freedom of thought and expression. Wilton Park is not a political propaganda machine.

With respect to Wilton Park's educational mission – in other words its underlying educational philosophy – perhaps one can start with the notion that three elements are present in most educational undertakings: materials or content; instructors or teachers; and learners or students. Given circumstances of available resources, time, facilities, and so forth, one tries to find the right combination of the three in order to have a successful educational enterprise. But it is also inevitable that one's educational philosophy will enter these considerations, and this will manifest itself in terms of which element will be given the greatest emphasis. In other words, will the process be content-centered or teacher-centered or student-centered?

Perhaps it is obvious from the discussion above that Koeppler and Wilton Park adopted a student-centered philosophy. Again, many reasons are undoubtedly involved here, but several seem to be central. First, the content approach runs counter to Koeppler's emphasis on the generalist rather than the specialist. By their very nature, modern industrial societies produce specialists in important positions, and therefore most conferences – as well as many if not most educational institutions – tend to serve the needs and interests of these specialists. Hence, content is emphasized in such institutions. In positioning itself –

that is, in addressing a need – Wilton Park attempted by design to be different from the typical conference center.

In addition, Koeppler knew that since Wilton Park participants would be diverse – not only in terms of nationalities and occupations but also in languages and politics – it would be exceedingly difficult if not impossible to present complex materials in a meaningful and understandable way in a short period of time. If a content approach were taken, much information would be almost literally thrown at participants but little would be absorbed. Under such conditions, how much learning would actually take place? Obviously, Koeppler believed, very little.

Like the content-centered approach, Koeppler also rejected the teacher-centered philosophy. No doubt remembering his own experience in Germany's interwar educational institutions, he knew that this approach did not encourage the free exchange of ideas and other democratic values. Taken to the extreme, as it was done in Hitler's Germany, the system was essentially authoritarian in nature. A joke heard at Wilton Park perhaps reflected the essence of the problem with the teacher-centered approach as seen by Koeppler. In English schools, when the teacher enters the classroom in the morning and says, 'Good morning, students,' the students respond by saying, 'Good morning, teacher.' In German schools, on the other hand, when the teacher says the same thing, the students respond by writing it in their notebooks!

In addition, Koeppler also knew that it was highly unlikely that Wilton Park participants, whose ages would be mainly from early thirties to late fifties, would find a teacher-centered philosophy acceptable. Unlike college undergraduates or other students, the participants would be people who were well established in their careers as professors, diplomats, business people, and the like, and hence not accustomed to any hint of being lectured at in their daily activities.

Of course, the student-centered approach – the learning-by-doing philosophy – has its problems as well, but Koeppler believed that they were manageable. Perhaps the most serious one was the time factor. One can now understand why he wanted three-week conferences, because it takes a considerable amount of time to break down the barriers among participants, something that is obviously necessary with interactive discussion as the main method of learning. And of course these barriers are many in number and formidable in nature. In the first place, most participants arrive at Wiston House as complete strangers to one another. If that were not enough in itself, there is a long list of other barriers, such as language, nationality, occupational, class, religious, political, educational, and bureaucratic – just to name a few.

So one of the main tasks at the conference is to break down these barriers as much and as swiftly as possible by developing the level of familiarity and trust among the participants to such a degree that they are willing to be honest, frank, and open with one another. In other words, a group of very diverse individuals who are pulled apart by the many differences mentioned above must somehow transcend those differences to become a community of learners.

This happens at Wilton Park. At least it happened at the conference I attended in 1979, but it took several days of hard work. My feeling is that the participants really began to come together on Wednesday during the Extra-Mural Visit to Camberley, though the place itself had very little to do with it. A visit to London would have probably had the same results. For what seemed to happen was that the participants now began to look upon themselves as a like-minded group – a group with a common purpose and with at least the beginnings of a common experience. In short, a bonding process began. As a result, the remaining two days of the conference brought about significant accomplishments.

What was achieved? To try to answer this simply stated yet difficult question, perhaps a few comments from past participants will help. From an American specialist in international relations:

> There is a certain type of social chemistry which occurs at Wilton Park. Part of it ... is the result of the lovely location. All participants seem pleased and relaxed to be in that kind of setting ... Conversational inhibitions therefore tend to drop away ... Moreover, the Wilton Park staff is extremely skillful at this kind of chemistry, creating a personal environment where the participants are almost immediately willing to start talking to each other.

From an American corporation executive:

> Nowhere else that I know of is there a forum where one may come to terms with political ideas and test reactions in a laboratory situation ... as one may at Wilton Park.

From a French lawyer:

> Wilton Park is a melting pot where prejudices and preconceived ideas dissolve and give way to a pragmatic view of the world, more realistic because it is more multinational.

And from a British civil servant:

> I am not sure that I learned anything new, but I certainly had my prejudices dented.[12]

Of the many, many comments I have read and heard about Wilton Park conferences for twenty years, these four probably come the closest to my own views. What our 1979 conference achieved, I believe, was to force its participants to examine such things as their narrow prejudices, assumptions, attitudes, habits of mind and world views, and to have some of them somewhat 'dented' if not changed. It would, of course, be expecting far too much to have participants change significantly such fundamental and basic things as these in only a week's time. Hence, the word 'dented' – or perhaps the word 'questioned' – seems about right.

Putting the achievement in more positive terms, the conference process activated the more cosmopolitan instincts of its participants. That is, it appealed to strong interests in international problems, ideas, movements, fashions, and cultures as well as to principles, rational discourse, and civility in dealing with them. In short, emphasis was on the universal rather than the parochial, on uniting the fragments with the whole rather than breaking apart. This idea of bonding together for a larger purpose was especially evident at the formal dinner concluding the conference where much of the ceremony emphasized an 'Old Wiltonian' theme: 'old boys (and girls)' forever tied together by the common Wilton Park experience.

A very memorable experience with the Greek Communist physician mentioned before illustrates this well. After the formal dinner, the conference participants gathered in the Common Room for some community singing led by the good doctor. Having been taken by his son to the Last Night of the Proms the day before the conference began, he had heard the crowd sing British patriotic songs at the Albert Hall in London and now conducted our group in a similar performance. The Spirit of Wilton Park seemed to be captured well that night when a Greek Communist led a diverse international body in singing 'Jerusalem,' 'Land of Hope and Glory,' and 'Rule Britannia!'

## *Special Relationship Appeal*

Perhaps this discussion gives some insight concerning the appeal of Wilton Park to people from the world over but provides little about the special relationship between Britain and the United States. What has been the special appeal, if any, to Americans? Several factors are important, and perhaps these are not unrelated to the fact that at least half of America's participants have had academic occupations.[13]

First, there is the collegiate ideal that Koeppler adopted mainly from the residential colleges at Oxford and that has flourished in the United States primarily in the small liberal arts colleges, such as Hendrix College, that dot the American landscape from coast to coast. Many American participants attended, taught in, and/or were familiar with one or more of these colleges before they went to Wilton Park. Hence, they understood the generalist approach to education and the goal of developing knowledgeable amateurs. In this sense, there is something very 'American,' if you will, about Wilton Park. It is *Alma Mater* for many of us.

Second, the Koeppler educational philosophy of student-centered learning-by-doing is also very American in nature. Whether the founder of Wilton Park ever read John Dewey's educational theories is not known, but he was certainly in tune with this great American philosopher, according to one former colleague who studied Dewey.[14] As known in educational circles, Dewey – among other Progressive and Experimental educators – made the learning-by-doing approach the centerpiece of American educational philosophy in the twentieth century. Most Americans going to Wilton Park have been exposed to this philosophy in one form or another during their lifetimes.

And third, there is the Koeppler method of discussion rather than instruction. Perhaps no other country has given greater emphasis to the method of interactive discussion in the classroom than has the United States. The point/counterpoint or dialectical method certainly has been used extensively and even more widely advocated in American education. Here, too, most Americans have felt very comfortable with Wilton Park's method.

Yet, there are certainly several factors present as well that are much more British than American in nature. One can only speculate that perhaps these appeal to American Anglophile propensities, or even American envies. At any rate they are elements of the Special Relationship.

First, the British sense of history is important. Being products of a 'new nation' looking to the future, Americans have a short history and for some of us a longer history rejected or at least denied by the Declaration of Independence and the American Revolutionary War, as the latter is called in the United States. Wiston House, as well as historical Sussex with the South Downs, helps Americans to reconnect with their own longer history and with the history of Western Civilization generally (see the next chapter). It is difficult to escape the feeling of continuity – of the past – of the unfolding of history itself at a Wilton Park conference just below the South Downs.

Second – to use Koeppler's words – 'Britain is the home of the self-denying ordinance, the arrangement by which the piper decides not to call the tune.'[15] The self-denying ordinance provides the basis for Wilton Park's academic integrity, making it a government-subsidized institution yet free from governmental interference. This quality, which Americans greatly admire, is seen perhaps most dramatically in the independent work of the British Broadcasting Corporation (BBC) which has served as the model for public broadcasting in the United States.

Third – and related to the second point – is the British sense of fair play, or as some might call it, sportsmanship. This gentlemanly attribute, so important to Alistair Cooke and associated with the British public schools and their games, is very much in evidence at Wilton Park conferences. The emphasis on all participants being drawn into discussions and other activities – no one being left in a corner by himself or herself – and on all points of view being listened to comes from this very British attitude. No attempt is made by the Wilton Park academic staff to impose a particular idea or attitude on anyone.

Fourth – and again related to the previous point – is the British sense of civility. In our own time, it has certainly become a cliche to refer to Britain as one of the most civilized countries in the world. Americans look with envy – and with disbelief – at the fact that most British police officers do not carry guns and in fact do not wish to carry them. Cliche or not there is certainly a sense of civility in Britain, largely absent in much of the United States, that manifests itself very strongly at Wiston House. All Americans who go there feel and appreciate it.

In summary, then, the first three reasons listed above are ones that are essentially 'American' and hence tie into the American experience at home, while the last four are basically 'British' but highly desirable for Americans. Looking at these British attributes closely, we see that they are fundamentally Helper values as identified in a previous chapter. The self-denying ordinance comes from the willingness to sacrifice one's own personal interests for those of others – in this instance the interests of one's nation for the higher interests of the world community. Fair play is of course directly related to the fairness value that is absolutely central to the entire configuration of Helper characteristics. The sense of civility comes from several values rather than only one, including broadmindedness, understanding and kindness.

Perhaps the sense of history stems not so much from one or even a cluster of Helper values but from one of her basic functions: nurturing. The chief transmitter of a society's values from one generation to another, the Helper is the central figure in the process of enculturation or socialization. As such, she selects from the collective memory those aspects of the culture worthy enough to be passed on to the next generation. She more than any other figure of the nuclear family is the conservator of the past for present and future generations. Hence, the Helper is the first history teacher of us all (see also the previous chapter).

It can be said, I believe, that these seven factors formed the core of the reasons why Wilton Park was a very important institution of the special relationship for Americans and perhaps for the British as well in the 1960s and 1970s, the Koeppler era. The past tense in the last sentence above is significant, for alas, by the late 1980s the Koeppler concept had ceased to exist, and Wilton Park had evolved into a very different institution. The change probably began as early as 1983 with the resignation of Director Tim Slack which was followed in the next several years by retirements and other departures of staff members from the Koeppler years. Not only was the institutional memory lost but the new director by design established a different concept.

Basically, he adopted a content-centered approach in a four-day conference format. In so doing, he and his successors in the years that followed changed or dropped entirely certain important parts of Koeppler's educational process. For example, the number of small group discussions was reduced and those that remained were usually chaired by a participant rather than by a trained leader from the academic staff. The Extra-Mural Visit – a key element in the bonding process – was downgraded to a short tourist excursion of a couple hours in length to a nearby town. And Koeppler's 'one-group' concept – that all participants would be actively involved in all things during the entire conference – was dropped in favor of allowing participants to enter and to leave the conference on any day they wished.

In fairness to the new director, as well as to his successors, he was almost certainly under intense pressure from the Foreign Office to make changes, mainly for financial reasons. Yet, he readily laid the ground-work for the repositioning of Wilton Park as a center for specialists who frequently know one another already from previous professional contacts rather than as a forum for a whole range of total strangers with diverse backgrounds. Koeppler's 'college' for the 'amateur éclairé' was on the way out. Hence, today Wilton Park seems less like an English or American liberal arts college with certain desirable British characteristics and more like a typical 'think tank' for specific policy matters. There is little apart from its beautiful setting and history that makes it unique.

As a consequence Wilton Park has declined as an institution of the Special Relationship. It is important to mention, however, that certain factors in the larger environment of the institution have encouraged this change as well. One of these is Britain's involvement in the European Union and the consequent re-orientation of Wilton Park to European rather than North Atlantic matters. Another is the end of the Cold War and the resulting reduction of security issues involving the United States on Wilton Park's agenda of conferences.

Yet, while Americans still come to Wilton Park when such issues are examined, the old enthusiasm of the 1960s and 1970s for general participation in all conferences has declined as seen in the virtual disappearance of the American Friends of Wilton Park as a national organization for recruitment. The nationwide network of Old Wiltonian devotees is gone. Hence today the American Friends is essentially an empty shell of its former self and could in fact disappear entirely within a few years. In addition the old American university networks with places like Baylor, a driving force for Wilton Park recruitment and support for many years, are not what they used to be. Again, the enthusiasm that was once there is gone.

For some, perhaps the Germans who still seem enthusiastic, the evolution of Wilton Park into a very different institution has not been very significant, but for Americans who experienced the Koeppler concept, it has meant something to be regretted. As the latter see it, the original institution as remembered is now gone. For those of us who knew it well from the 1960s to the early 1980s, Wilton Park has almost assumed a legendary quality in our memories. Perhaps, therefore, it is appropriate to turn to legend – British legend as interpreted in American music – for our lament about its passing. This is Camelot, the legendary court of sixth-century King Arthur, which was made popular in the United States by the Broadway musical of the same name and which became associated in the American mind with the brief and tragic Presidency of John F. Kennedy in the early 1960s. The closing lines of the title song seem appropriate here:

> Don't let it be forgot,
> That once there was a spot,
> For one brief shining moment
> That was known as Camelot.

If Old Wiltonians in America had the ear of the British powers-that-be, we might say only two words, the ones on a placard carried by a solitary figure during the equally brief and tragic Robert Kennedy Presidential campaign of 1968: 'Camelot Again.'

## Notes

1. Janet Pennington, 'A Brief History of Wiston House,' Wiston House Publication, 1990. Most of the historical information on Wiston House used in this chapter comes from this publication which is a revision of earlier ones.

2. 'Wiston House International Conference Centre: The Home of Wilton Park Conferences,' Wiston House Publication, no date.

3. Pennington, 'A Brief History of Wiston House,' 2.

4. Matthew Barry Sullivan, *Thresholds of Peace: German Prisoners and the People of Britain, 1944–1948* (London: Hamish Hamilton, 1979), 242.

5. 'Koeppler Trust,' Sir Heinz Koeppler Trust Publication, 1985. Most of the biographical information on Heinz Koeppler that follows comes from this publication.

6. Robert S. Sturrock to John Ziegler, 23 January 1996.

7. Heinz Koeppler, 'Frederick Barbarossa and the Schools of Bologna,' *English Historical Review* 216 (October 1939): 577–97. See also 'Koeppler Trust.'

8. Dexter M. Keezer, *A Unique Contribution to International Relations: The Story of Wilton Park* (London: McGraw-Hill Book Company, 1973). Most of the historical information on Wilton Park used in this chapter comes from this publication. While a conference participant, Keezer, an American and former president of Reed College, interviewed Heinz

Koeppler and other Wilton Park staffers and had access to the organization's files.

9. Ibid., 58.
10. 'Old Wiltonian Associations and Contacts,' *Wilton Park Journal* 53 (December 1976), 39.
11. Keezer, 56.
12. Ibid., 90–1.
13. 'Newsletter,' The American Friends of Wilton Park, Department of Journalism, Baylor University, Waco, Texas, 1980.
14. Robert S. Sturrock to John Ziegler, 28 March 1996.
15. H. Koeppler, *Purpose, Aims, and Methods of Wilton Park* (Wilton Park Publication, 1971), 16.

# Chapter VIII

# On the South Downs Way and Other Paths

And did those feet in ancient time
Walk upon England's mountains green?
And was the Holy Lamb of God
On England's pleasant pastures seen?

*W*henever I have taken to the rural public footpaths of Britain, I have been reminded of those opening lines of William Blake's 'Milton.' Perhaps they are better known as the lyrics of the famous song 'Jerusalem' from the popular 1980s film *Chariots of Fire*. While I can't say that my search for the 'special relationship' with Britain ever focused on those two questions asked by Blake, I have felt that my search in the British countryside has been much more mystical in nature than in any other area of inquiry. The hard evidences – the documents, the records, the books, and so forth – are just not there. Moreover, there is no institution as such to probe and analyze. By and large, most of my information came from the experiences of planning hikes and then walking the public footpaths that criss-cross Sussex, the part of rural Britain I know best. Hence, it is the public footpath, something rather rare in the United States, that is my vehicle in this chapter.

Why the public footpath? As suggested above, it was something unknown to me until I visited Britain, and I found in it certain very attractive things. In fact much of the answer to the question lies in the words themselves. In this case, the word public means public, not like the British use of that term with respect to certain famous schools such as Eton and Harrow which are in fact private. Thus, public paths are open to the public at large even though they may cut across private property.

Foot also means foot and not a vehicle of some sort, though occasionally bridle paths – sometimes even roads – and footpaths blend into one. But most importantly what the word foot suggests is that the system has been built on a human scale. The automobile or even the horse-drawn cart of yesteryear did not determine the nature of this 'thoroughfare' but walking humankind did.

And path means path, though sometimes because of the lack of use or other factors, it is difficult to determine literally where the path lies. Also its surface may consist of mud sticky enough to extract a shoe or two! But the important point here is that the word path means a way – a link if you will – to something else ahead and behind one's current location. In short, the public footpath ties people and places together in a most humanlike way.

When considering the ancient history of these pathways, which are still used today, one can understand why this is the case. Take, for example, the paths on the tops of the North and South Downs, the two ranges of low hills which extend across much of south-eastern England. During the Old Stone Age when Britain was still part of the continent of Europe, hunters, palaeolithic nomads, travelled to southern England in search of food, and no doubt walked along these chalk ridges because they were drier and less incumbered by trees than the swampy and forested lowlands. As the Stone Age passed into the Bronze Age, these hilltop tracks became in effect the roads linking together the first permanent settlements which were developed on the uplands as well. These tracks became quite long, though not usually as long-distance routes but by extension as the farms and fortified villages spread over more and more of the uplands where there was land clear of trees.

Occasionally these trackways left the highest ridges and ran along the lower escarpments of the chalk hills, though still above the forests that covered most of the land. One of these follows the escarpment of the North Downs and is known today as the Pilgrims' Way made famous by Chaucer in *Canterbury Tales*. However, it was trodden thousands of years before the middle ages by other pilgrims going in the opposite direction from Canterbury to the Salisbury Plain and Stonehenge. If the Neolithic people had a cultural and religious center, it was based on those great stones, and many of the ancient trackways of southern England seem to converge on the Plain. No wonder a sense of mysticism can overtake the walker of these ancient pathways! [1]

It certainly did soon after I embarked on my first brief walk on the South Downs in 1979 during a break in a Wilton Park Conference I was attending. Thus, I rather easily came to see myself as a modern pilgrim. As Sean Jennett points out in his *The Pilgrims Way*, I had tradition behind me to do so, for the word 'pilgrim' comes from the Latin word 'peregrinus' which means a foreigner. While he goes on to say that historically this meaning came not from the pilgrim himself but from the people in whose country he wandered, I was initially inclined to accept both points of view that I was indeed a foreigner because so many things in rural Sussex seemed so different from

America.[2] What I badly needed was a good local guide or even a guidebook, but being on my own without such, I had to take that first short walk virtually unassisted. That experience convinced me I would need some informed help before I undertook a major hike of the South Downs in the future.

## The Society of Sussex Downsmen

So I became a member of the Society of Sussex Downsmen, an organization founded in 1923. Today we would probably classify this organization as environmentalist in nature, not unlike America's Sierra Club though on a smaller scale, but originally it seems to have been more romantic in purpose as some lines from its early 'theme song' indicate:

> You may sing to me of the wolds of Kent,
> Of Devonshire lanes, and their sweet content,
> I know nothing of these to their detriment,
> Nor of Surrey's greeneree.
> You may praise if you will, the Northern dales,
> The Cotswold Hills, and the peaks of Wales;
> But give me the land of the Channel gales,
> The Sussex Downs for me!

And four additional lines from the song's chorus:

> Oh, give me cliffs of Beachy Head,
> On Blackdown's summit I'll make my bed;
> And I'll walk from Old Steyning to Chanctonberee,
> For the Sussex Downs are a-calling me!

This back-to-nature element runs throughout the song as the concluding lines show:

> And give me the note of the sweet sheep-bell,
> The song of the lark, with its magic spell,
> The peewit's call, and the gull's as well,
> On Rackham and Didling Down;
> For this is the dearest land to me,
> The land of the thorn and the tangled tree,
> The land that I call my own!

While the anonymous author of these lines will never pose a serious threat to a major poet like Kipling who also wrote about the Downs, he or she paints a rather compelling word picture of some of the sights and sounds of the hills which the Society hopes to preserve. In its own words the Society says that the object for which it is established is the 'preservation of the beauty and amenities of the South Downs in the Counties of East and West Sussex ... for the public benefit.' In view of my own interests, one of the 'subsidiary objects' of the organization easily caught my eye: 'To collect and preserve the literature, legends, folk-lore, folk-customs and history relating to the Sussex Downs.'[3]

Although I never became an active participant in this sizeable organization (over 2,500 members in the mid-1990s), I have followed with great interest via newsletters and reports its activities and suggested readings. These included listings and descriptions of sponsored guided walks and of books and pamphlets about various aspect of the Downs. The printed materials were most helpful in my trying to get an overview before considering specific areas for actual walks.

## An Overview of the Downs

The first thing I learned from my reading was that both the North and South Downs are rather long given the small size of south-eastern England. And though the major ways or pathways do not follow the entire lengths of the two ranges, they cover over one hundred miles each if one extends as guidebooks do the South Downs Way westward from Buriton to Winchester. In fact, one can say then that Winchester is the western terminus of both northern and southern ways while Canterbury and Eastbourne, the latter on the English Channel, serve the same function on the eastern ends, respectively.

Why Winchester in the west? In the first place, it was a very ancient settlement although its exact origins are unknown. It is known, however, that there was a sizeable settlement along the Itchen River just below the center of today's hillside Winchester long before the birth of Christ. This was called Caer Gwent, a Celtic name meaning the white town, and it was probably a fortified one. When the Romans seized it after their invasion in AD 44, the town was still flourishing, and they renamed it Venta Belgarum, the market town of the Belgae. Significantly, they made it the focus of a system of highways connecting with a number of other towns: Portchester, Southampton, Old Sarum, Cirencester and Silchester, among others. These communications centering on Winchester made it the obvious center and capital for the Saxon kings who won control of southern England after the Romans left and who founded the kingdom of Wessex. With the arrival of Christianity, Winchester ultimately became in the seventh century a cathedral city with the relocation there of the see founded by St Birinus at Dorchester-on-Thames.[4]

Perhaps most importantly for the development and use of the pathways, within two centuries of the relocation, Winchester became the goal of a popular pilgrimage to the grave of its saintly bishop Swithun. While not much is known about him, Swithun enlarged his cathedral and built a defensive wall around the precinct which provided additional shelter and safety when the Danes came raiding. According to Jennett, it was perhaps partly for this security as well as for the humility of his character that made the people of Winchester love him deeply. In fact, his essential humility made him ask that at his death he should be buried in some out-of-the-way grave on the north side of the cathedral, the side always regarded as less desirable because it was cold and away from the warmth and light of the sun.[5]

A hundred years after his death Swithun was so revered as a saint that his name was added to the dedication of the cathedral, and in 971 his body was transferred from its humble grave to a shrine behind the high alter. According to accounts of the time, the movement of the body was accompanied by various miracles, including a rainstorm that lasted forty days. It was thought that the showers were the saint's tears which were shed as a consequence of his removal to such an exalted place contrary to his wishes. Yet apparently the saint became reconciled to his fate, for additional miracles soon occurred at the new tomb. The result, as Jennett concludes, was that Swithun's shrine became the object of widespread national and even international pilgrimages, the most popular pilgrimage in England until the shrine of Thomas Becket came into vogue in Canterbury after 1170.[6]

Apparently this new development did not completely diminish the importance of St Swithun – at least among the devout pilgrims – during the middle ages, for they could now achieve two pilgrimages in one by following the northern pathway from Winchester to Canterbury or vice versa depending on where they started their pilgrimage in either England or on the continent of Europe. Hence, the pathway may have been rather heavily traveled by religious pilgrims going in both directions for centuries.[7]

Perhaps little needs to be said about the famous Thomas Becket in Canterbury, especially about his martyrdom, in view of the numerous accounts even into modern times through movie film and T. S. Eliot's popular play *Murder in the Cathedral*. But something should be mentioned about Becket's great pulling power – his ability to replace Swithun as 'number one' in the pilgrim mind. Or as Adam Nicolson asks: why was Becket 'thought of as a great saint?'[8]

Nicolson himself sees the answer lying more in politics than in religion, for Becket's 'holiness was almost entirely expressed in a political way.' By his martyrdom, which was essentially a political act, Becket guaranteed the independence of the church courts, an independence from King Henry II in particular and the Crown in general which lasted until the Reformation. And it was rather obvious at the time that Becket wanted to accomplish this through martyrdom because he had many opportunities to avoid this fate. However, displaying great courage and belief in his cause, he stopped his men from barring the cathedral door against the four assassin knights on December 29, 1170, and said those lines of martyrdom quoted again and again down through the ages shortly before he was killed: 'It is not fitting to make a fortress of the house of prayer. We came not to resist but to suffer.'[9]

However, in terms of great political theater, the kind that has the most impact on the public of the time as well as later generations, Henry's journey in July 1174 along the northern route, the part that became known as the Pilgrims' Way in the eighteenth century, to do penitence at Canterbury for Becket's death, is even more extraordinary than the murder. This event must have been something remarkable to behold, as well as to hear about down through the years: the King of England, one of the most powerful men of Europe who held his position by divine right, grovelling before the tomb of a cleric. What a powerful message that was!

In fact the whole story is very remarkable. Following his five-day journey along the Way during which time he lived on only bread and water, Henry put on sackcloth and ashes and went barefoot through the streets of Canterbury. His feet were cut so severely by the stony streets that a trail of blood was left along the way. Arriving inside the cathedral, he prayed at length, first in the north transept where Becket was murdered and then in the crypt before his coffin. After that, Henry's clothes were drawn down from his shoulders and he was flogged, five strokes from the prelates there, and three each from the monks of whom there were at least eighty. He then spent the night at prayer in the crypt, ending with a mass as day broke.[10]

With such a display of posthumous power to bring a king literally to his knees, it is no wonder that people came to believe Becket could work great miracles. Hence, at the center of the pilgrimages to Canterbury at the eastern end of the northern pathway was the cult of relics. As Nicolson indicates, to the medieval mind the spiritual beauty of Becket's life did not desert his physical remains at death. His body was as holy as the man had been alive and possessed miraculous powers of healing. To visit Becket's relics and be cured by them was almost invariably the aim of many pilgrimages.[11]

Yet, as Chaucer's characters in *Canterbury Tales* illustrate, the pilgrimage phenomenon cannot be reduced to this one cause alone. The journey itself could be imposed as a penance. Tourism, the sometimes suffocating pressures of medieval life itself, and ordinary human curiosity – among still other factors – must have also accounted for many of the pilgrimages.[12]

Again, as Chaucer's descriptions of his characters indicate, perhaps the style of the pilgrimage was just as important to the pilgrim as the substance. What was done could involve anything from the luxurious cortege of a penitent aristocrat to the dependence of a single pilgrim on charity along the way. As Nicolson observes, to go on foot was thought especially virtuous and to go alone was even better. No shoes brought the pilgrim nearer sanctity while those seeking the greatest humility could go naked as some fourteenth century pilgrims actually did![13]

Whatever the motivation behind or the style of the pilgrimage, one thing is known for sure: the Becket shrine became quite wealthy from the countless gifts of gold and silver and of rare and precious stones brought by many. Among them was a great ruby, the Regale of France, given by King Louis. According to Jennett, the Becket shrine was without parallel in brilliance and wealth.[14]

It remained so until 1538 when Henry VIII suppressed the monasteries. By that time the numbers of pilgrims had declined because the faith of old was changing. As Jennett observes, to a great extent the pilgrimage had become a habit, a custom, a frame of mind of the middle ages, and the middle ages were passing away with the impact of the Renaissance and Reformation. Taking advantage of the changing climate of opinion, Henry took his action and in so doing also targeted Becket's shrine. While some things survived Henry's attempt at total obliteration – including the saint's bones, so it is thought – the days of Becket as the greatest saint of the English Church were in the past.[15]

In concluding this discussion of the northern pathway, one can see, then, that the Christian religious pilgrimage was central to its use for many centuries. On the other hand, the southern pathway, primarily what is known as the South Downs Way today, seems to have had other uses as well, though this Christian element was there, too.

Perhaps a major clue to the other uses of the South Downs Way is seen in the fact that the eastern terminus is near Eastbourne along the Channel. Actually, it is probably more telling to use the names of Beachy Head and the Seven Sisters, the high chalk cliffs overlooking the sea, maybe the most spectacular sight along the southern coast of England. In this regard, it seems unfortunate that the so-called White Cliffs of Dover, which are lovely but not as awe-inspiring, have received greater publicity through film and song. World War II symbolism is very difficult to compete with.

By this reference to the Channel, I am not suggesting that the eastern end of the South Downs Way served as a gateway to England from the continent of Europe for Christian pilgrimages. Apparently ports further east, such as Dover, where the Channel narrows most were important in this regard. No, what I am suggesting is that the Downs, per se, may provide the answer as to why people from all ages came to use them. Hence, I must tell the rather complex story of how the Downs came about in the first place.

Briefly, from a geological perspective, the story can be outlined in the following way. During the first geological era, perhaps between 230 and 600 million years ago, volcanoes and earth movements in what is now England formed palaeozoic rocks upon which settled sedimentary deposits. Rivers washed down sand and gravel which in time formed sedimentary rock. The land then became submerged under the sea which in turn deposited greensand and gault clay on the rock. The temperature of the sea then rose, and the warmer waters became the home of countless marine animals called Foraminifera whose tiny shells formed the basis of chalk during what is known as the Cretaceous period, a time period lasting 72 million years.[16]

During the Eocene period, more sand and clay covered the chalk deposits and then, in comparatively recent geological times, violent earth movements pushed the land in southeastern England upwards into a huge dome above the sea. This is the area known today as the North and South Downs and the Weald, the latter the low land between the two ranges of hills. The subsequent erosive effects of water and wind tended to level the central area of the dome, the Weald, leaving only the outer slopes of chalk, the North and South Downs. Rivers, some of them now gone, cut through the chalk hills, mainly in a north-south direction, and about 6,000 years ago the sea broke through the narrow band of land that still linked Britain to the continent of Europe, creating Beachy Head and the Seven Sisters on the new coast.[17]

It may seem very strange that the chalk hills did not succumb to massive erosion as well, but it is precisely because water can percolate through chalk that the Downs have not been worn away. On the other hand, this characteristic of chalk has significantly influenced for millenia what people have been able to do on the Downs. Life has been dictated by the absolute lack of surface water and the strong acidity of the soil which resulted from its being constantly drained or leached.[18]

So as indicated at the outset of the chapter, these dry and rather barren chalk ridges provided early hunters from Europe an excellent pathway for their excursions into England more than 6,000 years ago. This natural highway remained such even after the physical break from Europe, for it was the recommended route for travellers going the breadth of Sussex until the coming of the turnpikes in the eighteenth century.[19]

Yet, even before the break came and long before the advent of Christianity, the arrival of the first farmers from Europe introduced certain religious and other practices that also had an impact on the use of the South Downs. In the first place, they built the early phases of both Stonehenge and Avebury, and therefore in so doing no doubt encouraged considerable foot traffic along the South Downs of pilgrims going to these religious and cultural centers. In addition, their culture, which has been called Windmill Hill, included the practice of burying at least the important dead in long barrows on the Downs, the construction of which required considerable cooperative manpower.

Some of these barrows, structures of shining white chalk, were over sixty yards long and more than three yards high. At the time of construction they were set on the brow of a hill from which they could dominate all around, but today they appear as merely low grassy mounds.[20]

As farmers of the Stone Age, these Windmill Hill people were much more interested in being permanent residents rather than mere transients on the Downs. Hence, they cleared whatever existing trees were necessary and constructed on the hills what are known as causewayed camps in which they lived and kept their domesticated animals.[21]

While these people certainly left their mark on the South Downs, it was probably the Bronze Age inhabitants that first altered their appearance most significantly. For around BC 2000, the tall, long-headed people who began to walk the chalk ridges introduced the custom of burying their dead in round barrows or tumuli, a custom that lasted to Saxon times. More than 400 of these tumuli have been located along the South Downs Way, and perhaps a thousand are in greater Sussex alone.[22]

Clearly having religious reasons behind their actions, these people at first buried their dead in a foetal position in the tumuli – perhaps for the return of the body to Mother Earth – with a pot of food beside them for the afterlife. Later, after cremation was introduced, they put the ashes of the dead in the food vessel. Called the Beaker Folk for this practice, little more is known about these religious people. Today their burial mounds are nothing but grassy 'warts,' as Nicolson calls them, often with a depression in their center where grave robbers and archaeologists have dug. But originally some of the tumuli may have been thirty feet high and brilliant white from their chalk construction before they were overgrown.[23]

While other religious practices had some impact on the use of the hills later on, defense needs somewhat altered the appearance of the South Downs during the next period, the Iron Age. The major contribution to the landscape of this more violent age was the hillfort of which there are nineteen, most of them very small stockaded farms. The largest by far is the Cissbury Ring, just north of Worthing, which is a rather massive sixty-acre fortress. The site itself had been in use during earlier ages for flint mining. The fort, like others of this later time, was intended as a refuge in time of attack, but this one has the most impressive earthworks on the South Downs. Dating from the third century BC, its defenses were renewed by the Romans as a protection against the Saxons. Apparently its inner rampart, chiefly constructed of chalk rubble, was secured in front by some nine to twelve thousand timber posts about fifteen feet high.[24]

Yet, in terms of size the Cissbury Ring is indeed the exception among the hillforts because as indicated before water shortages on top of the

Downs greatly limited the nature of habitations. Elaborate and innovative technology to obtain running water was still many centuries away, though perhaps the Iron Age people may have invented the dewpond, a small indentation in the ground sealed with clay to prevent water from rain and mists from seeping away. However, while many dewponds can be found today, it is thought that most of them are probably no older than the eighteenth century. Hence, large settlements, such as villages and much later the manors and other great houses, were built at the foot of the Downs where springs are available in abundance.[25]

Perhaps the most famous of all the hillforts is the Chanctonbury Ring, the best-known Sussex landmark located near Steyning, mainly because of the ring of beech trees following the perimeter which were, however, planted as recently as 1760. Unfortunately, this beautiful hilltop crown of trees was decimated during storms in the 1980s. The fort also has one of the most important strategic locations on the highest point in the area overlooking the Adur River and Arun River valleys which run north and south through the Downs. Excavation of the fort's interior this century revealed the remains of a small religious temple apparently used during the Roman occupation of Sussex.

In successfully growing wheat on the South Downs, the Romans also changed their appearance somewhat, though traditionally, again mainly because of the water problem, they have been used as pasturelands for animals, especially sheep. The famous South Down breed of sheep was developed which had short wool but meat lightly flavored from the wild thyme growing on the hills. In this century modern agricultural practices as well as other factors have brought more of the Downs under the plough.[26] Yet, one has the feeling that the earliest visitors to Britain would still easily recognize the South Downs if they could return today.

In conclusion, then, the southern pathway from Eastborne to Winchester – the South Downs Way and its extension – has been a major natural highway or link for many uses, including religious and defensive, mainly because of the nature and location of the Downs themselves. Most importantly the chalk composition of the hills has been the key: being relatively but not overly high and dry they have been excellent for traveling, especially walking; burying the dead, following religious practices; defending the area; and pasturing animals, especially sheep. On the other hand, the same characteristics of the hills have prevented or restricted many things, including large settlements of people who have had to build their homes in the valleys. Many, certainly those who have loved nature and the countryside, have not been unhappy about these limitations.

Perhaps Adam Nicolson has put his finger on an important difference between the northern and southern pathways in our time. He concludes his discussion of the former in the following way:

It is necessary to keep the historical idea firmly before one on the Pilgrims Way if the whole walk is not to disintegrate into something slightly ludicrous, particularly in Surrey, where you thread your way from golf course to back-garden to golf course again. It is all too easy to feel foolish standing in Guildford High Street in great boots and carting a rucksack. You cannot expect the exposure of other long walks on the North Downs today. To do so leads only to frustration and a hatred of suburban life. You must resolve either to love the putting greens themselves or carefully exclude them from your mind, filling it instead, as a medieval traveller would have done, with the strange story of Thomas a Becket.[27]

Fortunately, the South Downs Way has not reached this point, as yet, and it is hoped it never will because of its unique characteristics and the work of organizations like the Society of Sussex Downsmen.

## *The Walks*

With thoughts like these sticking in my mind, I decided to walk on the South Downs again. So questions such as where to begin and to end immediately came under consideration. Fortunately, the first question was easily answered when a Wilton Park staff member, who became a good friend, made his house, Cattle Copse, in the village of Upper Beeding available for my use while he and his family were away in June 1983. From Cattle Copse my friend has a short walk to the Downs near the point where the Adur River breaches the hills as it flows to the Channel.

Of course the second question was much harder to answer ahead of my arrival at Cattle Copse, though the limited amount of time I had available for walking certainly precluded any attempt to do the full length of the South Downs Way. In the end, without thinking in terms of specific mileage limits, I decided to focus on the Adur Valley, beginning and ending a series of relatively short walks, both on and below the hills, where the Adur breaches the Downs.

Perhaps something should be said first about the Adur River. Those of us whose concept of a river has been informed by excursions on the Mississippi at St Louis or even the Kaskaskia in southern Illinois have great difficulty using that term for the Adur at Upper Beeding. Upon arrival, the words 'creek' or perhaps 'rice canal' like the ones seen in Arkansas seemed to be much more appropriate. No doubt I offended some people early on in my stay when I called it a 'ditch.' Certainly, today's Adur is not like yesterday's.

Like other rivers of Sussex that bisect the Downs today – the Arun, Ouse, and Cuckmere which essentially cut the Downs into five blocks – the Adur was quite wide and relatively deep in the distant past before

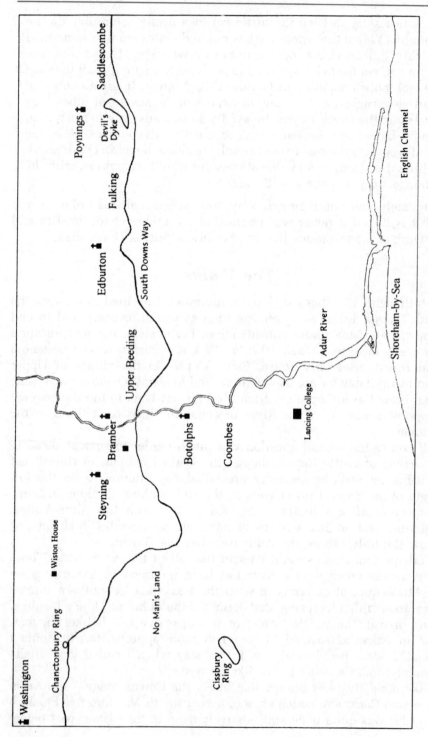

*Sussex: The South Downs Way and the Adur River Valley*

it began like the others to silt up very badly as a result of severe storms in the thirteenth century. River villages like Bramber and Steyning which today are about five miles from the Channel were once important Sussex ports. While I have seen people sailing along quite well in one-person kayaks on the Adur, I have doubts that vessels much larger fit the current dimensions of the river very well. On the other hand, its small size became part of the picture that began to unfold before me: many things in the Adur Valley were much more on a human scale than those in America.

Therefore, I began and ended that visit, like most of the others I have had there since, carless. I walked virtually everywhere I went and hence began my first stay by following a public footpath along the Adur from Upper Beeding to Bramber and then on to Steyning before returning to Cattle Copse. To readers unfamiliar with the area the first walk may sound like a major undertaking. But to those in the know, I certainly did not over-tax myself because the three villages, all quite small, are adjacent to one another with Upper Beeding on one side of the river and the two others on the other side.

## *Bramber*

Yet, each village is unique standing alone. Take Bramber. Crossing the road bridge that linked what Americans would call the main streets of Upper Beeding and Bramber, I found myself in the latter's 'The Street,' which I assume is its name because it appeared to be the one and only of its size in the village. Three sights along The Street immediately caught my eye: the ruins of the Castle, St Nicholas Church, and St Mary's House.

While little is left of the castle except part of the curtain wall and a few other bits and pieces, it must have been rather impressive on its mound overlooking the Adur when it was built shortly after the Norman Conquest in 1066. As headquarters for one of the six administrative areas of Sussex called Rapes, Bramber needed such a castle. It remained an important fortress until it was destroyed in the Civil War of the seventeenth century.[28]

St Nicholas, the nearby small church first built in 1075 as a chapel for the castle, is still intact, though little other than the nave remains of the original. It also suffered damage in the Civil War and again of a different kind when the Victorians tried to restore it last century.[29]

On the other hand, St Mary's is the pride of Bramber, often referred to as the best late-fifteenth-century timber-framed house in Sussex. Actually its foundations were laid in the twelfth century when the property was granted to the Knights Templar, but it gained royal recognition under private ownership during which time celebrated visits of Queen Elizabeth I and King Charles II are said to have taken place.

The latter's stay has also gained fame in detective literature: Sir Arthur Conan Doyle's Sherlock Holmes story, 'The Musgrave Ritual.' Significantly, one Alfred Musgrave, apparently a friend of Doyle, owned the house early this century.[30]

Today's St Mary's is the east wing of what was once a four-sided monastic inn comprising a central-galleried courtyard. It still has a number of fine panelled rooms, including the 'Painted Room' elaborately decorated for Queen Elizabeth's visit, and other period features.[31]

## *Steyning*

Following The Street north, I was soon in Steyning (pronounced Stenning) which I visited rather briefly before during a Wilton Park Conference. Historically and in other ways this village is the gem of the three. Recalling the Swithun and Becket pilgrimages, I was immediately struck by the fact that Steyning has a saint as well. He is Cuthman whose story dates from the Saxon period when the Christian faith was making inroads throughout much of England but paganism still remained entrenched in Sussex. According to legend, Cuthman was a simple shepherd boy, a pious Christian youth possessed of divine powers who on the death of his father traveled from the west bearing his ailing mother on a small cart – something like a wheelbarrow according to sketches – which broke down on reaching Steyning where he settled. Here he built a small wooden church on a site believed to have been just north of the present parish church of St Andrew.[32]

In local folklore, there are a number of other stories about the saint, two of which will be recounted now and another about his encounter with the Devil later on. Given the British interest in the weather, it is probably not surprising that these two involve the elements. According to the first story, when Cuthman's cart bearing his mother collapsed, some haymakers in a nearby field laughed, and the angry young man laid a curse on the field so that it rained every time its crops were harvested.[33]

In the second story, known as the legend of Fippa's Pool, when Cuthman found that his two oxen had been stolen by local widow Fippa's two sons, he yoked the boys to his plough. When Fippa angrily tried to put a curse on Cuthman, she was drawn up into the air by a whirlwind and deposited into a muddy pool.[34] Clearly Cuthman was not a fellow to be taken lightly!

The Steyning church founded by St Cuthman in the eighth century was rebuilt of stone by the Normans in the eleventh and adequately restored in the nineteenth. Today the parish church of St Andrew is still a beautiful Norman building, one of the best of its kind in Sussex, though probably it was once a much larger church, possibly cruciform.[35] Incidentally, the Normans used Caen stone which carves extremely well and which was easier to ship across the Channel from France than to haul English materials over land.[36]

This splendid church is indicative of the entire village: it is filled with over sixty outstanding buildings representing almost every century since 1100. These buildings are of such architectural or historic interest that they are included in the national schedule of buildings protected against demolition or unsuitable alteration. Hence, the second thing that struck me about Steyning is the continuity of its history before one's eyes. An American does not often have the chance to see history in this way. Unfortunately, my limited space does not allow me to do justice to this topic which, fortunately, has been considered elsewhere in books and pamphlets.[37]

Therefore, I'll mention only three important buildings along Church Street where a number of them are located. The first is Saxon Cottage, a very delightful National Trust thatched house with a 'cat slide' or long slope on one end. As a very popular Trust house dating from about 1500, it can be rented on a weekly basis but prospective users must plan a year ahead in most cases.

The Grammar School, built during the middle of the fifteenth century, began 'teaching little boys' in 1584. At one time the building was called Brotherhood Hall from its use by the Fraternity of the Holy Trinity, a guild of merchants.[38] The third building is a little further along Church Street at the edge of Chantry Green. It is Chantry House, a beautiful Queen Anne building and perhaps Steyning's architectural gem. The famous poet William Butler Yeats wrote many of his later works there.[39]

By the way, two other famous people, ones with American connections at any rate, are also associated with Steyning. James M. Whistler, the painter, was a frequent guest at another house on Chantry Green owned by a painter named A. F. Grace. William Penn, the founder of Pennsylvania, preached in Penn House, known as the Quakers Meeting House, in 1678, coming from a nearby village where he lived.[40]

While the building of St Cuthman's church in the eighth century does not mark the birth of Steyning, little is known about its early history before the Saxon period. With the Romans apparently showing little interest in the site, there is no definite evidence that it existed before that period. The Saxons developed the port and expanded the adjacent settlement into the nucleus of a village. Apparently Steyning became ideal for marketing wool, salt from the estuary, timber, and other natural resources. While never becoming large by contemporary standards – it has about 4,000 inhabitants today – it was by the eleventh century among the three or four largest towns in southern England with an estimated population of 1500. The Domesday Book of 1086 lists 123 houses.[41]

With its historic and architectural charm, Steyning was difficult to leave after this brief visit, but I vowed to return again and again, which I did, throughout my stay in Upper Beeding.

## *Upper Beeding*

Avoiding Bramber, I took a different route back to Upper Beeding by walking east through a residential part of Steyning before turning south. This route took me along a pathway through a pasture to a wooden bridge across the Adur. There were cattle on the north side of the bridge and a few horses on the south side with barriers preventing them from crossing. With the tide in, the Adur appeared much wider than before and several fishermen were perched rather high up on the diked banks, poles in hand. This short rural experience made me look forward to future walks in the countryside away from the villages.

Even before crossing the bridge and cutting across an open area at the entrance to Upper Beeding, I could see a couple of buildings of historic interest. One was St Peter's Church, parts of which dated from Norman construction in the eleventh century. It is thought that a church existed on the site before the Conquest. The Norman church became important in 1080 with the building of an adjacent Benedictine Priory which still stands today.[42]

While there were a few other buildings of historic interest in Upper Beeding, it was more of a dormitory village with many contemporary houses. Cattle Copse was one as well, but it had something that many homes in Bramber and Steyning did not: a great view of the South Downs across the back garden. Hence, when I wasn't out walking, I was sitting in the garden or near a window in the lounge taking in the beautiful, unobstructed view of those green and chalk hills to the south.

By the way, some readers may be wondering what is 'upper' about this Beeding if it is clearly, as I have described it, at the foot of the Downs next to the Adur River. And is there a 'lower' as well? Picking up on these questions, which also interested Hilaire Belloc about a century ago, Adam Nicolson, quoting that writer, states this paradox: Upper Beeding 'lies in a hollow, damp all the year round,' while Lower Beeding is miles away and higher up. Nicolson believes that the answer must lie in that the names probably mean that Lower is the daughter village of Upper.[43]

On the other hand, Belloc offers a much more colorful explanation in his book *The Four Men*. According to his account, when Adam with the help of Eve set out to name all the places of the earth, he desired to distinguish Sussex – 'late his happy seat,' the Paradise to be regained – from all others by some special mark. So he decided that whatever was high in Sussex should be called low and whatever was low should be called high.[44]

## The Walk to Chanctonbury

With this tour of the three villages as a warm-up, I was ready for my first long walk on the South Downs from Upper Beeding to Washington, a distance of about eight miles. This hike, which encompassed most of one block of the South Downs, has two important features mentioned before: the Cissbury and Chanctonbury Rings. Since the former is so extensive, I decided to forego a thorough trip there this walk, merely observing it from a distance for the time being. Hence, the Chanctonbury Ring, which rises to 783 feet as the dominant landmark of the area, was my primary objective.

Using a bridge for both man and beast over the Adur where the South Downs Way descends to the valley before rising again, I was prompted to recall that the river's name is relatively new by local standards. It was known as Bramber Water until 1613 when Michael Drayton used the new name in his poem *Polyolbion* in which he expressed belief that the Roman Portus Adurnis stood at its mouth.[45] In a mundane world poetry often loses out but not this time.

Just on the other side of the river and still in the valley lies Botolphs. It is the site of a deserted medieval village with only the church, half a dozen cottages, and an attractive Georgian farmhouse remaining. The church is worth a visit because it contains some Saxon work, including a splendid chancel arch.[46] It is worth a visit for another reason: during the course of my walks, I came to appreciate churches like this one – as well as others like St Nicholas, St Andrews, and St Peters mentioned before – as shrines along the way for the wandering pilgrim. While they never became the objects of my pilgrimage, they were wayfarer stations for physical and spiritual refreshment.

Continuing across the valley, I passed Annington Farm and Manor. The latter is an old house with a Georgian front while the former has a Horsham stone roof. Although flint which is in great abundance is one of the most popular building materials of old houses, Horsham stone, a Sussex laminated sandstone, has been used for roofing since medieval days but is no longer available. Thus, such a roof is prized and is a characteristic feature of many Steyning treasures.[47]

By this time it was apparent that the climbing had begun, and the South Downs Way signposts began to appear where there were junctions and intersections with other public footpaths or at other doubtful points. Occasionally there were concrete 'plinths' but more often than not wooden signs bearing the long-distance route symbol, an acorn, pointed in the appropriate direction like the long arm of a traffic cop.

As I continued my upward journey, I welcomed the next important landmark along the pathway: Tinpot Cottage. Having lived in Arkansas a number of years, I was familiar with that state's many colorful place names – such as Toad Suck Dam and Pickles Gap Road – and looked forward to an equally colorful explanation for the cottage's designation in my guidebooks. None could be found – clearly a missed opportunity.

A man who has walked the full length of the South Downs Way, Adam Nicolson, the grandson of Harold Nicolson and Vita Sackville-West of Sissinghurst Garden fame, believes that this part of the Downs leading to Washington and beyond to the Arun River is the best of all. Why? Because the hills now begin to grow in width to the south and walks on the many criss-crossing footpaths in that direction gives one, as he sees it, the 'impression of the Downs themselves driving a broad way westward through Sussex.'[48] I think he is probably correct in part, but I would place a little less emphasis on the highway aspect and at least some on the settlements. For although the South Downs Way continues as always to follow the northern edge of the hills, the vast top of the Downs here almost seems like a plateau where mankind must have settled for millenia and looked out to the Weald to the north and the Channel to the south.

Certainly as one looks south from near Steyning Round Hill, one sees large lynchets or terraces along the face of the Downs which mark the site of a settlement that seems to have been continuously inhabited and farmed from the Late Bronze Age until Roman times. And of course just a mile beyond the lynchets – through an area marked 'No Man's Land' on the map – lies the Cissbury Ring, the largest man-made structure in Sussex described before.[49]

I think it must be here that the human aspect of the South Downs is most strikingly apparent. Although there is scarcely a contemporary man-made building in sight, as I stood there I felt the historic presence of countless souls who had been there before. Certainly the existence of many tumuli scattered about the area gave weight to this feeling. In fact an urnfield was discovered nearby in 1949 with nearly three dozen urns inverted over cremated bones.[50]

As I was now about to begin my approach to the Chanctonbury Ring the human element was driven home even more. Although the Ring can be seen from a great distance – some have said as much as 35 miles away – I had lost sight of it as I started my climb from the valley. When it came into view again, the experience was absolutely breathtaking. Adam Nicolson has caught some of the feeling:

> the Ring is a magical place. From a distance the clump is like a solid, thick-trunked mushroom, and until you are quite close it appears impenetrable. Then, in a moment, it opens and the two-hundred-year-old trees separate from each other to allow you entrance.[51]

Since the Ring is on elevated ground, I felt like I was entering a great natural cathedral on a hill where people have come to worship for millenia and have buried their dead in the nearby churchyard below.

As indicated before, the trees are of course rather recent by local standards. They were planted on the hill by Charles Goring of Wiston House, located just below the Ring, when he was a boy. It is said that he carried bottles of water up the hill daily to keep his seedlings alive. Living to be ninety years of age, he saw his trees reach maturity, and at eighty-five, he celebrated his achievement in verse:

> How oft around thy Ring, sweet Hill,
> A Boy, I used to play,
> And form my plans to plant thy top
> On some auspicious day.[52]

Goring planted beeches, but others, such as ash, pine and sycamore, grew there as well. Unfortunately, a great storm in October 1987 decimated many of the trees, and it will be a long time before the great natural cathedral will be restored. On a brighter side, some much-needed tree-thinning has been carried out, and the 'inner chapel,' the site of a Romano-Celtic temple in the center of the Ring where coins and pottery dating to the first century AD have been found, is now easier to access.[53]

Just west of the Ring is a dewpond, which was rebuilt by the Society of Sussex Downsmen from the original constructed in the 1870s. It contains water-lilies, evidence of how well the pond retains water, and other plants for botanical study.[54]

At this point I descended the Downs for a good pub lunch at the Frankland Arms in Washington where I made plans for my return walk to Cattle Copse. I decided to go back to the Chanctonbury Ring for an additional rest stop and some spiritual refreshment in the natural cathedral before descending the Downs again near Wiston House for a brief visit with my Wilton Park friends. This became longer than anticipated because it was teatime. Therefore, I took a shorter walk back to Cattle Copse by way of Mouse Lane into Steyning and then across the pasture and the Adur as before.

## *The Walk to Shoreham-by-Sea*

If my first walk north into Bramber and Steyning had seemed like a stroll back in time, my hike south to Shoreham-by-Sea was more about the contemporary world. While historic sites were now and then in evidence, it was much more difficult to keep the past in mind because of our twentieth century way of life as seen in railroads, highways, parking lots, supermarkets, and the like. As I walked down the Adur Valley, I was often reminded of Adam Nicolson's statement quoted above about his experiences along the northern pathway.

As before I started my walk by crossing the Adur near Boltophs but then headed south on a footpath along the river. While Shoreham was my ultimate destination, my major interest along the way was Lancing College, a public school whose chapel is a valley landmark that takes second place only to the Chanctonbury Ring.

Moving away from the river to the west, I cut inland somewhat to visit Coombes first where there is a secluded little church. Unlike many others, the Coombes church is not dedicated to a saint or saints, but yet it is a fine example of an unspoiled downland church with a Norman nave and a chancel constructed only a century later. In 1949 some wall paintings dating from the twelfth century were discovered and restored.[55] As an American, I was impressed by the frequent appearance on the landscape of historic gems like this one, all within easy walking distance of one another. These shrines for the wandering pilgrim are long remembered and much appreciated.

Continuing my walk south, I soon arrived at Lancing College Chapel which is just as impressive nearby as it is from a distance. Said to be 190 feet long and 150 feet high, it is visible from many parts of the South Downs Way as well as elsewhere in the Adur Valley. Although begun in the middle of last century, the chapel is constructed in thirteenth-century French Gothic style – perhaps appropriate with so much Norman influence about – and apparently work is still being done on it. There are some fine modern tapestries inside. The founder of both the college and chapel was Canon N. Woodward who intended to build a number of English public schools and succeeded to some extent with Lancing and two others in Sussex alone.[56] The nineteenth-century Rugby tradition of Tom Brown was strong in southern Sussex as well.

But at this point twentieth century reality began to assert itself, for in view just across the river is what Colin Ulph aptly describes as 'the ugly scar inflicted on the downs by the Shoreham Cement Works.'[57] Obviously the more mundane aspects of life must go on as well, but certainly a less obtrusive spot could have been chosen for something that has significantly marred the landscape permanently.

Turning my gaze south, I moved off in that direction again for Shoreham, knowing that it would become harder and harder to search out and find those things of permanent value in the urban sprawl that was creeping along the southern coast. Fortunately a few things were still there to see in Shoreham, but I had to pay rather close attention to my map and Ulph's guidebook to find them.

Returning to the footpath along the Adur, I walked under the A27 road bridge and then crossed a rather quaint timber bridge, originally built in 1781, which it had replaced. Now back on the east side of the river again, I made my way through what is known as Old Shoreham to the church. Like the others in the area, this church of St Nicolas was worth the visit. The imposing Norman tower is impressive, but the Saxon nave and early English chancel are more memorable. Other internal Norman features, such as the tower arches, receive Ulph's short but enthusiastic approval with the word 'glorious' – quite appropriate.[58]

Not far away is another church, much less impressive, built not one hundred years after the first in what is known as New Shoreham which had to be built to get the port closer to the Channel when the Adur silted up. Shoreham is thus unusual in having two Norman churches.[59]

Perhaps the most interesting attraction near the commercially busy harbor is the Marlipins Museum which is in a twelfth-century customs house, one of the oldest surviving secular buildings in England. In the fourteenth century it was refaced with the present striking checkerwork of flint and Caen stone. Although primarily a maritime museum focusing on ancient Shoreham, Marlipins has an excellent collection of old Sussex maps.[60]

In his guidebook, Ulph advised a different return route to the east and away from the river, but I decided to follow the footpath along the Adur again because once I passed under the A27 bridge most of the unwanted urban sights were to my back. Only the awful cement works had to be faced again, but I was able to keep my eyes on the water most of the time to experience some simple and beautiful sights: numerous swans and other birds which were my escorts for part of the way back. Since the round trip was only about seven miles in length, I was back early enough in Upper Beeding for a late pub lunch at one of my favorites in the village, The Rising Sun.

## The Walk to Devil's Dyke and Beyond

The walk to Shoreham almost made me a back-to-nature convert. It was fitting, therefore, that my next walk would return me to the top of the South Downs but this time hiking east. My main objective was Devil's Dyke, a natural formation of a deep, dry valley. Since the very beginning, I had been looking forward to this visit as a result of my background reading into the rich legends and folklore of Sussex about ghosts, dragons, giants, and most importantly the Devil. Many natural features like the Downs are associated with the Devil in general and with his constant battles with the local saints in particular. One important battleground is Devil's Dyke where it is said the Devil attempted one night to breach the Downs in order to flood the Weald and all its churches. But he was frightened away before he could complete his evil deed that night by none other than St Cuthman who made the cocks crow early and an old woman who simulated the rising of the sun by holding a candle behind a sieve.[61] By the way another version of this story appears in Belloc's *The Four Men* in which the saint is Dunstan instead of Cuthman.

Although the walk along the South Downs Way from the Adur to

Devil's Dyke is only about five miles in length, it seems much longer. Perhaps the main reason is, as Adam Nicolson observes, that this stretch more than any other gives one a strong feeling of isolation, something for which the Downs are justly famous. He adds that some walkers really hate this feeling as apparently the good Dr Johnson, the famous Londoner did, who thought it was enough to make a man want to hang himself, if only he could find a tree! [62]

At least Dr Johnson is correct about the treeless nature of the terrain. The walker finds himself mainly following along white chalk tracks between fields of crops or pasture lands and occasionally crossing old roads coming up from the villages to the north and passing down the slopes to the Channel. Usually, often for the good, he sees virtually nothing of man's civilization along the coast in Shoreham's direction, only the grey sea. On the other hand, he does see some of the villages in the Weald below which the guidebooks try their best to make interesting enough for a descent now and then to an old church or the like, another shrine for the wandering pilgrim. But there is virtually nothing like this along the Way itself.

So whether one is a back-to-nature convert or not, one is inclined to start looking for the fauna and flora the guidebooks assure the reader are to be found along the Way. However, even with a pair of binoculars, I am rather embarrassed to say that most of the animals I observed fell into the well-known domesticated categories of sheep, cattle, and horses. Nevertheless, a variety of wild creatures apparently inhabit the Downs. Jennett lists about a dozen, excluding reptiles, with rabbits and hares being the most numerous as one might expect. Though I missed seeing any of these on this walk, I do recall observing many rabbits near Wiston House during a later visit. Jennett also mentions foxes, moles, stoats, and deer, yet admitting that he has never actually seen the last. That admission as well as his concession that many others, like badgers, are essentially nocturnal creatures missed by most walkers made me feel somewhat better about my meager list. [63]

I did have better luck spotting birds but lacking a field manual, I wasn't able to identify many with the exception of the obvious types like gulls, terns, and swifts. I certainly did not see a great bustard, a bird that has become nearly extinct on the Downs. According to Jennett, the famous naturalist Gilbert White saw many of them in his time near Brighton, measuring well over a yard in length and two yards in wing-span. [64]

The great variety of plants on the Downs is a huge subject by itself. Suffice it to say only that I was reminded of the years I spent living in the San Francisco Bay area where the range of climates within a few miles permits the gardener to try to grow countless types of plants but with success often depending on which side of the hill he lives on. So, too, seems to be the situation on the Downs.

As so often the case, blind expectations far exceeded actual perceptions. Devil's Dyke is indeed a deep, dry valley which is surmounted by a promontory fort consisting of a single rampart with an external ditch, as the guidebooks say. While I, as an American, did not expect something the size of the Grand Canyon, this trench – said to be a half mile long and 300 feet deep – is not overly impressive. One has a difficult time understanding why the Victorians in their enthusiasm for the place actually built a cable car across the valley and a funicular railway up from Brighton![65] Perhaps it is the view from the place which is said to be magnificent, though not on this hazy day, that inspired them to such great lengths. However, the one redeeming quality, the characteristic of so many things in the area, is the Dyke's human size. Walking up and down and around it is no major undertaking.

Though meeting a few other walkers along the lonely five miles from Upper Beeding, I decided to search out others by descending the Downs near Saddlescombe and returning via a road in the Weald through the villages of Poynings, Fulking, and Edburton, all of which stand at the foot of the hills.

Poynings (pronounced 'Punnings' locally) is a pleasant place with a sizeable fourteenth-century church which Jennett says may be compared with the so-called 'Cathedral of the Downs' of the same period at Alfriston in East Sussex.[66] Having visited the latter during walks along the Cuckmere River, I would have to disagree with him.

Fulking is noted for its famous downland pub with a streamside garden, the Shepherd and Dog, where good lunches are served. The stream is fed by spring water from the Downs which gushes from a fountain dedicated to the famous John Ruskin. According to Westacott, Ruskin greatly admired the downland sunsets from Fulking.[67]

Westacott also has several stories about the parish church of St Andrews in Edburton, a structure begun in the twelfth century which replaced a Saxon church founded by Edburga, Alfred the Great's granddaughter. With an American angle, one story is about a church window dedicated to the memory of George Keith, a rector there during his declining years in the middle of the eighteenth century. He seemed to have lived a very controversial life during his early years as a Quaker when he was jailed for his beliefs before going to America in 1683. Constantly involved in disagreements with his fellow Quakers in the colonies, he became best known for his important pamphlet on the evil of slavery, but his contentious personality brought him back to England where he was ordained in the Anglican church. Thereupon he returned to America to convince his former Quaker colleagues of the errors of their ways and to persuade them to become Anglicans like himself![68] He sounds like a true believer. In any event, St Andrews Church provided a much-needed rest stop for both physical and spiritual refreshment for a wandering and weary pilgrim before the last phase of the walk back to Cattle Copse.

Although I walked to other places this visit, including the Cissbury Ring and destinations along the Adur to the north, I returned to Upper Beeding on two other occasions in later years to retrace many of these same steps as well as to explore new areas. Obviously, I greatly enjoyed these experiences when they occurred but even more so after I had some basis for comparison following walks along the Cuckmere from Seven Sisters to Alfriston and along the Arun River near Arundel.

Being a walker in America as well, I easily concluded that many things, from the superficial to the essential, are significantly different between the two countries. Some of these are obvious to the reader while others may not be, but space limits that which can be mentioned in what follows.

## The Special Relationship

The basic differences will be discussed in the context of the 'special relationship' because some very desirable aspects of the British experience need to be emphasized. But first, a few general considerations about differences between the Old and New Worlds are in order for perspective.

In trying to identify the essential difference between Europe and America, one commentator has said America is Europe with all the walls down. This is a significant insight, but as a historian I tend to generalize the basic difference in this way: the New World looks to the future while the Old to the past. With these tendencies the two have gained much, but they have also lost much through the years. Concerning the study of history itself, for example, America has forgotten much of its own – if it was ever learned in the first place – and Europe cannot forget much of its past, or at least the favored version of each group. Putting these tendencies in social science terms, America has emphasized the instrumental approach to life: getting things done, solving problems in the most efficient and effective way possible. Hence, it is not surprising that Pragmatism as put forward by William James and John Dewey is usually called the American philosophy. On the other hand, Europe has emphasized the ceremonial approach: conservation of the existing status quo with deference to such things as tradition, rank and cultural values. These tendencies have manifested themselves in the international relations, the main area of interest here, of these two regions as well. Negative results can be seen in such things as a rudderless America which has difficulty in defining its world role and a quarrelsome Europe which has yet to find a formula for permanent peace.

It has seemed to me, therefore, that the New and Old Worlds could obtain some mutual benefits by becoming more attuned to the tendencies of the other. In other words, a balance could be struck in our approaches to history, to the instrumental and ceremonial and to international relations. Perhaps both worlds would be improved.

For me, as this book has argued throughout, the best strategy for America to adopt to gain the needed balance in international relations is through a 'special relationship' with Britain so we can reconnect with those important elements, the Helper values, which were rejected at the time of the American Revolution. Walks on the footpaths of Britain like those I have described can help Americans make the needed connections, I believe.

Consider first the purpose and use of footpaths in the two countries. While American footpaths seem to be seen primarily as avenues of escape – many are called nature trails for example – the British public footpaths, though no doubt used by some walkers for that purpose, are basically connecting links as they have been for centuries. As indicated at the beginning of the chapter, these paths tie people and places together in a most human-like way – they foster community because they are there, because they are ubiquitous. Such an ever-present pathway is only a few yards away from Cattle Copse and other homes in the Sussex villages. In America, on the other hand, most people must *drive* miles to a similar pathway for a special, not an everyday, outing. The public footpath in Britain, unlike in America, is part of that country's way of life.

As such, it should also be seen there as a cultural institution, much like the family or the university, which prescribes and proscribes certain behaviors. The pathway establishes a process, a procedure for interaction, of which its users are a part. Hence, a walker feels the impact of the pathway on himself, and in turn he affects it and other users. A common – a shared – experience takes place.

Perhaps an example will illustrate part of the process that occurs. One of the consequences of walking the pathway is that of meeting and sometimes overtaking many other people doing the same or resting nearby. Usually, this encourages face-to-face and often eye-to-eye contact and perhaps nods, smiles, or even verbal greetings. Maybe a short conversation results. A genuine human interaction occurs, something more and more missing in our daily lives as we go about our usual routines.[69]

This, then, is one of the things Americans can learn from British practice: that the pathway provides a process for unity – for community – rather than a means of escape. Hence, the real importance of the public footpath lies not so much in the fact that it exists here or there but in its use for common experiences that bring about desirable consequences for humankind.

But just as important Americans can learn that these British public footpaths tie people to the past – to their history. No doubt *some*

American trails, especially those used by Indians and early pioneers, attempt to do the same, but they are not as successful because the important man-made things of the past, such as buildings and other structures, are not in evidence like those in Sussex. Of these the very old churches with features dating from many centuries past stand out. Yet, simple things are often just as important in reminding one of those who have gone before: the well-worn stone path and steps into these churches, for example.

Unfortunately, Americans have not really made good connections with the Indians in the same way one sees in Britain with regard to ancient peoples there. Some have seen racism in this failure, but I see the explanation in Margaret Mead's interpretation in Chapter I. Americans take the third generation stance towards the Indians: they are simply out-of-date and should be passed by. Don't take them seriously, don't look back.

Although all the old buildings in places like Steyning and the many churches throughout the Adur Valley foster historical links, the Downs themselves carry the sense even further back with evidence of hillforts, tumuli, and the like. But even more important is the chalk itself. To reach down to pick up a handful of chalky soil – the dust of ancient creatures – along the many miles of pathway is to reach back to life in very early times, to the primeval. There is no comparable experience to be had in the United States.

But perhaps the best way to illustrate what I am talking about is to refer back to a previous discussion about the Chain of Being metaphor so important to the Tudors and to some modern legal scholars. I think that metaphor describes the role of the public footpath in Britain better than anything I have come across. In this sense the footpath should be seen like the law: something that holds the community together and something – in its personification as a woman, the Helper – that identifies its role as the preserver and propagator of the cultural and historical values of the community. And like the law, the footpath is Janus-like: it leads us both backward and forward.

The last word on the essence and importance of the public footpath in Britain to our being will be given to Hilaire Belloc who wrote about it at the turn of the century. In his now classic account of the Pilgrims' Way in *The Old Road*, Belloc sees the pathway, which he calls The Road, as one of the primal things of mankind. After listing other primal elements of our human manner, which move us, such as the camp, the refuge, and the hearth, he considers The Road in the following:

> Of these primal things the least obvious but the most important is The Road. It does not strike the sense as do those others I have mentioned; we are slow to feel its influence. We take it so much for granted that its original meaning escapes us. Men, indeed, whose

pleasure it is perpetually to explore even their own country on foot, and to whom its every phase of climate is delightful, receive, somewhat tardily, the spirit of The Road. They feel a meaning in it; it grows to suggest the towns upon it, it explains its own vagaries, and it gives a unity to all that has arisen along its way. But for the mass The Road is silent; it is the humblest and the most subtle, but ... the greatest and the most original of the spells which we inherit from the earliest pioneers of our race. It was the most imperative and the first of our necessities. It is older than building and than wells; before we were quite men we knew it, for the animals still have it today.[70]

## *Notes*

1. For a discussion of early communications in Britain, see Keith Mossman, *The Shell Book of Rural Britain* (Oxford: Alden Press, 1978), 178–81.

2. Sean Jennett, *The Pilgrims' Way: From Winchester to Canterbury* (London: Cassell & Company, Ltd., 1971), 17.

3. *Seventy-Third Annual Report and Balance Sheet, 1996* (Hove, England: Society of Sussex Downsmen), 2.

4. Jennett, 67.

5. Ibid., 67–8.

6. Ibid., 68.

7. Ibid.

8. Adam Nicolson, *The National Trust Book of Long Walks* (London: Weidenfeld and Nicolson, 1981), 104.

9. Ibid.

10. Ibid., 105.

11. Ibid., 104.

12. Ibid.

13. Ibid.

14. Jennett, 53.

15. Ibid., 54.

16. H. D. Westacott, *The South Downs Way* (Harmondsworth, England: Penguin Books Ltd., 1983), 14.

17. Ibid.

18. Nicolson, 130.

19. Ibid.

20. Sean Jennett, *South Downs Way* rev. ed. (London: Her Majesty's Stationery Office, 1977), 9.

21. Ibid.

22. Ibid., 10.

23. Nicolson, 131–2.
24. Ibid., 132; David J. Allen, *Sussex: Shire County Guide* 2nd. ed. (Aylesbury, England: Shire Publications, Ltd., 1987), 14.
25. Nicolson, 132.
26. Ibid.
27. Ibid., 105.
28. Allen, 17.
29. Ibid.
30. *St. Mary's, Bramber, West Sussex* (Hove, England: Laceys Ltd.), 2–3.
31. Ibid.
32. Harry Ford, *Steyning: Conservation Area Guide* (Steyning: Steyning Society, 1980), 2.
33. Allen, 59.
34. Ford, 30.
35. Ibid., 29.
36. Nicolson, 142.
37. See bibliography in Ford, 33.
38. Ibid., 24.
39. Ibid.
40. Ibid., 12, 27.
41. Ibid., 1–2.
42. Colin Ulph, *Southdown Walks* (Shoreham-by-Sea, England: Colin Ulph, 1981), 39.
43. Nicolson, 142.
44. Hilaire Belloc, *The Four Men: A Farrago* (London: Thomas Nelson and Sons), 83–4.
45. Westacott, 50.
46. Ibid.
47. Ford, 6.
48. Nicolson, 143.
49. Ibid.
50. Jennett, *South Downs Way*, 73.
51. Nicolson, 144.
52. Jennett, *South Downs Way*, 74
53. Ibid.
54. Ibid., 75.
55. Ulph, 21.
56. Jennett, *South Downs Way*, 108; Nicolson, 142.
57. Ulph, 21.
58. Ibid., 25–6.
59. Allen, 59.
60. Ibid., 35.

61. Ibid., 11.
62. Nicolson, 140.
63. Jennett, *South Downs Way*, 21–2.
64. Ibid., 21.
65. Allen, 14.
66. Jennett, *South Downs Way*, 66–7.
67. Westacott, 48.
68. Ibid.
69. Hilaire Belloc, *The Old Road* (London: Archibald Constable and Company, 1904) and his *The Four Men*, mentioned previously, provide significant insights about the nature and outcomes of this process of interaction among pathways and their users. Of course, not to be overlooked is Chaucer's great classic *Canterbury Tales*.
70. Belloc, *The Old Road*, 3–4.

# Chapter IX

# London: Some Churches and Theaters

Graffiti on London Walls –
In 1956: 'God is dead.'
In 1996: 'God is gay.'

Graffiti may give a hint about the nature of a place, but perhaps these two lines of London graffiti observed forty years apart tell more about the times than the place itself. Certainly the well-known Existentialist movement immediately after World War II, which tended to popularize the 'God is dead' slogan, is associated more with towering French figures like Sartre and Camus in Paris than with any comparable ones in London. Yet, based on my first visit to London at Christmas time in 1956, I felt that much of the mood of the city – whether permanent or passing, I didn't know which at the time – was captured in that first line of graffiti. Although the war had been over for eleven years, London still seemed to be locked into something like a wartime mentality. Outwardly this was definitely the case because of its appearance as well as that of its people.

For example, much of the area around St Paul's in the City section was still flat from the wartime bombardment. Even some of the other sections of London that had not been hit hard were still showing evidence of destruction. I remember well the gutted shell of a building across the street from my small hotel just off Russell Square in Bloomsbury.

The people themselves seemed to be still dressed – and not very well – in the clothes of the 1930s and 1940s. The trendy stylishness that would make London one of the great attractions for many, but especially the young, was still many years in the future. No, London itself seemed to be dark, dreary, and dirty that Christmas, and the Londoners tended to reflect these unhappy conditions to a great extent.

As is well known by travellers to the British capital since the 1960s, London is much different now, suggesting that the first line above only reflected the mood of the time and not a permanent condition of the city. Thus, perhaps the second line is also reflective of the current time and not the place. Certainly the gay scene of the 1990s is big if not universal and London is part of it, though probably not to the extent of San Francisco and several other cities.

Therefore, if this London graffiti is essentially an expression of the mood of the periods, what about the nature of the place? What is its essence and can this be captured in a few words on a wall? A short, neat answer is a tall order for most things but especially so for a huge, sprawling city like London. However, circumstances of limited space and time require me to try to fill it. So for me, the line of graffiti I would write on a London wall to identify the place at all times is this: 'God is alive, and She can be found in London.'

First of all, a brief explanation about the pronoun used above is in order. If one is going to anthropomorphize God, which we usually do in Western Civilization, it seems appropriate enough as we do to begin with a consideration of the three figures of the nuclear family described in Chapter I: Father, Mother and Son. Traditionally, of course, we have selected the first for the role of God, but the second is more in keeping with my view of God when the terms Hero, Helper and Rebel are considered as well. The attributes of the Helper – including such things as understanding, fair, honorable and kind – seem much more God-like today than those of the Hero. Hence, my pronoun choice. Some might object to this choice, but it seems to be in line with the recent stand of British Methodists and some other groups. In a sense, then, for me the search for the Special Relationship in London is really a search for God. Certainly this gives some direction for such a difficult undertaking.

As the product of a village in Middle Western 'frontier' America, it may seem out of character for me to seek God in a big city like London. After all, our Jeffersonian/Jacksonian agrarian folklore argues that God is most likely to be found not in the 'evil and corrupt' city but rather in the rural and small-town countryside where one has a close association with the land. Hence, the 'Godless' city should be avoided. Yet, at the close of the twentieth century, the city – whether we like it or not – is more and more with us, and therefore the issue is not so much one of how to avoid it but how can it be made more liveable and workable – more God-like, if you will – for the huge numbers of people who have little choice about where they must live.

Clearly, some cities are already more liveable and workable than others. London is one of these. Why? The complete answer to this question is so long and complex that volumes are needed, but my limited space permits the consideration of only four themes in this chapter and the next that I think are central to London's success. These are London's churches, theaters, villages, and parks. The first two are discussed in this chapter.

Social scientists tell us that there are at least a half dozen or so essential life functions that all communities must perform reasonably well to be viable now and into the future. Perhaps nurturing the young is at or near the top of the list but not far down are psychic support and effective communication. In talking about these in Western societies, we usually focus on religion and language. These two are not only keys to London's success, but they are also important to the Special Relationship. Certainly very close religious and language connections between Britain and America are historical facts. In keeping with my institutional approach, some specific churches and theaters will be sketched.

## The Churches of London

If searching for the Special Relationship in London is tantamount to seeking God, the obvious place to start looking is the church. During my initial visit to London in 1956, I, like most tourists, went first to the huge, the impressive, and the well-known: Westminster Abbey, St Paul's Cathedral, and Westminster Cathedral – but even the lesser-known Southwark Cathedral. It was not until later trips that I developed an interest in small churches and with that a growing understanding of their importance for the Special Relationship. The definitive event was a visit to the Guildhall area one quiet Sunday morning with some British friends who pointed out the gutted ruins nearby of St Mary the Virgin, Aldermanbury, a Christopher Wren church. Though not one of the great architect's masterpieces, this congregationless church had been fire-bombed during World War II and seemed to be destined for slow decay into complete ruins if not outright destruction first by commercial interests who seemed to have the upperhand in development at that time.

Yet, it soon became known, thanks to the efforts of the President of Westminster College in America and a few others, that the church was going to be saved though not by Britons only but by Americans too and not for London but for Fulton, Missouri, where the institution is located. College officials had been looking round since 1946 when Winston Churchill gave his 'Sinews of Peace' or as it came to be known his 'Iron Curtain' speech in Fulton for a suitable way to commemorate that famous event. They conceived the idea of shipping the church stone-by-stone to Missouri and re-erecting it on the college campus. With the enthusiastic support of Churchill himself and many other prominent people on both sides of the Atlantic, money for the project was raised rather quickly and the foundation stone was laid by the Bishop of London in October 1966, though Churchill did not live to see this event. Only a few years later, the completely rebuilt church along with its undercroft containing a museum and library was recognized as an important symbol of the Special Relationship at its reconsecration by the Bishop of Dover in May 1969. My enthusiastic support of this project prompted me to read about and to visit many other London churches during the following years.

My early reading made one thing clear: the most striking fact about the churches of London is their huge number. In his latest edition of *A Guide to London Churches*, Mervyn Blatch immediately acknowledges this problem in his opening pages in saying that he was confronted by two questions at the outset. They were 'Which parts of London?' and 'Which churches?' Essentially, he answered them by focusing on the Cities of London and Westminster, the eleven enlarged inner boroughs formed in 1965, and pre-nineteenth century buildings. He also included later churches of special architectural, historical and social interest in those geographical areas. In so doing, he still listed about 150 churches, 42 in the City of London alone and another 27 in the City of Westminster, the two areas I know best. While I cannot claim to have explored all sixty-nine churches, I have visited the sites of many of them, often of course finding their doors bolted from within. I will mention about a dozen of the ones I came to know and like best during a series of walks over the years, but first some general statements about the reasons for so many churches need to be made.

Perhaps the huge numbers of churches in America are easier to explain than they are in Britain. For Americans, the direct descendants of the Protestant revolt, the abundance of different denominations and the prevailing attitude that 'if you don't like any existing churches, start your own' help to explain the situation in the United States. But for Britons, things have been different, for traditionally – even before the Reformation during Medieval times – there were many churches. Why? In considering the reasons for the numerous City churches alone, John Barron and Alexandra Moore see much of the answer in the wealth and royal connections of the great religious foundations and of the City merchants and noblemen. The foundations had the land upon which to build additional churches for ordinary people and the merchants and nobles had the resources to endow them. In addition, older parish churches created new ones, such as the four churches dedicated to St Mary formed from St Mary Aldermary.[1]

Significantly, Barron and Moore also point out that the churches were more than just religious institutions for the people of London. Such things as plays and dances were held in them, and maypoles, as well as the dress worn by Morris Dancers, were stored in churches. Stocks and pillories were frequently placed inside churchyards, and archery practice occurred there where yew trees, still found today, supplied the best wood for bows. Water conduits and cisterns were often church property and were usually located near churches so that the water could be blessed.[2]

The churches themselves were often involved in the resolution of

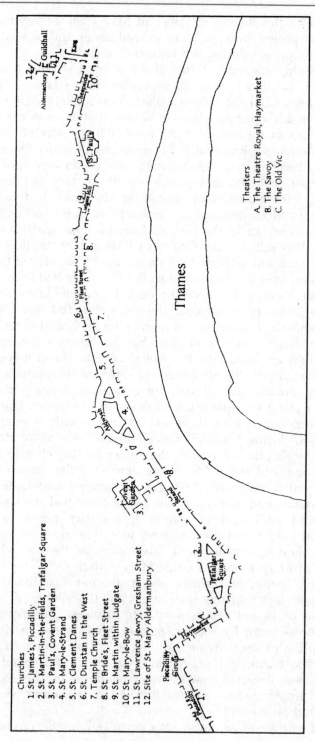

Churches
1. St James's, Piccadilly
2. St Martin-in-the-Fields, Trafalgar Square
3. St Paul's, Covent Garden
4. St Mary-le-Strand
5. St Clement Danes
6. St Dunstan in the West
7. Temple Church
8. St Bride's, Fleet Street
9. St Martin within Ludgate
10. St Mary-le-Bow
11. St Lawrence Jewry, Gresham Street
12. Site of St Mary Aldermanbury

Theaters
A. The Theatre Royal, Haymarket
B. The Savoy
C. The Old Vic

*London: A walk from St James's, Piccadilly to the site of St Mary Aldermanbury.*

criminal and other judicial matters. Many churches had been granted the right of sanctuary, though a person in sanctuary was not permitted to be supplied with food in the hope that the avenger and hunted would come to terms quickly. The same churches were Courts of Justice as well with legal contracts being ratified by the altar.[3]

The medieval City churches were involved in economic matters, too. They were often local banks whose strong chests can still be seen in some churches today. In times of danger to the community, they were warehouses for goods that might otherwise be stolen or destroyed by raiders.[4] In performing such a range of functions over and beyond the religious only, the churches were more like community centers that served the needs and interests of the people generally.

Of course, many churches – or at least their sites – had very long religious histories. When Christopher Wren rebuilt many London churches after the Great Fire in the seventeenth century, he often did so on some very ancient foundations. Examples will be given in the discussion below. The point here is that from the British point of view there have often been sound historical reasons for constructing and reconstructing – sometimes centuries later – churches on certain sites. This sense of history is very striking to an American.

As indicated, many of the churches have been designed by great builders like Wren. Hence, there have been sound architectural reasons for their construction and reconstruction, especially after World War II, even though some, like St Mary the Virgin, no longer had congregations. Preservation of the cultural heritage in architecture is important, too. One is also reminded of Churchill's observation that we shape our buildings, and they in turn shape us.

It seems, then, that there are a number of reasons for the existence of so many churches in London today, and each has one or more in its background. Perhaps the two churches – they are actually in Westminster – that maintain the community center tradition better than most are St James's, Piccadilly, and St Martin-in-the-Fields, Trafalgar Square, which are only a rather short walk from one another in central London.

## St James's

Another visit recently to St James's underscored for me Mervyn Blatch's observation that the church's home-like 'brick exterior set in its peaceful garden and the stately interior make a striking contrast to the bustle outside' in Piccadilly.[5] This statement quite correctly puts the church in the category of others in London that 'provide havens of tranquillity and spiritual sanctuary in the midst of the pressure, bustle, and hurry' of a great city, as Eddie George puts it.[6]

But to leave things there would be to miss much about the current mission of the church. Actually a cursory look round during my visit suggested that some of the bustle of local activity now emanates from within the church itself as well as its garden. While a few people sat in meditation and prayer inside the sanctuary, the hall outside and the garden area beyond were places of 'commerce.' Christmas cards sponsored by a host of charities were for sale in the hall and the Piccadilly Market featuring various things such as arts, crafts, knitwear and gifts was attracting potential customers from the street into the garden. At 1:10 p.m. that same day a free piano recital of classical music was also scheduled, something, like the Market, that seemed to be an almost daily occurrence during the week. Also in operation, in this case every day of the week, was the Wren Cafe which advertised itself as 'London's finest vegetarian wholefood cafe' and which offered take-away and private catering services as well. Certainly, religious services were held that day as part of the almost daily Midweek and Sunday Services schedule, but the list of events described in the monthly brochure available to visitors suggested that the various activities – both religious and secular – in and sponsored by St James's went far beyond what has been described above. Clearly, this beautiful Wren church is even more so because of the functions it performs for the community.

Although detailed descriptions of the history and architecture of St James's are best left to the guide books, a few points should be made here. Perhaps because St James's was the only church built by Wren on a completely new site and on one of considerable area, he felt it was necessary to state why he limited the size of the new church. Blatch quotes him as saying the following:

> The Romanists, indeed may build larger Churches, it is enough if they hear the Murmur of the Mass, and see the Elevation of the Host, but ours are to be fitted for Auditories. I can hardly think it practicable to make a single Room so capacious ... as to hold above 2,000 Persons, and all to hear the Service, and both to hear distinctly, and see the Preacher.[7]

Yet, the church has a feeling of spaciousness and width, perhaps in part to the presence of north and south aisles and galleries on three sides which, as Blatch observes, 'curve round the west end as in a theatre.' It is this theatre-like sense of the place as well as its elegance of the proportions and the refinement of the decoration which 'impart an air of much distinction' to the church.[8] Hence, as a work of interesting church architecture alone, it is worth a visit.

## St Martin-in-the-Fields

Often called the 'parish church of London,' St Martin-in-the-Fields is perhaps the most cosmopolitan church in all of Britain, drawing people from around the world in large part because of its 'ever-open Door' and concern with the less fortunate. It is appropriate, therefore, that its namesake is St Martin who, according to legend, met a beggar while riding in bitter winter weather towards Amiens and though penniless himself, cut his cloak into two and gave half to the beggar. The emblem of St Martin showing him dividing his cloak appears on lamp posts and door handles in the parish.[9]

It was, however, during World War I that the present reputation of St Martin's became firmly established, thanks in large part to its minister 'Dick' Sheppard who as a military chaplain had witnessed the horrors of war on the Western front. He kept the church open for young soldiers as they arrived back from France at nearby Charing Cross Railway Station. Thus, St Martin's became known as a beacon for those who need help or consolation – with no strings attached. One of the literary heroines of the war, Vera Brittain, later wrote a book, *Story of St Martin's*, which widely publicized Sheppard's work.[10]

A complete listing of the current community services of the church would be very long indeed but the following examples of recent developments should suffice: the expansion of its well-known Social Care Unit; the opening of a Chinese community center; the availability to the general public in the crypt of a cafe, gallery, and bookshop; and lunchtime and evening concerts several times a week.[11] The last-named continues the long music tradition of the church which is best known worldwide through the recordings of the famous Academy of St Martin-in-the-Fields founded in 1958.

Probably the most photographed of London churches today because of its ideal location on Trafalgar Square, the current St Martin's, the third on the site, dates from the early eighteenth century, a point in time almost a hundred years before the construction of the square itself. The new building, designed by James Gibbs, was actually erected in a run-down area mainly because a replacement was needed for the existing unsafe Tudor church. With a capacity of only 400 people, this old church was also too small for a parish of 40,000. Blatch notes that the improvement resulting from the Square's construction in 1820 had one disadvantage: 'it drew attention to the awkward placing of the steeple behind the pedimented portico on the west end of the church proper.'[12] Be that as it may, few photographers and others have apparently been put off by this design 'flaw.'

Blatch also mentions another criticism from the past. This one describes the church's interior as being 'a little too gay and theatrical for Protestant worship,' a remark probably stemming mainly from the 'graceful plasterwork executed by the renowned Artari and Bagutti which provides sparkle and much visual pleasure.' This effect is heightened by the way the 'nave curves round to embrace the small, narrow chancel and by the royal "boxes" at the east end.'[13] Recalling the theatrical appearance of St James's interior, the modern community-minded critic, who favors the use of churches for concerts, plays and the like, probably sees something positive here, I believe.

As the above suggests, there is a link between St Martin's and the Crown, something that may seem surprising in view of the church's current mission. Buckingham Palace does lie in St Martin's parish, but even before it became a royal home King Charles II was baptised in the Tudor church and King George I was the first churchwarden of Gibbs's church.[14] Since such things may seem like events of the distant past, perhaps some would easily dismiss their significance. Yet, apparently the links with royalty are still very close and as such seem appropriate for a community-minded institution of this type. Like St James's, St Martin's is an excellent example of the Helper in action.

## St Paul's, Covent Garden

During my walks of the churches, my next stop is usually St Paul's, Covent Garden, a short distance from Trafalgar Square. While past visitors may have some difficulty recalling the church's interior, if they even took time to find the main entrance on the western end, few can forget the great portico on the east front which serves as a classical backdrop for events in Covent Garden. 'Backdrop' is indeed the right word because of St Paul's long association with the – and as a – stage. Who can forget the opening scenes by the pillars of Shaw's *Pygmalion* or its musical version *My Fair Lady*? Or for Covent Garden visitors the 'stage' before the pillars where street performers entertain the lunchtime crowds?

Hence, what one has in St Paul's is something different from St James's and St Martin's: a church that is identified with a particular craft or profession of the larger London community. But again service to the community is evident as the mission of the church.

No complete listing of St Paul's theatrical associations will be attempted, but a few examples are worth mentioning. W. S. Gilbert, of Gilbert and Sullivan fame, was baptized and the great Ellen Terry, among other actors, was buried here. Panels on the screen at the western end of the church remember some recent stage personalities, such as Charles B. Cochran, Ivor Novello, and Leslie Henson. Blatch also likes to recall that Samuel Pepys watched a Punch and Judy show at the church in 1662. A thriving parish church today, St Paul's continues to be the headquarters and spiritual center of the Actors' Church Union.[15]

Perhaps traditionalists of church architecture find this Inigo Jones creation hard to accept. In fact some have likened the exterior to a box with a big lid on it, 'not unlike a large version of a Swiss chalet' or worse. Others have thought Jones rather pretentious in that the proportions of the building were stated to be those of Solomon's temple in Jerusalem. According to accounts of the time, Francis Russell, the fourth Earl of Bedford, engaged Jones for the creation of a splendid Covent Garden piazza with a church as 'the focal climax of the whole design' but then told Jones out of financial considerations that it should not be much better than a 'barn.' To which the great architect apparently replied: 'Well then, you shall have the handsomest barn in England.'[16] Perhaps Jones was as good as his word; it is certainly unique to say the least.

## St Mary-le-Strand

Walking from Covent Garden towards the river and turning left on the Strand, one soon sees what Blatch calls 'two great galleons sailing down the highway.' These are, to continue the sea metaphor, the 'island' churches of St Mary-le-Strand and St Clement Danes, 'authentic' churches according to traditionalists.

Whatever one feels about church architecture, few would probably quarrel with the proposition that in St Mary's James Gibbs has designed one of London's most beautiful churches, certainly its loveliest Baroque church, on its small island site in the middle of the Strand. A Scottish Roman Catholic who had studied in Rome, Gibbs came under the influence of Carlo Fontana, Surveyor to the Pope, and designed St Mary's ceiling similar to two of Fontana's churches in the Italian capital. Blatch observes that St Mary's is the most Italian in feeling of Gibbs's churches – so much so that it has been called an 'expatriate Roman.'[17]

Whether Roman or British or cosmopolitan, St Mary's has its historical roots in an area seen as the center of early Saxon London and on a site of a Saxon church dating from at least the eleventh century. Not much more of significance is known about this period other than that Thomas Becket was made the church's rector about 1151 while he was still a layman. Four hundred years later, the King's uncle, the Duke of Somerset, had the still existing church demolished to make way for the construction of his famous mansion, Somerset House. The dispossessed congregation was forced to go to the Savoy Chapel nearby, but quite remarkably kept their identity for over 150 years and returned to the original site when Gibbs built the new church in the early eighteenth century.[18]

Perhaps this type of loyalty to place, along with the beauty of Gibbs's church, helps to explain in part why, despite the great changes that have occurred in this area of London during the past 200 years, St Mary's continues today to function and prosper with a growing congregation. It should also be noted that in 1984 St Mary's became the official church of the former Women's Royal Naval Service, known as the Wrens. *The Book of Remembrance* near the organ records the names of the Wrens who died in service since World War I.

I must confess that connections between religious and military institutions have always been somewhat troublesome for me, and I remain of two minds about them. Perhaps because of the historical linking of church and state in Britain, this is seen as acceptable there, but for an American coming out of the strong tradition of separation of the two, such connections are harder to accept. Yet, in view of what was said above about St Paul's, perhaps military organizations, like other crafts and professions, are entitled to 'their' churches as well, especially if the purpose is to honor the dead for their service and sacrifice for the community.

## St Clement Danes

Certainly one of the many connecting links between St Mary's and St Clement Danes, its sister church on the next island in the Strand, is the military association. It is in fact even much stronger with St Clement's because the latter is the 'Central Church of the Royal Air Force,' according to the visitor's guide. This designation came about in 1958 when the RAF restored the church after its near destruction during World War II bombing. More than 125,000 names of RAF men and women who gave their lives since 1911 are recorded in ten *Books of Remembrance* displayed throughout the church. In keeping with the Special Relationship, another book containing the names of 19,000 members of the United States Air Force who died while serving in Britain during World War II is located in the American Shrine beneath the north gallery. Still another British ally of the war is honored in the north aisle where a memorial is set in the floor to the Polish Squadrons that flew with the RAF.

The most striking feature of the Remembrance is also located in the church's floor. This is the huge rosette formed by the badges of the RAF and Commonwealth Air Forces. There are over 800 squadron and unit badges sculpted in Welsh slate embedded in the floor.

The international dimension is in keeping with the church's early history as its name suggests. According to tradition at least, the original building was erected in the ninth century by Danes residing in London who, having married English wives, were permitted by the authorities to live between Westminster and Ludgate in London. As seafarers, the Danes apparently chose the name of Clement because this one-time Bishop of Rome was the patron saint of mariners. Throughout the centuries that followed, the church was rebuilt several times with Sir Christopher Wren designing the present structure in 1682 and James Gibbs adding the steeple to Wren's tower in 1719.

While Wren's exterior is still very much in evidence, the 1958 rebuilding of the interior by W. A. S. Lloyd carries the latter's stamp as well. Lloyd has provided the church, Blatch believes, with an interior of great richness, 'lighter and more spacious than before and with a striking contrast of dark oak and white columns with richly decorated arches.'[19] It is indeed a very moving sight.

When one rebuilds a church for the purposes of an organization, there is always a price to be paid. In this case, St Clement Danes ceased to be a parish church of its own and was joined to its sister St Mary-le-Strand. Yet it still serves that other function Eddie George mentioned above: a haven of 'tranquillity and spiritual sanctuary' in a busy modern city. And no doubt oranges and lemons will always be associated with St Clement Danes because the ancient rhyme is still rung on its bells, though the fruit ceased to be carried through its churchyard to market many, many years ago.

## St Dunstan in the West and Temple Church

When one continues walking along the Strand and suddenly realizes that the thoroughfare has become Fleet Street, it dawns that Temple Bar has been passed and that the City of London has been entered. Although St Bride's is the next destination, two other churches beckon for attention: St Dunstan in the West and Temple Church, the latter a short stroll off the street towards the river. Thus, the main problem of a London walk of churches becomes quite apparent: too many churches for too little time.

But both of these churches deserve passing comments. St Dunstan's has become a truly international community church, an ecumenical model for us all. It offers the following range of worship services: Romanian Orthodox, Armenian, Coptic, Syrian and Indo-Syrian as well as Lutheran, Old Roman Catholic and Nestorian. One of the oldest Livery Companies of London, the Cordwainers founded in 1272, is still connected with St Dunstan's as well.[20]

Originally built by the Knights Templar and consecrated in 1185, Temple Church, though restored many times since, retains many of its original features, including a round nave. Hence, it is considered one of the finest examples of early Gothic architecture in Britain. Blatch even asserts that the church is the most important survivor of Knights Templar churches in Europe and a 'remarkable example of the transition from the round Norman arch to the upward-pointing Gothic style' side by side. For centuries the church was the private chapel of London's lawyers after they became tenants in the Temple, and today it is still connected with the legal profession, belonging to two of the Inns of Court.[21]

In these two London City churches, then, one can see an interesting contrast in service. On the one hand, there is a macro community approach and on the other a micro one, both very important given the nature of the modern city.

## St Bride's, Fleet Street

Like the Temple Church, St Bride's is just off Fleet Street and thereby suffers some of the same consequences from being hemmed in. In the latter's case, it is the difficulty of seeing its celebrated wedding cake spire which now can be enjoyed only from a distance. Having been struck by lightning on several occasions, the steeple has also been the center of controversy, the most famous of which occurred between King George III and his soon-to-be-rebellious colonist, Benjamin Franklin, who was living in London at the time. An argument developed between the two after the King called in the Doctor of lightning rod fame for advice concerning what form of conductor should be used on the spire. Franklin advised the use of pointed ends but George insisted on blunt ends. This difference of opinion led to comments of the day about 'good, blunt, honest King George' and 'those sharp-witted colonists!' [22]

Actually the church's current name dates only from the last century when it was changed from St Bridget, the name of the Irish saint second in fame only to St Patrick. Born about 453, she was noted among the Irish for her many miraculous powers, including the ability to change well water into beer. Why her name was chosen for the church on this London site, a most unusual circumstance, is apparently not known, but speculation abounds. One story suggests that she was so honored because on at least one occasion the water in the churchyard's well turned into beer on St Bridget's Day. Another says that the name was given by the early Irish settlers in the area. In any event, it is thought that this site was the first place in London where Christ was worshipped. [23]

By the fifteenth century, four churches had been built successively on the site, and the one standing at that time became connected with printing, thus beginning the well-known tradition of St Bride's association with 'Fleet Street,' the British press. Although most newspapers have actually moved out of Fleet Street, St Bride's is still considered the 'journalists' church' for various functions, including weddings and funerals. Among the many memorials to members of the press in the church is a plaque installed by the Overseas Press Club of America to commemorate journalists from this country who have died in overseas service.

Yet to stop with journalists only would be to miss a larger dimension, for the church's location at the center of what can be called 'Literary London' has resulted in associations with many 'greats' of English letters who lived in the area: Pepys, Milton, Johnson, Goldsmith, Wordsworth, Keats – to mention only a few. [24] So themes mentioned at the outset and identified with St Paul's, St Clement's, and Temple Church are repeated with St Bride's.

The current church, which was badly damaged during World War II and restored in 1957, was designed and built by Wren in 1680 to replace the structure destroyed in the Great Fire. Noting that the great architect's building has been called a 'madrigal of stone', Barron and Moore believe that St Bride's is one of Wren's finest works. Few would probably disagree with their final assessment that the 'warm and intimate atmosphere' of the church 'together with the natural light and sparkling interior, uplifts the soul.'[25]

## St Martin within Ludgate

Within the City of London, it is of course difficult to escape the 'towering' influence of Wren! Moving along Fleet Street in the direction of Ludgate Hill, the walker finds his eyes drawn to Wren's great masterpiece, St Paul's Cathedral, and hence he is likely to miss one of his smaller gems along the way, St Martin within Ludgate, located halfway up the hill. To avoid doing so, Barron and Moore suggest that walkers along Fleet Street who might become mesmerized by the overpowering presence of St Paul's dome should keep in mind that it is neatly bisected by St Martin's 'graceful leaden tower' which, though now almost hidden by ugly office buildings, can still serve as a beacon to the church.[26]

The visitor's guide to St Martin's waxes even more poetic about the steeple and the church's interior.

With its slender, elegant and feminine spire, St Martin's is truly a jewel beside the noisy, frenzied, Ludgate Hill, but within, there is enchantment, peace, and always evocative genius of its architect and builder.

Later on the guide becomes a little more matter-of-fact:

Wren's interior concept is delightfully simple. The main body of the church is nearly a perfect square and is spanned by an intersecting barrel-vault supported by four free-standing columns. These are of the Corinthian order, painted with capitals and picked out in gold. The roof spanning in the center is cruciform in design; the timbers are in the oak of old England.[27]

Of course much more can be said about this beautiful little church, but the sad and ironic fact about it, as well as about a number of other City churches, is that it has no congregation. There are no Sunday services. On my recent Sunday visit, the only reason the church was open was that a solitary volunteer from a London suburb had come many miles to make it available for visitors. She expressed the belief – and one hopes she is correct – that the building of new apartments in the area will mean a congregation for the church in the future, something that happened with St Giles as a result of the Barbican development. Perhaps City living will become a desirable thing once again. St Martin's is ready.

Yet, when open during the week, as it usually is, St Martin's is truly a haven of peace, comfort and joy from the bustle of the City. Its offerings of midday Holy Communion on Thursdays and music recitals on Wednesdays draw people from the nearby office blocks. The church also claims that it is the Chapel of the Middlesex Yeomanry and the Honourable Society of the Knights of the Round Table. It has close associations with the Guild of Freeman of the City of London and the Worshipful Company of Scriveners and Stationers. Lastly, the Central Criminal Court and the Worshipful Company of Chartered Accountants have their annual Carol Service in the sanctuary.

## St Mary-le-Bow

Walking on to Cheapside, I headed for St Mary-le-Bow, perhaps the best known of all City churches worldwide because of its bells. There are in fact twelve Bow Bells, each with its own name – including Katherine, Fabian and Cuthbert – and they help to perpetuate the legend that a Cockney or true Londoner is one born within their sounds. Actually, the word 'Bow' probably refers to the arches of the crypt under the church rather than to the bells or even the church itself.[28]

Although the foundations of the church are built on the remains of a Roman basilica, the Norman crypt, the oldest parochial building in London, is still very much in evidence, having even survived the Blitz of 1940–41 that destroyed the church. It is in this crypt that the Court of Arches, the supreme Court of the Province of Canterbury, has continued to meet since the twelfth century. Until 1847, the whole church was under the control of the Archbishop of Canterbury.[29]

While the link with Canterbury is still strong, the City connection is even stronger. Both the Worshipful Company of Grocers and the Worshipful Company of Arbitrators are associated with the church. Perhaps the church's most important ongoing contribution to contemporary London life is its celebrated 'Bow Dialogues,' which have been a feature of church activities for the past thirty years. Each week the rector invites distinguished guests from diverse backgrounds to participate in a forty-minute discussion conducted from two pulpits. The midday dialogues on Tuesdays are usually attended by more than 100 people.[30]

Although the church's life is rather subdued today, its past has had its share of sensation, due no doubt in part to its location on the edge of what was once an important open market in the heart of a very crowded city. On at least two occasions – one involving the roof and the other the steeple – parts of the church fell on people below, killing them. But certainly the most sensational event occurred in 1284 when a quarrel over a woman led to Lawrence Duket, a goldsmith, who was probably seeking sanctuary, being hanged inside the church! This atrocious act necessitated stopping up the doors and windows with thorns until the building had been purged of this desecration.[31]

With bells the church's main claim to world fame, it is fitting that the steeple where they are housed is one of Wren's greatest creations, a project that took seven years and huge costs to complete. The tower has two main stages, the belfry and the spire, with the latter described very succinctly by Blatch. It consists

> of a circular colonnade of 12 columns thrusting upwards by means of flying buttresses to a square stage, also with 12 columns, and completed with an obelisk spirelet of Aberdeen granite which is topped by a copper ball and the famous dragon weather-vane nearly nine feet long, all in the most harmonious proportions.[32]

Since the church required complete rebuilding after World War II, the interior, though following Wren's original structure, has been arranged to meet contemporary needs with flexible seating, a free-standing altar, and the cross raised overhead. One has a sense of openness and adaptability with a minimum of furnishing to enable the sanctuary to be used for various purposes, both religious and secular, to fill community needs.

## St Lawrence Jewry

Only a very short walk is needed from Cheapside along King Street to Gresham Street for the last church on the tour, St Lawrence Jewry, near the Guildhall. This church is the official civic place of worship of the Corporation of London.

Given the Christian nature of much of London's history, Jewry seems a strange name for the 'official' church. At least two theories have been presented in explanation. First, it is thought that the word refers to this section of the City where the Jewish population lived from the time of William I until their expulsion by Edward I in 1290. A second theory is that 'Jewry' is a corruption of 'jus, juris,' the center of the Roman city close to the amphitheater, which was in what is now the Guildhall yard. In any event, the church's close proximity to the Guildhall, especially with the removal to Missouri of St Mary Aldermanbury from across the street, has made St Lawrence the logical candidate for its present role, which was assumed in 1957.[33]

While this Wren church suffered some irreparable damage in the Blitz, it has been described as 'the most beautiful of the restored interiors' of London. A 'hall' type interior, the church nevertheless has two chapels, one on the north side called the Commonwealth Chapel and the other at the west end called the Tower Chapel. The first memorializes the City's role in the development of the British Commonwealth and the other is a replica of that which was used temporarily for services after the Blitz until the church was reopened.[34]

Many of the church's furnishings reflect its association with the City government. The Lord Mayor's pew is at the front on the right side and other pews are designated for the Queen's Sheriffs, the Court of Aldermen, and the Esquires. These are used when the Lord Mayor and other officials of the Corporation attend the church twice a year for state functions. The City flag is displayed on the south sanctuary wall and the City coat of arms is seen on the choir gallery.[35] Again, as a separation-of-church-and-state American, I find this association a little too close for comfort.

Although St Lawrence is the official civic place of worship, there are weekday services as well as more secular activities, such as music recitals and talks by prominent speakers, open to the public. Annual services are held by several city companies, too, including the Loriners, the Haberdashers and the Girdlers – the last company since 1180.[36] The church is also used by countless daily workers in the area as a place for quiet, spiritual refreshment away from the hectic pace of City life.

## The Site of St Mary Aldermanbury

My tour of these churches of Westminster and the City ends when I walk across the street to the small garden where St Mary Aldermanbury once stood. I have come full circle. A little rest time in the garden encourages some reflection on what has been seen and felt on the tour. My ultimate conclusion is that these architectural gems – with their long religious histories and their community associations and services – offer the people of London much psychic support and help to maintain public morale. One can understand why they have been preserved and rebuilt again and again for centuries. They are an important part of the British heritage and the American heritage as well. Certainly the experience of the walk – a reconnecting experience with some of America's past – prompts an American to think in this way.

But the garden itself, the church site of St Mary's since the twelfth century, has an effect as well. The thought that the last church on this site now stands in America makes the British-American connection, the Special Relationship, seem even stronger. By the way, when I visited that church in Fulton, Missouri, that feeling returned as thoughts about it and the previous churches on the London site were recalled. The most memorable of these is the fact that John Hemminge and Henry Condell, parishioners of St Mary's and actor friends of William Shakespeare, collected and published his works for posterity after his death. It is also believed that Shakespeare, who lived nearby, probably worshipped in St Mary's, too.[37] The Shakespeare connection seems quite appropriate as well because he is still the most produced playwright in America. And for the British, he is 'the Briton of the millennium,' according to a recent BBC poll.

## *London Theaters*

Numbers again. If the large number of London churches presented a problem, the same can be said about theaters – and certainly the productions in those theaters. Just from my own personal experiences since 1956, there are over 100 productions in more than thirty-five theaters to consider. Perhaps some would say that the answer is easy and can be found in the previous paragraph: simply focus on Shakespeare. After all, he is the greatest playwright of the English-speaking world, and his spirit, as well as his plays, are still alive and well in London. If God is sought through London theater, She, or perhaps He in this case, can be found in Shakespeare – so the argument goes.

Few would deny that Shakespeare is a special case no matter how one approaches the London theater. Certainly his plays are encountered all the time and at virtually every venue in London. Although Shakespeare was mainly associated with the Old Vic when I arrived in 1956 and now with the Barbican and the National Theatre, his plays can appear almost anywhere both indoors and outdoors around London. The recent completion of The Globe seems to assure that for years to come. While Shakespeare certainly stands on his own merits and will be around as long as the London stage, much of the current promotional credit goes to one group. What eventually became known as the Royal Shakespeare Company, which for a century was the driving force for his plays in Stratford-upon-Avon, became such as well in London in the 1960s when it established its first base at the Aldwych Theatre. The company solidified its strength with the move to the new Barbican Centre in 1982. Hence, Shakespeare's place as an important part of the London stage seems very secure indeed.

Yet, to focus only on Shakespeare would be unfortunate, for while of extraordinary importance to the London stage, he is perhaps more illustrative or symbolic of the Special Relationship than its essence. In other words, its essence is something else. Perhaps an anecdote about a stage production of one of Shakespeare's plays will help to make my point.

In 1986, my older daughter and I attended a performance of *The Merry Wives of Windsor* at the Barbican. About halfway through the first act, I noticed that she had her eyes closed, something very unusual for a devotee of Shakespeare. I asked whether she was ill or merely tired, and she replied neither but was trying to cope with a major flaw in the production. For her and for me as well, Shakespeare's language had been all but compromised in an attempt to 'modernize' the play – in other words to make it like television. Far from being strict traditionalists, we, who can accept modern dress and other changes, were appalled by the use of gimmicks and the tired cliches of television and the movies.

For example, during one scene an actor dressed as a policeman rode a bicycle on stage and, sure enough, he fell off. Some thirty years before, several Scottish friends pointed out to me that this was standard practice in British comedy films, something they found ludicrous and hackneyed.

My daughter had it right. Shakespeare's main strength and much of his appeal stem from his use of the language – English, the mother tongue, if you will – and obviously a large part of the Special Relationship is about the common language of Britons and Americans. One is reminded about a prediction Otto von Bismarck, the great German Chancellor of last century, made about this one. The single most important fact of the twentieth century, he said, would be that the British and the Americans speak the same language. While one should probably temper this remark somewhat with Oscar Wilde's quip – that is, that the British and the Americans are divided by a common language – Bismarck is correct in seeing that language is one of the key factors in Anglo-American relations.

Few would deny that both written and spoken English are important in communication, but having spent much of my lifetime as a lecturer, I am convinced that the latter, especially in an appropriate setting, is much more influential in the lives of most people. Who can doubt the power of Churchill's wartime speeches and Franklin Roosevelt's Fireside Chats! For me, then, it is the use of the spoken word on stage – an appropriate setting indeed – that makes the London theater a focal point in my search for the Special Relationship.

In addition to Shakespeare, there are obviously many more playwrights who have made important contributions to the language of the London stage. My favorites among contemporaries are Tom Stoppard and Peter Shaffer. But being a historian, I shall look to the past and consider, along with Shakespeare, Wilde and W. S. Gilbert, two theatrical giants of the same period 100 years ago. Rather than focusing on the men themselves, I shall look at them indirectly by considering the theaters where they rose to great public acclaim: the Old Vic, the Haymarket and the Savoy.

Since these theaters are only three among about three dozen, something should be said about the big picture first. Two walks around London's West End help to locate about thirty of the most important theaters. While a map will show that the theaters are scattered about somewhat, it is rather remarkable how many of them are within easy walking distance of one another.

Essentially, my first walk is a circle with Leicester Square in the middle. It begins in Haymarket, actually at the lower end to include the Theatre Royal and its neighbor across the street, Her Majesty's. Moving north, the Comedy can be seen a short distance down Panton Street to the right, after which another glance in the same direction down Coventry Street at the top of Haymarket locates the Prince of Wales. A left turn on Coventry leads into Piccadilly Circus and the Criterion. Now begins the long stroll up Shaftesbury Avenue with short excursions off the street now and then to locate theaters on side streets. This is the case with the Piccadilly at the start before the walk up Shaftesbury past the Lyric, Apollo, Gielgud (until recently the Globe) and Queen's, all in a row on the left side of the street.

A left turn on Greek Street to Old Compton Street a short distance away leads to Prince Edward. A right turn and another short walk along Old Compton brings the walker to Charing Cross Road. The Phoenix is up that road to the left, and where it intersects with Shaftesbury Avenue a little to the right is the Palace. A short distance up Shaftesbury again and a right on Earlham Street leads to a cluster of theaters on side streets in a small area: Cambridge, Ambassadors and St Martin's.

Returning to a main road, this time to Monmouth Street which leads into St Martin's Lane going south, the walker passes the Albery, Duke of York's and Coliseum. A right turn on William IV Street and another right on Charing Cross Road takes one past the Garrick and Wyndhams. Finally, just a short walk across Charing Cross and into Leicester Square leads to a bench for a much-needed rest!

My second walk is something of a circle as well. It begins in the Strand and moves east to Aldwych and doubles back by way of Covent Garden where a short walk down Southampton Street leads to the Strand again. A number of theaters are to be seen along the way: Adelphi, Vaudeville, Savoy, Strand, Aldwych, Duchess, Drury Lane, Fortune and Royal Opera House.

While these two walks take in the vast majority of theaters in Central London, a few others, including well-known ones, are clustered in other regions. For example, south of the River Thames can be found the National Theatre complex with several theatres together, the Old Vic, the Young Vic, and the recently completed Globe. The area near Victoria Railway Station has three others.

## The Old Vic

Despite its problematic history and its uncertain future, the Old Vic will always be a sentimental favorite and the most symbolic of Shakespeare. Had I seen my first London production of a Shakespearian play elsewhere, this might not be the case, but the splendid performance of *The Merchant of Venice* there in 1956 is long remembered.

As suggested above concerning the theater's location, perhaps the crux of the Old Vic's historical as well as its contemporary problem is its address in an uninviting area some distance from Waterloo Station. Readers, who like my London students have walked to the station late at night after a performance, know the uneasy feeling of the journey. Paradoxically at the time of the theater's founding, its location was seen as an asset. Apparently the choice of site was influenced by the completion in 1817 of Waterloo Bridge that gave easy access to the still largely rural area south of the Thames which had been known as Cupid's Garden. An additional asset was the fact that the theater was named the Royal Coburg in honor of its chief patrons, Princess Charlotte, King George IV's only child, and Prince Leopold of Saxe-Coburg.[38]

Immediately after its opening in 1818, the Coburg attracted the upper classes of London society. But having no patent, the theater had to limit its performances to melodrama, pantomime, and music shows in general. Despite having appearances from some 'names' of the day – the great clown Grimaldi, the famous musician Paganini, and the well-known actor Edmund Kean – most classical actors performed elsewhere.[39] Hence, the Coburg's appeal to the public was rather limited.

In 1833, its name was changed to the Royal Victoria Theatre in honor of the young Princess, but melodramas remained the principal offering. One writer describes the theater's clientele at the time as being 'local people,' but Charles Mathews is less discreet:

> The lower orders rush there in mobs, and in shirtsleeves, frantically drink ginger-beer, munch apples, crack nuts, call the actors by their Christian names, and throw them orange peel and apples by way of bouquets.[40]

This comment reflects what had happened to the area south of the river: its development 'as ill-favored slum accommodation, not enhanced by the building of Waterloo Station in 1848,' as one writer puts it. Moreover, the theater's reputation was not improved in 1858 when sixteen people were trampled to death as a result of a false fire alarm.[41]

There followed a series of closings and reopenings, usually involving changes to the theater's interior. Reflecting the spirit of the times, the New Victoria Theatre, as it was now called, soon became a temperance music hall for the working classes in 1880 and acquired still another new name: the Royal Victoria Temperance Music Hall and Coffee Tavern.[42]

While this development might seem the beginning of the end for a theater, it was actually a new beginning for the Vic, thanks in large part to two dynamic women: Emma Cons and her niece Lilian Baylis. Apparently Cons had two main missions in life, that of securing housing for the working classes and achieving total temperance. The theater became her vehicle for the latter. On two nights of the week, she attracted people to the Vic by music hall performances and tried to encourage them to return other nights for temperance meetings, lectures, and ballad recitals. She had great success. Out of the recitals grew 'operatic extracts in costume,' a limited staging of opera which by 1914 had given the theater the reputation of 'the home of opera in English.' By the way, the lectures evolved into Morley College, a working men's academy housed backstage until it moved to its own campus in 1923.[43]

Lilian Baylis joined her aunt's operation in 1898 and took complete charge when Emma Cons died in 1912. With a stronger interest in theatrical productions, Baylis negotiated a theater license and tried popular drama without success. Not knowing what to do next, she said she made one last effort: 'In despair, I turned to Shakespeare.' Out of desperation the real birth of the Old Vic occurred. Her most significant decision was to hire Ben Greet, an experienced actor-manager, as her director of productions and between them they established the Old Vic Shakespeare Company. During the next half century, this company developed, first, a local, then a national, and eventually an international reputation for excellence.[44]

Many factors produced this excellence, but the list of outstanding directors and actors, rather than money, surely ranks first. In addition to Greet, the directors included Robert Atkins, Harcourt Williams, Tyrone Guthrie, Ralph Richardson, and Laurence Olivier. The actors, too numerous to try to list them all, were a Who's Who of the London stage: Richardson, Olivier, Sybil Thorndike, Edith Evans, Peggy Ashcroft, John Gielgud, Alec Guinness, Michael Redgrave, and Charles Laughton – among many others.

War is another factor in the rise of the Old Vic's fortunes. According to Jim De Young and John Miller, the outbreak of World War I in 1914 proved to be the theater's 'salvation' in attracting a loyal following. In offering Shakespeare during a time of great national crisis, Baylis gave Londoners something they longed for – something they failed to get from the commercial managements of the other West End theaters that turned 'to light escapist fare' throughout the war.[45]

Apart from theatrical substance, it is of course difficult to know precisely what Londoners found in Shakespeare to satisfy their needs. In a general way, perhaps the plays were fulfilling the more traditional role of the communication arts as a mechanism by which human cooperation and unity can emerge from the realm of imagination into social life. This is likely during time of war. Yet one feels that the very critical nature of the time called forth something even more significant: the plays as providers of psychic support and enhancers of public morale. In other words, they became something like religion, a secular religion, perhaps. Certainly, as we have seen, the line between church and theater in Britain is very thin indeed, and hence the Old Vic very likely became a place for spiritual uplifting.

Again, perhaps one can only speculate about what Londoners found at the Old Vic, but one senses that it had something to do with the Elizabethan Age, including the Chain of Being and the other factors discussed in Chapter VI. The Helper was sought, and She was found.

On the other hand, when World War II came along the Old Vic's fortunes began to decline. The theater was forced to close after being bombed in 1941 and was unable to reopen until 1950. Although the Old Vic Company continued to offer outstanding productions at the New Theatre (now the Albery) in London and elsewhere during this time, the changes of venue prompted questions to be raised about the Old Vic's future as a post-war theatrical center. In addition, the idea of a new National Theatre with a specially recruited company under Olivier's direction was gaining much support.[46]

In the end the decision was made to create the National Theatre Company, and the only major benefit for the Old Vic was to be named its temporary home in the early 1960s. In 1963 the last Old Vic Company performance was given, and the National Theatre Company remained at the theater until it moved into its new South Bank complex in 1974.

Thus ended the great Shakespearian years of the Old Vic and its old identity. With the Royal Shakespeare Company performing Shakespeare at the Barbican and the National Company presenting many of his plays as well not far away, the Old Vic's raison d'etre seems to have disappeared. Perhaps this demonstrates well that Shakespeare is indeed bigger than any one theatrical institution. Yet will the Old Vic, the sentimental favorite, survive? So far it has, thanks in large part to the efforts of the Peter Hall Company which has presented a repertoire of classics and new plays. Whether this effort can be sustained – given the theater's location and the departure of Shakespeare – remains to be seen.

## The Theatre Royal, Haymarket

One of London's oldest theaters, the Haymarket is my favorite because in so many respects it represents what a great theater ought to be, and at the same time it also symbolizes better than any other what London theater is in fact. In short, there is a coming together of the ideal and the real in the history of the Haymarket. One can argue that the theater's many difficulties during its first 100 years illustrate the hard realities of London's theatrical history while its many successes during the last eighty or so years show what theater should be. In many respects the almost 100 years in between these periods present a mixture of the two, and Oscar Wilde personifies this mixture better than anyone else connected with the theater. Late last century the Haymarket shared Wilde's great stage successes and then witnessed his personal tragedy, which was of course a tragedy for London theater as well.

Only in his middle forties when he died a broken man, Wilde seemed to be at the height of his creative powers just before the scandal occurred. While certainly not on Shakespeare's level, he was perhaps the most talented playwright in the English-speaking world at the time and added much to the language of the theater. Before considering his contributions and his appeal to Londoners, something will be said about the Haymarket's history.

Opening almost three centuries ago, the Haymarket — known as the Little Theatre in the Hay at the time — had no license for productions at the outset. Thus, John Potter, its builder, had difficulty in letting it to the acting community, but finally in the 1730s the great Henry Fielding began to manage it — at least for a short time. Presenting some of his famous satires about politicians of the day, Fielding soon crossed the line in his biting portrayal of Sir Robert Walpole. The political outrage that followed led to the passage of the Licensing Act of 1737 which had a great impact on London's theaters for the next two centuries.

Briefly, the law did three things. It limited the number of theaters to those currently holding patents, required all new productions to get an authorization from the Lord Chamberlain, and empowered that official to prohibit any individual theatrical performance. This great power of censorship, perhaps the darkest side of London's theatrical history, remained part of British law until 1968 when the Lord Chamberlain's authority to approve manuscripts and license plays was finally abolished.[47]

The immediate effect of the law on the Little Theatre was its closure and many thought its demise. Yet, by 1747, the theater had been reopened through the ingenuity of Samuel Foote. He managed to flout the licensing laws by taking admission money for refreshments served during performances.[48]

Somehow continuing to operate for years in this questionable way, Foote finally got his break — literally — for a royal patent in the 1760s through the help of the Duke of York. It all started when the Duke persuaded Foote to ride a wild horse which threw him off and caused him to have a badly broken leg. The break was so serious that Foote's leg had to be amputated. As compensation the Duke obtained the patent which enabled the theater to be open during the summer months for Foote's lifetime.[49]

With all the great actors of the day beginning to perform in the newly named Theatre Royal, it seemed that the royal connection assured the Haymarket a much brighter future. But this association brought tragedy as well in 1794 when twenty persons lost their lives and many others were injured by the crush of a vast crowd pressing to see the

King attending the first command performance at the theater. Eleven years later the Life Guards had to be called out to disperse rioting tailors incensed by the performance of the satirical play titled *The Tailors*.[50]

As the first 100 years of the theater's troubled life came to a close in 1820, it was appropriate that the old theater building closed and a new one was erected a little further south on Haymarket, providing a vista from St James's Square. This new beginning was very dramatic indeed, for the great Court architect John Nash was commissioned to design the new building, which still stands today.[51]

The theater's second 100 years were indeed much better. One of the high points was the period of time from 1853 to 1878 when actor John Baldwin Buckstone managed the Haymarket. A theatrical favorite and friend of Queen Victoria, Buckstone devoted his life to the theater and its 200 productions with 'scarcely one failure and many unusual successes,' according to one account. Among his great successes was *Our American Cousin* which ran 400 nights. About the same time Ellen Terry made her theatrical debut there at age fifteen.[52]

Buckstone's name is still associated with some of the great folklore of the London theater. It is said that his ghost, a benign presence, haunts the Haymarket and has been seen by many actors and theater staff over the years. His activities include opening and closing doors, walking the hallways, resting in dressing rooms, and sitting in the royal box.[53]

Much more controversial was the management of actor Sir Herbert Beerbohm-Tree from 1887 to 1896. Brother of Max Beerbohm, Tree had gained fame for his lavish Shakespeare productions which included the use of live rabbits and a horse. While managing the Haymarket, he built his own theater, Her Majesty's, opposite which later featured a drama school. In time this school evolved into the famous The Royal Academy of Dramatic Art.[54]

At the Haymarket, Tree is remembered most for productions of two new plays by Oscar Wilde. These are the premiere performances of *A Woman of No Importance* in 1893 and *An Ideal Husband* two years later. Although the scandal in Wilde's life did not become public knowledge until the latter play had moved to another theater, Wilde's flamboyance and the banning of his biblical play *Salome* in 1892, among other things, had already made him a controversial figure before the former production appeared. Whether difficult or not, Tree's decisions to produce the plays brought success from the public if not from the critics.

While not as successful as *Lady Windermere's Fan* in 1892, *A Woman of No Importance* ran for 118 performances at the Haymarket, only closing to enable Tree to honor a prior commitment. Two short anecdotes, the first about opening night and the second about the following night, illustrate how well the play was received. After great applause and calls for the author at the final curtain on the first night, Wilde brought the house down with his brief statement: 'Ladies and gentlemen, I regret to inform you that Mr Oscar Wilde is not in the house.' Attending the second night, the Prince of Wales was observed greatly enjoying himself and commented to Wilde afterword: 'Do not alter a single line.'[55]

On the other hand the critics were very cool, perhaps because Wilde was offering something new and even revolutionary for the London stage. They responded in the same way to *An Ideal Husband* which prompted George Bernard Shaw to chide them as follows:

> They laugh angrily at his epigrams ... They protest that the trick is obvious, and that such epigrams can be turned out by the score by anyone light-minded enough to condescend to such frivolity. As far as I can ascertain, I am the only person in London who cannot sit down and write an Oscar Wilde play at will.

Shaw concluded:

> Mr. Wilde is to me our thorough playwright. He plays with everything: with wit, with philosophy, with drama, with actors and audience, with the whole theatre ...[56]

*An Ideal Husband* was an immediate public success as well. This time the Prince of Wales attended opening night, and when Wilde remarked that he might have to shorten the play, the Prince apparently replied, 'Pray do not take out a single word.' The play ran for 111 performances at the Haymarket before a scheduled transfer to the Criterion where it ran only two weeks – a casualty of Wilde's arrest and trial.[57]

Thus, after the scandal became public, even Shaw's words of praise could not help to save Wilde's plays or Wilde himself. Fortunately, the passage of time and the changing attitudes of critics and the public – especially the latter towards homosexuality – have given perspective to see the accuracy of Shaw's assessment. Therefore, 100 years after Wilde's plays opened at the Haymarket, they returned to both critical and public acclaim in the 1990s.

Of all the recent comments about Wilde's plays, those by Director Peter Hall seem the most accurate to me. In an article for the *Guardian* in 1993, Hall, who focused mainly on *An Ideal Husband*, had things to say about Wilde which applied to much of the playwright's entire work. According to Hall, love and forgiveness are at the heart of Wilde's philosophy. For him

> care and understanding of other people were an integral part of love; so was tolerance. And so, above all, was forgiveness. All this had

been evident in his work for many years in his plays ... the public had enjoyed their mockery of the hypocrisies of society. They had also found them surprisingly goodhearted. It is the warmth, rather than the wit ... which still ensures that the plays are popular. People like to spend an evening with a sensibility that is so markedly generous and compassionate, and whose sense of the ridiculous keeps him from sentimentality.[58]

Although Wilde was Irish by birth, Hall sees great understanding of the English character in his plays. He also shows insight about Wilde's use of language.

All Wilde's characters are extravagantly emotional and are naturally egocentric. But they do not show their feelings or release their emotions; that would be un-English. They speak witticisms instead. The more emotional they become, the more extravagant the wit. It is a type of English stiff-upper lip, and it informs all Wilde's theatre. Beneath the wit, there's always an intense emotional reality.[59]

It has been said that the purpose of religion is to afflict the comfortable and comfort the afflicted and that seems to have been Wilde's purpose as well. Perhaps it is significant that Wilde was received into the Catholic Church the year before his death. At any rate, in terms of the metaphors of this book Wilde's sympathies clearly lay with the Helper rather than with the Hero or Rebel. The Helper personifies the types of values Wilde honored in his plays: love, forgiveness, care, understanding and tolerance. On the other hand, the Hero and Rebel are types inclined towards the hypocrisies Wilde mocked: the ones who indulge in such things as self-love, self-righteousness and self-importance. Hence, Wilde's plays represent very well what the Haymarket in particular and the London theater in general are all about at their very best. A hundred years after Wilde's plays opened Londoners recognize this.

Limits of space preclude recounting much additional history of the Haymarket during the twentieth century. However, some examples of playwrights and actors associated with their productions at the Haymarket will illustrate why there have been many successes. In addition to Wilde, there have been plays by Shakespeare, Congreve, Shaw, Chekhov, Pirandello, Rattigan, Tennessee Williams, Albee, Pinter and Stoppard. Among the actors, only a few of the better-known names include the following: John Gielgud, Ralph Richardson, Alec Guinnes, Michael Redgrave, Wendy Hiller, Margaret Rutherford, Vanessa Redgrave, Maggie Smith, Peter Ustinov, and Derek Jacobi.

## The Savoy

If Oscar Wilde can be used to represent the best of the Haymarket, Gilbert and Sullivan certainly play the same role for the Savoy Theatre. In fact for me, the Savoy serves mainly as a symbol for Gilbert and Sullivan operas rather than the place for them. All London productions I have seen have not been there but in four other theaters: Princes (now Shaftesbury), Westminster, Sadler's Wells, and Cambridge.

As well known by all Savoyards, Richard D'Oyly Carte financed the building of the Savoy Theatre in 1881 for the production of Gilbert and Sullivan operas. The first public building in London to be lit by electricity, it opened with *Patience*, which had transferred from the Opera Comique, and *Iolanthe* followed in 1882. Two years later came the productions of *Princess Ida*, *The Sorcerer* and *Trial by Jury*. The stage hits continued with *The Mikado* (1885), *Ruddigore* (1887), *The Yeoman of the Guard* (1888) and *The Gondoliers* (1889).

With this team of three enjoying great success year after year, it seemed that their prosperity would mount indefinitely. However, in 1890 Gilbert quarrelled with Carte about, of course, money. The former became annoyed over the costs of the production of *The Gondoliers*, especially by a bill for expensive new carpets. When Sullivan supported Carte, the partnership broke up, but two new productions of poor quality followed: *Utopia Ltd.* in 1893 and three years later *The Grand Duke*, an outright failure and the last collaboration of Gilbert and Sullivan.[60]

While most Savoyards have their favorites among the fourteen operas, I have found it rather difficult to rank order them. However, with background in law, government, and military service, I put *Iolanthe*, *The Mikado*, *Trial by Jury*, and *H.M.S. Pinafore* high on my list. Certainly my legal training has got me in touch with Gilbert who read law as well. Thus, I have passed along to my students many of Gilbert's witty and insightful lyrics. Perhaps their favorite lines – they are indeed mine – are these from *Iolanthe*:

> The Law is the true embodiment
> Of everything that's excellent.
> It has no kind of fault or flaw,
> And I, my lords, embody the Law.

Since most of my students planned to be lawyers, I made sure they were familiar with many lines from *Trial by Jury*, especially these:

> All thieves, who could my fees afford,
> Relied on my orations,
> And many a burglar I've restored
> To his friends and his relations!

In America, Gilbert's insights have informed both lawyers and judges, even some at the highest levels. For example, United States Supreme Court Chief Justice William Rehnquist has used Gilbert's lyrics in at least one of his important opinions that I know. By the why, who in this world of television can deny the impact of Gilbert and Sullivan on the Chief Justice after seeing his yellow-striped, G. and S. inspired judicial gown during the impeachment trial of President Bill Clinton!

Of course, countless other examples concerning the law could be given. But Gilbert's insights extend to other institutions as well, as these two verses from 'When I Was a Lad' (*H.M.S. Pinafore*) show:

> I grew so rich that I was sent
> By a pocket borough into Parliament.
> I always voted at my party's call,
> And I never thought of thinking for myself at all.
> I thought so little they rewarded me,
> By making me the ruler of the Queen's Navee.
> Now landsmen all, whoever you may be
> If you want to rise to the top of the tree,
> If your soul isn't fettered to an office stool,
> Be careful to be guided by this golden rule –
> Stick close to your desks and never go to sea,
> And you all may be rulers of the Queen's Navee.

Why are such lyrics so appealing? I think many if not most of Peter Hall's remarks about Oscar Wilde apply to Gilbert as well. In particular, here, as with Wilde, there is mockery of the hypocrisies of society, but it is done in a good-hearted way. There is warmth – not anger – and, yes, compassion and forgiveness as well. It is no coincidence, I believe, that Wilde and Gilbert wrote and enjoyed great success at the same time near the end of last century. And, of course, Gilbert and Sullivan had great fun in satirizing Wilde and others in the aesthetic movement in *Patience* – which delighted Wilde no end.

While Wilde and Gilbert are alike in many ways, I think at least two of their differences account for much of Gilbert's appeal, especially in America where Gilbert and Sullivan have enjoyed a larger following than Wilde. The first can be seen in the lyrics above: they are very clever but they are also easy to understand. In other words, Gilbert wrote for everyman – the common man while Wilde wrote for a more sophisticated audience. As Shaw pointed out, Wilde is philosophical and hence much more intellectual. Gilbert is not and hence many more Americans can relate to him.

The other difference concerns the focus of each. Wilde is much more interested in individuals while Gilbert emphasizes institutions. Certainly the latter has important individual characters, but as the lyrics above suggest Gilbert goes beyond them to such institutions as the law, the military and the government. In *Iolanthe*, for example, both Houses of Parliament are targets of his barbs. Now certainly most Americans are not very knowledgeable about such institutions, but Gilbert and Sullivan make it clear that they are being satirized. One does not have to be very sophisticated about Parliament to appreciate their humor.

I have known a few Britons who have had problems with this aspect of Gilbert and Sullivan. Many years ago, an elderly London couple tried to persuade me during my first visit there to see Julian Slade's very popular *Salad Days* rather than *Iolanthe*. They found the political satire of the latter too difficult to cope with during Britain's declining years of the 1950s, especially at the time of the Suez Crisis. Yet I think their views stemmed mainly from that difficult time, and if they were alive today, they, too, would see more value in Gilbert than Slade.

It seems to me that Gilbert and Sullivan remind us in their charming and good-hearted way that all institutions have – in the terms of the social scientist – both instrumental and ceremonial aspects, and when the latter become too strong, undesirable things can happen. So let's not take ourselves and our institutions too seriously; let's be able to laugh at ourselves. Like Wilde, it's the Helper rather than the Hero or Rebel who is honored by Gilbert and Sullivan.

The Savoy Theatre has had a life of its own these past 100 years. In fact, the ending of the Gilbert-Sullivan-Carte association did not immediately affect the nature of the Savoy's productions. From 1897 to 1903 comic operas by other composers were staged but without great success. Things improved somewhat with a run of Shaw revivals and two seasons of Shakespeare between 1912 and 1914 by Harvey Granville Barker. Yet the theater's subsequent productions, which included some Gilbert and Sullivan revivals, achieved more success with standard comedies and farces than anything else, including comic operas. For example, in 1918, *Nothing but the Truth*, a farce by James Montgomery, began the first of its 578 performances. Noel Coward's comedy *The Young Idea* had a good run in the 1920s, and beginning in 1941 *The Man Who Came to Dinner*, with Robert Morley, had a record 709 performances. Never achieving the status of the Haymarket for great theater, the Savoy has nevertheless made important contributions to London's theatrical history. However, it will be remembered most for that short period of Gilbert and Sullivan classics.[61]

## Conclusion

Many London churches and theaters are very important institutions which help to make that huge, sprawling city liveable and workable. I have discussed only a small sample of them, but I hope my examples have given others some insight about the nature of their importance. Perhaps only personal experience can give a sense of their real importance to people who live and work there. But my conclusion is this: as an American makes face-to-face contact with these institutions – as he explores them, reads about their histories, and participates in their functions and activities – he can gain some understanding of the nature of the Special Relationship between Britain and the United States. For these institutions at their best exemplify and enhance all those Helper values mentioned before – those values at the heart of the Special Relationship.

## *Notes*

1. John Barron and Alexandra Moore, *City of London Churches: A Walkers' Guide* (Winchester, United Kingdom: Barron and Moore, 1998), ix.
2. Ibid.
3. Ibid.
4. Ibid.
5. Mervyn Blatch, *A Guide to London's Churches*, 2nd ed., (London: Constable and Company Ltd., 1995), 223.
6. Barron and Moore, vii.
7. Blatch, 219.
8. Ibid., 222.
9. Ibid., 233.
10. Ibid., 237.
11. Ibid.
12. Ibid., 235.
13. Ibid.
14. Ibid., 236.
15. Ibid., 255.
16. Ibid., 253–4.
17. Ibid., 242.
18. Ibid., 240–1.
19. Ibid., 206.
20. Barron and Moore, 217–18.
21. Blatch, 171.
22. Ibid., 58.
23. Ibid., 55.
24. Ibid., 58–9.
25. Barron and Moore, 225.
26. Ibid., 229.
27. 'St Martin Within Ludgate.'
28. Blatch, 127–8. See also *The City of London Churches: A Pictorial Rediscovery* (London: Collins and Brown Limited, 1998), 164–5.
29. Barron and Moore, 189.
30. Ibid., 190.
31. Ibid., 189.

32. Blatch, 128.
33. Ibid., 95.
34. Ibid., 97.
35. Barron and Moore, 162.
36. Blatch, 100.
37. Ibid., 190.
38. Jim De Young and John Miller, *London Theatre Walks* (London: Applause Books, 1998), 203.
39. *An Ideal Husband Programme* (Bristol, England: Proscenium Theatre Publications, 1996), no page number.
40. *An Encyclopaedia of London*, revised by Godfrey Thompson, 1970, s.v. 'Theatres.'
41. *An Ideal Husband Programme.*
42. Ibid.
43. Ibid.
44. Ibid.
45. De Young and Miller, 204.
46. *An Ideal Husband Programme.*
47. De Young and Miller, 109.
48. *The London Encyclopedia*, s.v. 'Haymarket Theatre.'
49. Ibid.
50. *An Ideal Husband Programme* 6, no. 98 (London: Theatreprint Ltd.), no page number.
51. Ibid.
52. Ibid.
53. De Young and Miller, 110.
54. Ibid., 107–8.
55. *An Ideal Husband Programme* 6, no. 98.
56. Ibid.
57. Ibid.
58. Ibid. Reprinted from the *Guardian.*
59. Ibid.
60. *The London Encyclopaedia*, s.v. 'Savoy Theatre.' See also *The Authentic Gilbert and Sullivan Songbook* (New York: Dover Publications, Inc., 1977), xi.
61. *The London Encyclopaedia*, s.v. 'Savoy Theatre.'

# Chapter X

# London: Two Villages and a Few Parks

*T*he experiences of reading many accounts about and walking numerous times through two London villages, where I have stayed, and five of its parks are recounted in this chapter. My main objectives in my undertakings were to learn about their identities and their very essences because each is quite unique in many respects but yet alike as sources of Helper values, the heart of the Special Relationship. As such sources, they have helped to make huge and sprawling London a workable and a very enjoyable city to visit and to live in. Their identities developed from a number of factors coming together: historical, geographical, sociological, political, economic, psychological, educational, cultural and religious – among others. Largely based on my impressionistic 'feel' of the places, my approach has been to assign a particular identity to each and to build a case for such by selecting from those numerous factors examples that I believe illustrate my point as well as the Helper values.

## Village London

How many books have been titled 'Village London' or something similar? As I write there are three such in front of me published in 1978, 1990, and 1997, but I imagine they are only the tip of the iceberg. Clearly the notion of London as a collection of villages has been around for such a long time that it is generally accepted as being true. Less agreed upon, however, are the answers to such questions as: How many are there? And what are their borders? For example, one of my books lists 25 villages and another has 21 with only 5 of these in both. And boundary lines for those listed seem to follow the imaginations of the writers. Yet, what appears to be most important about 'Village London' is the concept rather than the details, the image rather than reality. In short, what people carry around in their heads.

At any rate, like studies of London's churches, theaters, and parks, large numbers of villages preclude much more than a few samples in a book like this. Although my choices are made on the basis of where

I have stayed numerous and lengthy times, the selections are not easy to make among such places as Bloomsbury, Kensington, South Kensington, Notting Hill, Pimlico, Muswell Hill, Brixton, Kew and Richmond. Those familiar with these villages or their immediate neighbors will understand the difficulty of choice because of the unique characteristics of each, though some may think that in a few instances such are not very desirable. Whatever the case, my selections are Bloomsbury and Kensington with a few words also about two neighbors of the latter.

## *Bloomsbury*

Perhaps not surprising my first question about Bloomsbury concerned location. Where is it? In fact, is it really there somewhere or is it merely a state of mind? Actually, it seems to be both. However, when I think of it geographically, there are several ways of locating it on London's map. In terms of London's boroughs, Bloomsbury is the most southern part of Camden; in terms of London's postal zones, it is WC1; and in terms of streets, it is bounded on the west by Tottenham Court Road, on the east by Gray's Inn Road, on the north by Euston Road, and on the south by three: New Oxford Street, Bloomsbury Way and Theobalds Road. Now some Londoners might argue with this, especially my southern boundary, but my reluctance to follow High Holburn further south stems from the resulting division of two Inns of Court: Gray's and Lincoln's. By defining Bloomsbury in this way, its center is pretty much where I think it should be and that is Russell Square, the crossroads or 'village green,' as I see it.

Although there are several other important squares in this area – Bloomsbury Square among them – Russell Square is not only important in terms of location but also in size. One of London's largest squares, it jumps out at you from every map. But there are other important defining elements of this area which help to give it its character. These include the British Museum, the University of London, hospitals, and hotels, especially the smaller ones where students have often stayed. Perhaps it is not surprising then that for me, an academic, Bloomsbury no matter how it is defined geographically always conjures up the general theme of London's academic and intellectual life, a very definite state of mind. Hence the 'Bloomsbury Intellectual' is a defining type of the area, both in reality and in its stereotypical form as seen in Nicolas Bentley's cartoon characters and George Mikes' description in the latter's famous book of humor, *How To Be An Alien*.

Historically, the intellectual theme has not always been the case – far from it. Part of Bloomsbury is recorded in *Domesday Book* as having vineyards and woods for 100 pigs! The name itself seems to derive from Blemondisberi, meaning the 'bury' or manor of Blemond, after

William Blemond, who acquired it in the early thirteenth century. On its southern border his son had Blemond's Dyke dug which surprisingly was still evident in the nineteenth century as a common sewer.[1]

Much of Bloomsbury's early history is about the manor and its owners. For example, by the early fourteenth century the manor was held by Edward III who later gave it to the Carthusian monks of the London Charterhouse, located some distance to the east. After Henry VIII dissolved the monasteries, Bloomsbury ended up in the hands of Thomas Wriothesley, Earl of Southampton, in 1550. A century later, the 4th Earl built Southampton House, and Bloomsbury Square was laid out afterward to its south as an appropriate setting for such a magnificent place. This began the aristocratic influence in the development of the area which lasted for two centuries.[2]

The main force in this development was the powerful Russell family, already established in Covent Garden to the south. That family acquired an interest in the area when Rachel, Lady Vaughan, the widowed daughter of the Earl of Southampton and heiress to Bloomsbury, married William Lord Russell, second son of the 5th Earl of Bedford. He became heir to the Russell fortune when his elder brother died in 1678. Though the family experienced some political setbacks leading to William's death, his son, who became the 2nd Duke of Bedford, and Rachel inherited the Southampton Estates and the Russell fortune. Successive Dukes, including the 3rd and 4th who married granddaughters of Sarah Churchill, 1st Duchess of Marlborough, engaged in a number of construction projects that transformed the physical character of Bloomsbury into a very fashionable area.[3]

It was in fact Sarah Churchill who was influential in getting the name of Southampton House changed to Bedford House and thereafter the names of Bedford and Russell began to appear on more places in Bloomsbury as development ensued. An early project was the building of Great Russell Street to link Bedford House and Bloomsbury Square with Tottenham Court Road.[4]

During the eighteenth century one of the most important developments in Bloomsbury was undertaken by Gertrude Leveson Gower, the widow of the 4th Duke of Bedford. She built Bedford Square, one of the great Georgian squares of London, and Gower Street, a main north-south artery through Bloomsbury.[5]

When Gower's son, the 5th Duke, came of age, he was not interested in living in Bloomsbury and had the great Bedford House demolished in 1800, a sign of the changing nature of the area. In its place the famous James Burton built a terrace of houses, the first of a number of Bloomsbury projects he would complete. Later, under the 6th Duke, Burton and the even more famous Thomas Cubitt pushed development north and east with the result of an irregular but controlled and planned series of handsome squares and roads. It was during this time in the

London: Two Villages and a Few Parks

nineteenth century that Bloomsbury became the favorite area for intellectuals, especially writers, painters and musicians, as well as for lawyers who appreciated the close proximity to the Inns of Court.[6]

Actually the intellectual nature of the area began to form during the previous century with the founding of the British Museum. Opened to the public in 1759, the Museum began its life in Montagu House, another great house of Bloomsbury built shortly after the construction of Southampton House. Like the pulling down of that house, then bearing the Bedford name as noted above, the conversion of Montagu House into something other than a home for aristocrats was indicative of the changing nature of Bloomsbury. In this case, it marked the beginning of the appearance of major institutions devoted to learning. During the next two centuries, Bloomsbury would become dominated by the University of London and other learned institutions as well as by hospitals and their schools of medicine. As early as 1866 a resident of the village could describe it as 'a very unfashionable area, though very respectable.'[7]

While middle-class respectability may have been felt by this resident last century, no doubt he or she would have revised that view at least somewhat for the current one, as suggested by my allusion to the 'Bloomsbury Intellectual' in Mikes' book of humor. Perhaps this stereotype of the twentieth century's 'typical' resident developed mainly from the so-called 'Bloomsbury Group,' an association of friends, mostly writers and artists, who lived and/or met in the village. Among the best known of the Group were E. M. Forster, Lytton Strachey, John Maynard Keyes, and Virgina and Leonard Woolf. Apparently the Group started meeting after Virginia and her sister and brothers moved from – to quote Roger Hudson – 'their oppressive family home in Kensington,' following the death of their father, Sir Leslie Stephen, in 1904 to 46 Gordon Square in Bloomsbury. This liberating event and the bringing together there of her brother Thoby's friends of the secretive society known as the Cambridge Apostles laid the foundation for the Group.[8]

The intellectual glue that held the Group together came from the writings of contemporary Cambridge philosopher G. E. Moore. He believed that

> by far the most valuable things ... are ... the pleasures of human
> intercourse and the enjoyment of beautiful objects ... It is they ...
> that form the rational ultimate end of social progress.[9]

Whether the Bloomsbury Group should be held responsible for the 'Bloomsbury Intellectual' stereotype is open to debate, but obviously the Group itself has passed into history, though scholars will no doubt also continue their debates about its significance.

Although the intellectual theme has been mentioned by many writers, at least one has ignored it altogether. In her essay on Bloomsbury in *Village London*, published in 1978, Mary Kenny, a native of Dublin, Ireland, focuses on factors that remind her of home. As a resident of Bloomsbury, she feels that the admirable Georgian houses and squares, which are much like those in Dublin, help to define the essence of the village. In addition, also like Dublin, she finds Bloomsbury 'curiously classless, being neither associated with upward mobility nor with urban decay.' Its true character, she believes, is rooted in tradition but essentially an ethnic one from abroad. According to Kenny,

> there are people whose grandparents were born in the same street. You don't often get that sense of continuity in London. The Italian community, which is the ethnic mark of Bloomsbury, has been living in this part of London since the seventeenth century, when the Italians first came as fencing masters.[10]

Since Kenny's essay seems very impressionistic, it would probably take the efforts of a professional social scientist to verify or refute this argument. Yet, from a cursory count of institutions, there seems no doubt that those of learning and medicine dominate the village today. And one can add that they do so at some cost to tradition – whether aristocratic or Georgian or Italian – because of the addition of new and the modification of old buildings to accommodate these professional endeavors.

Certainly the British Museum and Bedford Square are cases in point. With respect to the former, so many private collections as well as purchases and gifts had been added to the Museum by the early nineteenth century that Montagu House along with temporary structures nearby were filled to overflowing. In 1823, therefore, work began on an extensive building program which led to the demolition of Montagu House and its replacement by the huge building there today with its classical Greek facade and portico.[11]

Fortunately, Bedford Square has had a better fate than Montagu House, but sadly it is the only complete Georgian Square left in Bloomsbury. Yet like Montagu House early on, the Square lost its original purpose as a place of residence by the middle of this century when the interiors of most of the lovely houses were converted to offices for mainly architects and publishers, though apparently the latter have recently moved away.[12]

While changes like these can be lamented, it is fortunate, as Kenny indicates, that they have not produced decay but actually positive results. Generally, I believe this has been the case where institutions of learning and medicine have developed and expanded in the centers of cities this century. I have seen this personally elsewhere in Britain, notably in Dundee, and in the United States as well. So while there have been some unhappy costs, the benefits to the community have clearly outweighed them. Perhaps this is the best we can do in most cities today.

Although most of my many stays in Bloomsbury during the past forty years have been for intellectual and academic reasons, two others should be mentioned as well. My first visit at Christmastime in 1956 can be explained by what Kenny calls the point-of-entry theory about where one resides in London. That is, I stayed in Bloomsbury because it is served by a railroad station – in this case King's Cross – where I first arrived from Scotland. My small hotel on Guilford Street just off Russell Square was not far away. Had I arrived at Victoria Station instead, my first hotel would have probably been in Pimlico. Once in Bloomsbury, I quickly learned a second reason for staying there: 'it's near the *centre* of everything,' as Kenny puts it.[13]

Certainly that last reason also brought me back again and again to Bloomsbury no matter my point-of-entry during subsequent visits. Yet, I eventually came to lament the fact that while Bloomsbury and Central London became very familiar I never felt quite at home even after staying there for over 2½ months with a group of students as described in Chapter II. Why?

The main reason, I believe, is that unlike extended stays in other London villages, I have never resided in a house or flat, only hotels. Although these have ranged from the large, including the Russell, to the very small, I have usually stayed in the latter, the kind with the bathroom on the next floor or landing and the breakfast room in the basement. While the resident landlords, their families and the staff have often been very hospitable, the 'outsider' feeling is always present. There is something very comforting, settling, and even homelike about having two or three rooms of your 'own' in a house or flat and shopping in neighborhood stores for provisions even if little cooking is actually done. While never actually becoming a resident of the village, there is the feeling of moving in that direction, something I never experienced in Bloomsbury.

Since my many Bloomsbury hotels have been located on virtually every side of Russell Square, though only one on the square itself, I have crossed the 'village green' many times, tipping my hat occasionally to the statue of the 5th Duke of Bedford in appreciation for his family's contributions to the village. While much could be said about these walks from the square past various institutions, such as the British Museum, limits of space restrict consideration to two which exemplify best of all the presence of Helper values in Bloomsbury: the University of London and Great Ormond Street Hospital for Sick Children.

Since much has been said in previous chapters about the relationship between the university and Helper values, only a few things unique to the University of London will be mentioned here. Started in 1826, the university actually began as University College, a place founded by a number of advocates of religious toleration including the famous utilitarians James Mill and Jeremy Bentham, the poet Thomas Campbell, and some leaders of London's Jewish community. They wished to provide an institution of higher education for non-Anglicans excluded from Oxford and Cambridge. Supporters of the Church of England referred to it as 'the godless college in Gower Street' and opened King's College in 1828 as a rival.[14]

In 1836 the British Government stepped in to create the University of London and eventually both colleges – as well as a number of others along with various schools and institutes elsewhere in London – came under the university's jurisdiction. Thus, by this century the university became a collection of institutions which, though scattered about London, were held together at its center in Bloomsbury. The construction of the Senate House near Russell Square in 1936 more than symbolized this.[15]

There is an American connection here, though for several obvious reasons little is usually said about it. Some American money, a grant from the Rockefeller Foundation, was secured to help finance the Senate House which was designed by Charles Holden. Unfortunately, according to Roger Hudson, Holden lost his usually excellent touch with this building. Seeing a 'modernist-totalitarian tendency' in its design, Hudson points out that it was not only used by the British Government for its Ministry of Information during World War II, but it was also taken by George Orwell as his model for the Ministry of Truth in his novel *1984*! While Hudson's comments seem rather harsh, I think it is fortunate that the building does not completely dominate the area since the British Museum is nearby, but there is no doubt that the architecture of the village has not been helped by the Senate House.[16]

On a much lighter side, founder Jeremy Bentham willed his body to University College with instructions that his skeleton should be 'put together in such a manner that the whole figure may be seated in a chair usually occupied by me when living.' His wishes were carried out to the extent that his clothed skeleton with a wax face can be seen in a glass-fronted box at the College today.[17] Through the years, many students on Hendrix College's London Program at nearby Birkbeck College have taken a few minutes to 'visit the Great Jeremy,' as they put it.

While Britain's great residential colleges are located in smaller cities elsewhere in the country, the collection of institutions in Bloomsbury and the rest of London serve to unite in their own way the village as an intellectual community and Greater London as well to some extent. With so many forces pulling communities apart in our time, academic institutions serve an important countervailing role, and there seems to be evidence the University of London is doing that. Hail, Alma Mater!

With their schools of medicine, hospitals have a link with the

University, but they – at least one in particular – deserve special mention when considering the sources of Helper values. Great Ormond Street Hospital for Sick Children is only a short walk to the east from Russell Square. One among several hospitals in the area, London Hospital for Sick Children – as it was originally called – was founded in 1851 on the inspiration of Dr Charles West who was appalled at the bleak outlook for sick children in London. There was at the time no children's hospital in London – in fact none at all in England – and out of the 50,000 people who died annually in London, 21,000 were children under ten years of age. A study carried out in 1843 showed that of the 2,363 patients in all the hospitals of London, there were only twenty-six under the age of ten. Hence, Dr West's conclusion was that children were to all intents and purposes excluded from hospital.[18]

To meet the needs of sick children, Dr West and some colleagues began their work at 49 Great Ormond Street, a rented house that had once been the home of a royal physician. Soon they added a second house next door which had, like the first, extensive gardens. By the 1870s a new building was under construction in the gardens, and the old houses were eventually demolished. Twenty years later a new block was opened, bringing the bed numbers to 240 – an extraordinary forty-year development starting from nothing. Greatly impressed by the work of the hospital, Sir James Barrie became one of its famous benefactors when he gave it his copyright of *Peter Pan*.[19] Perhaps it is no coincidence that Dickens House where the great novelist wrote *Oliver Twist* and other works about children is only a short distance away in Doughty Street.

The twentieth century has witnessed much rebuilding and extensions of the hospital's mission and services to children. During the interwar period, for example, the main hospital block was rebuilt with the foundation stone having been laid in 1933 by the Princess Royal who had been a nurse there. After World War II, the Institute of Child Health developed in collaboration with the University of London and the Department of Health.[20] It is difficult to find a better example of Helper values in action in Bloomsbury and perhaps in all of London.

## Kensington

If Bloomsbury is as much a state of mind as a specific place, Kensington is certainly a better example of a geographically identifiable village which eventually became surrounded by a westward-moving London. Yet the key to its identity today in my mind is still writer Leigh Hunt's famous description in the 1850s: the 'old court suburb.' This name stems from the fact that William III, badly plagued by asthma attacks from the fogs along the Thames, moved his court from Whitehall Palace to a healthier Kensington in 1689. He did so after acquiring Lord Notting-ham's huge house and transforming it into Kensington Palace. The Palace is still the most important landmark of the village today despite the fact that major figures of court deserted it after George II's death in 1760. However, lesser royals, such as Princess Diana who resided there at the time of her death, have helped to perpetuate the court identity of the village.[21]

Not unlike Bloomsbury's early years, Kensington's history before the old court's arrival had aristocratic beginnings in the Middle Ages. After the Norman Conquest, the de Vere family from France, who became the Earls of Oxford, added the manor of Kensington to their other lands before the end of the eleventh century. Since the manor's name appears in the *Domesday* survey of 1086 as Chenesit, it is thought that it was known as Cynesige's farm prior to the Conquest. The fact that a priest is also mentioned suggests that a church had been on the manor from Saxon times.[22]

The Earls of Oxford remained lords of the manor until the early sixteenth century by which time the original lands had been subdivided. Apparently some subdivision occurred as early as the 1100s when one of the first de Veres granted a portion of Kensington to Abingdon Abbey near Oxford out of gratitude for medical services performed by the abbot for a family member. The abbey's property became a separate manor, known as Abbots Kensington, and gave its name to the local parish church, St Mary Abbots.[23]

Even after the end of the Middle Ages, Kensington remained largely rural in character and became noted for its market gardens and nurseries in its southern area. Hay for the London market was produced in the north. However, much of the prosperity enjoyed by the village – which grew up at the junction of today's High and Church Streets – came from its location on the Great West Road. The traffic between London to the east and important counties to the west made the village a key stop along the way.[24]

The departure of the de Veres and the destruction of Abingdon Abbey in the sixteenth century led to most of Kensington becoming the possession of Sir Walter Cope around 1600. Hence the aristocratic influence continued – and even more so. Starting a trend for the use of the higher ground between the present High Street and Notting Hill Gate, Cope built himself a large mansion, a fine country house with a view across the fields to the Thames and within a short distance of London. Completed in 1606, this later became known as Holland House, and Campden House, among others, soon followed. Of course the best known today was the mansion built by Sir George Coppin, subsequently acquired by the Earls of Nottingham, and even later still transformed into Kensington Palace.[25]

Apparently the arrival of William's court in the late seventeenth century not only brought the gentry and 'persons of note' to Kensington, as one observer of the time says, but it also stimulated local trade and employment. Yet the period of court residence did not cause a tremendous growth in the size of the village, believed to have been around 1,000 inhabitants in the 1690s but only about 8,500 a century later. Perhaps some might argue that the court brought quality rather than quantity because the village became known for its private schools. Kensington also attracted some short-term visitors to its healthy climate and well-known gardens.[26]

Actually the transformation of Kensington from a rural village to a city 'village' occurred during the nineteenth century. It grew from less than 10,000 in 1801 to 176,000 in 1901. As the farms and market gardens of the early 1800s disappeared, they were replaced by street after street of new houses in mainly estate developments. By and large the new well-off Victorian middle classes filled these houses, and the smart shops and emerging department stores, such as Barkers, soon followed. Modern transportation, most importantly the underground railway which arrived in 1866, made both living and shopping in Kensington desirable and easy.[27]

Although the court's role in all of this nineteenth-century development was at best minimal, the figures of Prince Albert and Queen Victoria should not be overlooked. Their impact on what today is called South Kensington is difficult to exaggerate. Seemingly it all started with an idea, apparently conceived by one Henry Cole of the Public Record Office but often attributed to Albert, to inform the world of Britain's great scientific, technological, and commercial achievements of the century. The idea was implemented through the Great Exhibition of 1851 which was housed in the famous Crystal Palace erected in Hyde Park just for the occasion. Albert, a driving force for the project, presided over the Royal Commission appointed to raise money. The Exhibition was a great success with attendance by over six million people who paid £356,000 for admission. These funds were used to establish the South Kensington Arts Centre in particular and estate development there in general.[28] The long-term outcome of this undertaking, though Albert saw little of it because of his untimely death in 1861, was the great complex of schools, museums and learned institutions there today, including the Science Museum, the Natural History Museum and of course the Victoria and Albert Museum — among others. Perhaps because of his early death and the tributes to him by a grieving Victoria and others, Albert, now in statue form in his memorial across the street in Kensington Gardens, seems to symbolize it all. As David Piper observes:

Under his canopy, Albert sits facing south, like a father-figure, brooding over the whole complex ... packed into the slope below him – there can hardly be a greater cultural density anywhere in the world. The whole complex is a magnificent expression of Victorian confidence in the education of mind and soul, in the propagation of knowledge, and Albert himself is not unjustly sited as its figure-head.[29]

Although Victoria's eighteenth-century predecessors were largely responsible for most of the other royal developments in Kensington Gardens, which will be discussed later in this chapter, she had strong attachments to the village, especially its palace where she was born and spent her youth. Hence, Kensington, after it attained metropolitan borough status in 1900, was accorded the title of 'Royal' the following year.

In addition to the presence of some royals in Kensington Palace this century, perhaps another noteworthy sign today of the 'old court' is seen along Palace Green and Kensington Palace Gardens, a north-south street just to the west of the Palace. The rows of vast mansions on both sides of this private street house many diplomats accredited to the 'Court of St James.' In other words, these huge nineteenth-century houses, which were once the homes of aristocrats and wealthy businessmen who liked the 'royal neighborhood,' are now the embassies of a number of countries. A walker along this secluded street encounters few people, but the plaques on the walls and iron gates indicate that behind them in the mansions are numerous officials from such places as Russia, Israel, Egypt and the Czech Republic.

If elements of the 'old court' identity are still present in Kensington today, a couple of other factors have helped to preserve it geographically as a village. One of these is in fact Kensington Gardens which by covering the entire area from Bayswater Road on the north to Kensington Road on the south provides a solid wall of open space to the village's east. A similar wall exists to its west in the form of Holland Park which extends from near Holland Park Avenue on the north to a short distance from Kensington High Street on the south. Therefore, the village has two 'buffer zones' preventing encroachments from those directions. While it lacks such natural barriers to its north and south, Kensington has perhaps benefitted somewhat from its immediate neighbors in those directions.

As mentioned above, South Kensington has added the great cultural complex of schools, museums and learned institutions between Kensington Gardens and Cromwell Road. Recalling the Helper values of Bloomsbury with its British Museum and other institutions, one sees a very worthy counterpart in this complex. As a result, Kensington's attraction as a village is enhanced by its southern neighbor – thanks to a great extent to royal influence last century.

Perhaps it is much harder to determine how Kensington has benefitted from its northern neighbor Notting Hill. As recently as the early 1960s, E. R. Wethersett, in his revised edition of Harold P. Clunn's well-known and authoritative *The Face of London*, has this to say about the area:

> Situated on both sides of Notting Hill Gate and centered around Kensington Church Street on the south and Portobello Road on the north is Kensington's ... squalid hamlet, comprising a rookery of mean streets and small houses.

He goes on to say, however, that fortunately 'action is now being taken and much of the slum property is being pulled down.'[30] In the years since, the area has been greatly improved, as I can testify personally from several stays in flats near the upper end of Kensington Church Street.

Yet the contrast between that area and what one sees further south along Kensington Church Street is still quite great. There are numerous ways of getting at this contrast, but perhaps two examples will be sufficient. Walking south along Kensington Church Street, a busy traffic thoroughfare but with few pedestrians, the visitor encounters one upscale shop after another, especially those featuring expensive antiques, something for which the area is noted. On the other hand, should the walker proceed north instead – across Notting Hill Gate, along Pembridge Road for a short distance, and into Portobello Road – he finds himself in a vastly different world. Emma Tennant provides one of the best brief descriptions of this other well-known place I have seen. On Saturday, the main market day, Portobello Road, she says,

> becomes the most entertaining street in London. Innumerable stalls selling antiques, fruit, fakes, clothes and all sorts of incredible junk, plus a wild mixture of people wandering along in search of bargains – sixties-style hippies, visiting film stars, Rasta men with dreadlocks and woolly hats, old ladies poking among the discarded vegetables. Lots of buskers, too – shaven-headed sitar players, steel bands, a blind organ grinder with a parrot on his head. Whole drab street transformed into something ... outrageously picturesque ...[31]

It is significant, I believe, that there is a connecting link between these two descriptions of opposite worlds. Though the prices are far apart, the sale of antiques in both places is symbolic of how counterpoint can exist if not in complete harmony at least not in complete discordance either. There seems to be a live-and-let-live attitude here, a mutual toleration of contrasting outlooks and styles, that benefit both villages. Perhaps one begins to understand some of the reasons for the great outpouring of grief among all classes at the death of the 'People's Princess.' Diana was the most famous resident of Kensington, but one could imagine her visiting the market regularly as well. Obviously, the Princess of Wales was a person who moved easily between these two worlds and in the minds of many, was trying to show the way for others to do the same.

The second example of contrast is the Notting Hill Carnival, something hard to imagine in Kensington. Founded in 1966 as a local pageant and fair, it has become a huge Caribbean carnival held annually on the August Bank Holiday. To the unfamiliar the word 'Caribbean' gives a hint as to what has been seen as problematic about this event. To those who know the area and its history, racial problems, though not as great as those in Brixton, in times past have been part of the context for the event as well. Describing how things had evolved in Notting Hill with respect to the carnival by the late 1970s, Emma Tennant has written that

> every year the carnival hangs like a frown over the brows of the police and the organizers. It's difficult to enjoy a party atmosphere when scrutinized by what seems to be the entire police force, but if they do insist in turning out in such numbers at the occasion of a party, then they should be less discriminating ...[32]

Happily, the tensions of the late 1970s have eased over the years, and even the police are much more relaxed now than before. So here, too, an attitude of toleration has developed between the villages, and they have learned to live side-by-side even at Carnival time.

Although the intersection of Church and High Streets is the center of Kensington, the 'village green,' is elsewhere. The obvious choice is Kensington Gardens but as described later in the chapter, the Gardens seem to stand apart from the village. Hence, Holland Park is a better selection, though it, too, has some sense of self-importance. Given its 54-acre size and configuration, the park provides the opportunity for the most enjoyable of all walks the village has to offer. Staying near the northern end of the village, I have usually entered the park just off Holland Park Avenue near the Greek Embassy and here, unlike the southern approach from High Street, the feeling is obvious that this is almost a world of its own rather than part of a village. Perhaps the main reason for this is the variety of things which surround and seem a part of what remains of Holland House, a once splendid Jacobean mansion built on one of the natural terraces above the Thames Valley. During World War II, the house was nearly destroyed but for its east wing which has been restored and forms part of a youth hostel.

Though not much of the great house is left, its surroundings have been preserved and enhanced, evolving from the original formal gardens alongside a wilder area of woodlands to the north where I enter the grounds. With some ten woodland enclosures altogether in the park, the Beech Enclosure, which the walker encounters first along excellent paths, is planted with beech trees and holly plants that have reached huge proportions. Perhaps most visitors spend little time in the woodlands and head for the several beautiful individual gardens – including the Dutch, Kyoto, Dahlia and Iris – in the vicinity of the old house. The white peacocks in the Japanese garden help most decide where to go first. But all of these gardens are only part of a much larger complex which forms a very attractive whole that pulls in people from the village and elsewhere. For example, an open-air theater stages operas and concerts during the summer and the Orangery and Ice House feature art exhibitions and other events. The Ecology Centre also has displays and exhibitions, and a nearby sports field attracts the very energetic. In short, Holland Park is more than a park – it is a community center.

For those familiar with Holland House's history, there is something of the 'old court' feel about the Park as well – though with an ironic twist. That is, because of a scandal, Lady Holland, the wife of the 3rd Lord Holland (Henry Fox, 1773–1840), was ostracized from the Royal Court but undaunted she decided to establish something of a rival court of her own. She was so successful that Holland House became the center of London's literary and political society early last century. Such literary giants as Byron, Macaulay, Scott, Wordsworth and Dickens came as well as political leaders like Melbourne, Palmerston and a host of other Whig politicians who eventually formed the Liberal Party.[33]

The Hollands were indeed an influential and a very colorful couple, and thus there are many fascinating stories about them. My favorite concerns Napolean whom they met in 1802. So impressed by the great man, they gave him their unfailing support thereafter, even to the extent of sending him jars of plum jam, more than 400 books, and a refrigerator when he was exiled on Elba.[34]

An institution near Holland Park complements its cultural activities. This is the Commonwealth Institute, founded in 1887 as the Imperial Institute to commemorate Queen Victoria's Golden Jubilee and moved to its present location in 1962. It is housed in a building of striking design which incorporates materials from the Commonwealth countries. The building's spacious galleries display exhibitions on every Commonwealth country and examples of fine art, sculpture, craftwork and tribal art from them. The Institute conducts a broad range of educational programs including poetry recitals, music and drama.[35]

Given the royal identity of Kensington, it is very fitting indeed that the Institute is located in the village, but it is also appropriate for another reason. As mentioned above, Kensington became noted for the proliferation of schools in its past, especially private schools that occupied many of the large houses that were built over the years. This activity has continued down to the present and institutions like the Institute have added to this educational tradition of the village.

Perhaps anti-royalist readers have cringed at my attempt to identify Kensington as 'old court.' Perhaps some others have accepted my designation but find the village undesirable because of its characteristics. While never a royalist myself, I nevertheless find the sense of noblesse oblige and the willingness to reach accommodation with others very attractive in the royals' contributions to the development of Kensington and its surroundings. As discussed at some length in Chapter IV about Alistair Cooke, these characteristics are highly desirable no matter who is involved. Whenever the advantaged members of society understand and act upon their obligations to the disadvantaged, good things happen in the long run. Kensington is an example of this, and as we shall see next, Kensington Gardens and several other Royal Parks illustrate this as well.

## London Parks

Many of London's parks are another part of the great legacy handed down to Londoners by royalty – as well as by aristocracy like the Dukes of Bedford – because of the attitude of noblesse oblige. These parks should also be credited with making the huge metropolis more liveable and workable, especially more attractive. However, here too, the numerous parks of all kinds, both Royal and non-Royal, present a formidable problem. A few numbers will provide some perspective on the scope of it. In his book on London's parks, Hunter Davies estimates that Greater London encloses an area of over 600 square miles within which are found 45,000 acres of parks and open spaces. These range from the mammoth 2,500-acre Richmond Park to many tiny one-acre open spaces that are little more than large gardens or playgrounds. Stating things a different way, Davies calculates that there are about 1,000 plots of grass throughout London which are known as parks. Yet, what may be somewhat surprising is that within the City itself, the famous one-square mile, he found only 35 acres of open space, mainly small gardens, squares, walks and churchyards. With but 8 acres total, the Barbican is by far the largest single area there.[36]

Obviously, it would take a book to describe all the parks in Greater London. I consider less than half a dozen here, and these are selected mainly from the list of Royal Parks located in Central London which I have come to know well during the past forty years. Unlike Richmond Park as well as Hampton Court Home Park and Bushy Park which cover 1,000 or more acres each, my Royal Park selections, along with one from the City of Westminster, are relatively small in size individually but are virtually connected with one another to form a continuous park area with pathways from Kensington to the City. Hence, it is possible to walk, as I have done, from Kensington Gardens to Blackfriars Bridge while crossing only four roads and going under two others along the way. This is extraordinary in the heart of a huge city. My discussion, therefore, is about Kensington Gardens, Hyde Park, Green Park, and

St James's Park among the Royal Parks and Victoria Embankment Gardens of Westminster.

## *Kensington Gardens*

Having rented flats near the upper end of Kensington Church Street for many stays, I usually start my walks of Kensington Gardens at convenient Black Lion Gate near the north-west corner along Bayswater Road. But perhaps the best place, at least the most dramatic place to begin is at King's Arms Gate near the south-west corner along Kensington Road. Why? Because the impressive tulip tree-lined Dial Walk beginning there takes one to Crowther Gates of Kensington Palace, the place where hundreds – perhaps thousands – of mourners left their flowers following Princess Diana's death. This sea of flowers was seen on television throughout the world. When last I was there, more than a year after the Princess' death, small groups of people still gathered silently at that site for a few moments to remember and to take pictures even though the faded flowers were long gone.

The fact that Kensington Palace is here suggests much about the history of the park, perhaps the most royal of all. Through the years various royals have certainly done much to shape its contemporary character. Starting with what was part of Hyde Park in 1689, William III was the first to develop it as something unique when he commissioned Sir Christopher Wren and Nicholas Hawksmoor to convert Nottingham House to his country palace and to create beautiful gardens for himself and his household alongside. Twenty-six acres of Dutch gardens, including parterres, were laid out around the Palace. Apparently William's wife, Queen Mary, a garden enthusiast, was largely responsible for the adoption of the Dutch style. Her sister Anne, the next Queen, extended the garden even further, creating two features still in evidence today: the Orangery and the Sunken Garden, though the current form of the latter dates from this century.[37]

It was, however, Queen Caroline, wife of George II, who put the most significant royal stamp on the gardens as seen today. She had the Serpentine dug out which was later extended as The Long Water. Not satisfied with only one body of water, she also had a somewhat circular basin created – known today as the Round Pond – whose waters could be viewed from the windows of the Palace. Caroline also had her gardeners plant some magnificent avenues of trees that extended into Hyde Park which probably help to define more than anything else the larger character of the Gardens today. It has been said that the Queen's spending reached £20,000 in 1730's currency, a huge sum by the standards of the day.[38]

Initially public access to these splendid gardens was limited to weekends, when the King and Queen were away, but even then formal dress had to be worn by visitors and certain lower-class types, including soldiers, sailors and liveried servants, were excluded altogether. Since adjoining Hyde Park was much more democratically run, resentment grew among some of the 'rabble' and eventually after subsequent monarchs no longer made the Palace their main residence, the Gardens were opened to all 'respectably dressed persons' the year round.[39]

Several things apart from the Palace itself still give a royal 'feel' to the Gardens. The statue of the young Victoria carved by her daughter Princess Louise is one, but certainly the Albert Memorial stands above everything else in more ways than one. Over 170 feet high, this memorial recently restored to all its glory and now featuring a goldleafed Albert like the original, has been an object of controversy since its unveiling last century to the pleasure of Queen Victoria. I shall not enter that debate in these pages, but perhaps Mark Twain's comment about the memorial suggests where I stand: 'In all this grave and beautiful land, I have encountered only one genuinely humorous idea: the Albert Memorial.'[40]

Two other rather curious monuments suggest not only the royal but also Britain's imperial past. The first is 'The Statue of Physical Energy,' a huge statue standing at the focal point of six tree-lined paths in the middle of the Gardens. The work of G. F. Watts, this equestrian statue with its naked male rider is a duplicate of the original which stands in Cape Town as a memorial to Cecil Rhodes. Like the Albert Memorial, this one has also prompted critical remarks about various aspects, including the positioning of the rider's thumb on his forehead. Hunter Davies speculates that the rider could be making 'some sort of rude sign,' or engaging in 'a bit of ham acting' or 'simply someone who has lost his way.'[41] Again, like the Albert Memorial, this one seems more a monument to the Age of Victoria than anything else.

The other curious monument seems to fall into the same category. This is the 'unspeakable,' as Davies calls it, Speke Monument, the 'most boring statue' in London.[42] This pointed, blank column of polished granite is a memorial to the Victorian explorer of Africa, John Hanning Speke. Perhaps the monument's plainness as well as the few terse words about Speke at its base is designed to express neutrality in the controversies surrounding Speke's disputed claim to have discovered the source of the Nile and his death: accident or suicide. At any rate, much better sense was used here than with Energy in finding an unobtrusive place for it.

Certainly much happier thoughts are associated with the Gardens' most famous statue, Peter Pan, though it has had its share of criticism as well. But perhaps negative comments have been outweighed by positive ones because of the child-like innocence involved. Hence, while someone like Geoffrey Young may complain that the statue's 'tortuous design oozes rabbits, mice, squirrels, and bronze fairies,' he mercifully concedes that the 'ensemble is intended for children' and acknowledges that even the rabbits' ears are as likely 'to be tweaked' by adults. Such comments are evidence that most critics realize by now that both the statue, which also depicts Peter with his pipes, and Sir James Barrie's play about a boy who never grew up, are nearly sacred in the public mind in Britain and elsewhere. It is interesting to note that when the statue was unveiled unofficially in 1912 in what was to be a temporary place, popular opinion would not allow it to be moved elsewhere.[43] Peter Pan belongs in Kensington Gardens, that is for sure.

Even though the monuments to the rich and powerful of the past are there, too, one has the sense that the Gardens are really much more child oriented. For in addition to Peter Pan's statue, there is a playground with another widely known child's delight near its center. This is the Elfin Oak, the huge stump of a dead oak tree carved with fairies and goblins. It is thought that the Oak originates from a poem written by Thomas Tickell in 1772 about an Elfin King who had his home nearby. This fairy mythology associated with the Gardens was perpetuated by Matthew Arnold in 1852 with his poem 'Lines Written in Kensington Gardens.' One line from this poem reads as follows: 'In my helpless cradle I was breathed on by rural Pan.' Davies speculates that this line may have, as he puts it, 'sparked off' Sir James Barrie who loved the Gardens and children.[44]

To the walker of the Gardens the most ubiquitous signs of child orientation are, of course, the children themselves. While they are of all ages, perhaps one tends to notice the very young, the toddlers or babies still in their prams, being cared for by their mothers or nannies. They can be seen in all areas of the Gardens. Yet Davies believes that a favorite gathering place of many nannies, though they are harder to identify today because few wear uniforms, is along the Flower Walk, the 500-yard path which leads from the Albert Memorial towards the Palace. Here in this carefully planned setting of beautiful plants, perhaps the best in London, the nannies both young and old, gather on the benches to chat while caring for their charges.[45] Although the presence of many nannies reflects the upscale nature of Kensington and other nearby areas, one has the feeling that these lovely Gardens attract all classes.

There seems no doubt that the Gardens have a certain magical power to pull in visitors of all classes, both young and old, from nearby as well as from around the world. Whether this power comes from the fairies, the flowers, the trees, or any number of other things, one can only speculate, but the feeling is there that this is no ordinary park; it is a very special place for all people. The feeling is so good that I can spend hours just strolling its length and breadth.

# *Hyde Park*

Most people probably cannot tell for sure where Kensington Gardens ends and Hyde Park begins, although crossing the Serpentine Bridge or the West Carriage Drive gives one a feeling that a change of significance has occurred. That feeling is encouraged by different sights and sounds such as galloping horses, football games, and tennis matches usually in action along the southern border of the Park. While many trees are still present, the great avenues of Kensington Gardens have largely given way to large open areas and the thirty-two watery acres of The Serpentine. Perhaps the words 'Gardens' and 'Park' have captured well the essence of the differences between the two.

While the Gardens may be the more beautiful, Hyde Park wins easily in terms of total acreage: 360 to 275. In a historical sense, it also takes top honors because, as suggested above, Hyde Park was there first. The site became royal property in 1536 when Henry VIII, during the dissolution of the monasteries, seized the land around the manor of Hyde, which belonged to the Abbots of Westminster, and fenced it to make a private park for the royal hunt. Henry's idea was to give himself a continuous stretch of hunting territory from his Palace at Westminster near the Thames to the slopes of Hampstead in the north. For the next century Hyde Park remained a Royal Park for hunting until the Stuarts, James I and his son Charles I, opened it to the public.[46] Bless them.

During Cromwell's brief rule, Hyde Park was sold in three lots but returned to royal ownership with the Restoration and reopened to the public as before. Immediately, it became a popular meeting place, but its present physical character was probably shaped more by royal action in the eighteenth century than by public usage. Again, Queen Caroline did more than anyone when she had the Serpentine dug. The lake was created from the old River Westbourne and a chain of small ponds, and hence its depth is variable, falling off to as much as 20 feet in places. Boating on the Serpentine's water by all – ranging from the royals to the commoners – has characterized its history since George II and Caroline sailed yachts there on May Day 1731, the grand opening. Another great gala occurred in 1814 with the re-enactment of the 1805 Battle of Trafalgar. Yet these two high profile events are the exceptions rather than the rule, for ordinary people have been the main users of the lake, like the rest of the park, over the years.[47] Hyde Park is indeed the people's park.

In addition to the areas set aside for the public's sports, other places in the park show its democratic character. The well-known Speakers' Corner near Marble Arch is certainly one of them. This is the traditional spot for anyone to speak on almost any subject to anyone at any time – though activities occur mainly on Sundays. While free speech is defined rather broadly here, the ground rules forbid sedition, treason, blasphemy, obscenities, and incitement of racial hatred. How this place became such a platform is not known, though some maintain that the tradition has its origins in certain other infamous practices nearby. These are the public hangings of Tyburn Tree, the gallows for two centuries until they were moved to Newgate in 1783. This haunted place, as Young calls it, saw the death of many, few of whom were really hardened criminals but only the poor down on their luck. But being condemned, they did have the right to speak before their execution, and perhaps free speech became institutionalized there as a result.[48] While many disagree with this interpretation, those who like to see some good coming out of so much evil may accept it.

Perhaps most visitors to Speakers' Corner today understand something about the place although at least one famous American did not until after she mounted her own soap box there. The speaker was feminist and anarchist Emma Goldman who obviously took both her ideas and her hecklers there too seriously, clearly things to be avoided at Speakers' Corner. According to her autobiography, when Goldman attempted to answer the latter, her replies only 'kept the crowd in spasms' and so she gave up on this rather sour note: 'My work meant too much for me to turn it into a circus for the amusement of the British public.'[49]

Related to the notion of Hyde Park as a place of free speech for all is that of free assembly. Challenging Trafalgar Square as the spot for huge mass demonstrations and marches in London, the Park has accommodated crowds of hundreds of thousands on many occasions of public protest as it did for the anti-nuclear marches in the 1960s.

While Trafalgar Square or even Piccadilly Circus may seem like the center of London, Hyde Park not only has the size for mass gatherings but also the better location. It is near London's major shopping center, Oxford Street, and the smart shops and museums of Knightsbridge and South Kensington. It also serves as a short cut for many Londoners going to and from work and for many visitors housed in the numerous hotels nearby. Hyde Park is the crossroads of London, the 'village green,' if you will.

Seeing it as such, Davies spent a day recording the foot traffic through the Park. The first to arrive in the morning are the swimmers at about 5:30 for the Lido on the Serpentine. At about 6 a.m. 'scores' of runners arrive for their morning jogs. An hour later come the dog-walkers, soon followed by a steady stream of commuting workers for the next two hours. From 10:30 to about 2:00, visitors as well as London's own very old and very young occupy the Park. Then at 4 the first of the commuters reappear, on their way home, followed at about 6 by the joggers again. At one time 'scores of prostitutes' as well as their clients, used to be the most numerous evening visitors but since 1956 laws have forced them elsewhere. In this age of the homeless, many people attempt to sleep overnight in the park, though the police often keep them moving.[50]

With sizable open green areas, lake, playing grounds, freedoms, location, and the like, it would seem that Hyde Park needs nothing more to sustain it as the people's park. Yet something should be said about two other factors: its gardens and its icons to patriotism, if that is the right word in this day and age.

Young describes the south-east corner of Hyde Park as a 'hotbed of horticulture for a century and a half.' Apparently it all started with the Victorians who were delighted with the botanical discoveries being made throughout the British Empire and who therefore enthusiastically attempted to grow the newly introduced plants, many of which were native to hotter climates, in greenhouses for bedding out in the warmer months. They held display competitions at this corner for the best bedding schemes. Today the consequences of these efforts can be seen in the magnificent carpet bedding and flower gardens near Hyde Park Corner.[51] My favorite is the necklace of small rose gardens where the species and varieties of the numerous roses are all named.

The preliminary work for these wonderful displays is carried out in Hyde Park's own nursery composed of twelve immense greenhouses which together cover three acres not far from the West Carriage Drive. Some 500,000 plants are produced each year for bedding out in this and other Royal Parks, government gardens, and indoor displays. There are 2,000 varieties of 200 different species grown, including, for example, ten different shades of begonia alone.[52]

From the historical record, the feeling of British patriotism that one senses in Hyde Park probably stems from the place called the Parade Ground near Speakers' Corner where Queen Elizabeth I reviewed her troops and Cromwell had the front line of his chain of defenses during the Civil War. Since the casual visitor is not usually aware of this, how are such feelings explained when they appear? No doubt other Hyde Park Corner sights are largely responsible. The most conspicuous is, of course, Apsley House, now the Wellington Museum, the huge neoclassical home of the Duke of Wellington, one of Britain's greatest military heroes and statesmen. Near the house is another classical heroic sight, Apsley Gate, with its horsemen motif based on a frieze from the Acropolis. If these are not enough to get the patriotic juices flowing, a bronze statue a short distance away of a naked Achilles, some 18 feet high, whose head is said to resemble that of the Duke, should help.

Actually, there is an interesting story about the statue and its origins that concerns serious patriotism but contains some humor which shows, like activities at the Speakers' Corner, that the Hyde Park British can keep things in perspective. Apparently it all began in 1814 when during the course of an official celebration in the Park to honor Wellington, along with Nelson, a lady decided 'to strip off' and have a swim but was restrained and hurried away by some older ladies. So upset by this 'disgusting incident,' a group of women, later called the Committee of Ladies, decided to open a public appeal for money to erect a suitable monument to the greatness of the Duke. Soon enough funds poured in to have the noted Sir Richard Westmacott produce the statue cast from 22 French cannons captured during battles with Napoleon. However, it was immediately apparent when the statue was erected in 1822 that the Wellington head, with its 'colossal male body striking an heroic pose' had a problem lower down on its anatomy where it was 'decidedly under endowed.' Cruikshank and other cartoonists of the time had a field day with the statue's modest fig leaf. Since that time the leaf has been twice chipped off with the current one dating from 1963.[53]

If the long-dead Duke, so honored with these monuments, is the personification of nineteenth-century British patriotism in Hyde Park, perhaps another icon connects this past with the present. This is the Household Cavalry housed in the nearby Hyde Park Barracks. One can frequently see a troop of them in their splendid attire of the past riding along Rotten Row on their way to perform duties, mainly ceremonial, often to the great delight of camera-toting tourists from the world over. This, too, is a curious blend of the serious and the humorous, perhaps the best way to view twentieth-century patriotism as well.

## *Green Park*

I usually enter Green Park via the subway from Hyde Park Corner after my jaunts through Kensington Gardens and Hyde Park itself. By using the subway I have had to cross only one road so far, West Carriage Drive, the dividing line between the Gardens and Hyde Park, and will not have to cross another until I leave Green Park. Since the Drive is not a major road, I have the feeling all the way through these three parks that they are really one, though their underlying characters are certainly significantly different.

If Kensington Gardens is a beautiful, magical, and royal-like place for children of all ages, and Hyde Park is a crossroads 'village green' for and of the people, Green Park is a quiet, understated, and even overlooked park that is perhaps seen too often as little more than a corridor and rest stop between Hyde Park and St James's Park. It deserves better, but there is no doubt that it suffers by comparison with its splendid neighbors.

While Green Park is a quiet and tranquil place today, despite its location like a slice of pie between two very busy streets, Piccadilly and Constitution Hill, its history after Henry VIII's death is quite different. Up to that time the park was a somewhat swampy meadowland that Henry had acquired for grazing and hunting, but his daughter,

Mary I, had it fortified to deal with the opponents of her marriage to Philip II of Spain. It was fortified again during the Civil War of the next century. After the war Charles II turned 36 acres of the land into a formal park complete with a network of pathways, a deer enclosure and many young trees. Unfortunately, the park, known then as Upper St James's Park, attracted mostly highwaymen and many duellers taking shots at one another.[54]

By the eighteenth century the park was still a very noisy place when it was used for military parades and fireworks displays, the latter – especially one – becoming its chief claim to fame. For it was here that King George II staged his famous Royal Fireworks Celebration of 1749, the occasion for which Handel composed his even more famous music of a similar name. In keeping with the triumphal nature of the celebration – the signing of the peace treaty ending the War of the Austrian Succession – Handel employed 100 musicians, including 40 trumpeters and 20 French horn players, to match the 100 cannons assembled by the King. For the performance in the park, the musicians were congregated on a stage in the beautifully decorated Temple of Peace, an immitation Doric temple constructed of wood over 400 feet long and 100 feet high. However, when the first rockets were set off amid the firing of cannon, the building caught fire, causing two arches to collapse. But in the tradition of good theater, the show went on and the King stayed until midnight.[55]

Yet triumphalism in the park seemed to be an invitation for disaster to strike. When another huge temple, the Temple of Concord, was built in 1814 to celebrate a century of Hanovarian rule and victory over Napoleon, a mysterious fire one night burned it down. Next day a crowd, feeling cheated out of its entertainment, severely vandalized the park.[56]

Smaller disasters seemed to plague the park from time to time during the rest of the nineteenth century when ballooning enthusiasts who used it as a launching area had their inevitable accidents. Even Queen Victoria, whose coronation fireworks display there somehow came off well, had frightening experiences when being shot at on three separate occasions by people judged to be insane.[57] The duelling tradition living on?

Despite its past – which does not seem to be prologue here – Green Park is today a popular place for quiet short walks and peaceful outdoor lunches. The charm of this small park – only 53 acres in size – lies in its trees and its rural atmosphere, though others see little or no charm at all. For example, Davies reports that even some of the park employees dismiss it as being of little importance with at least one gardener referring to it as 'dog shit island!'[58] While dogs certainly do their thing in the park, perhaps such comments really stem from the fact that Green Park has no flower beds, lakes or other fancy ornamentations like the other parks which gardeners love to show off. In addition the casual observer is much more likely to see larger numbers of barren patches and mounds of left-over soil here than elsewhere – signs of a park considered less than a showplace.

But for me there is something quite charming about a park in the heart of a great city that has the feel of the countryside, a natural feel if you will. Such a place provides urban weary visitors with some welcome and needed relief. Yes, the formal gardens are beautiful to experience, but there is a certain artificiality about them, like so much of the city, that becomes tiresome after a time. Green Park provides an escape to the rural and the natural, a refreshing change along the path through the city.

## *St James's Park*

More often than not writers consider Green Park and St James's Park together for various reasons, not the least of which is that the former has been seen as part of the latter as suggested above. Certainly many historical events have been shared as well. There is no doubt today, however, that they are separate entities if for no other reason than that they are cut off from one another by The Mall, London's most important royal street. This is only the second road I have had to cross since entering Kensington Gardens, which will be three miles back after completing my walk through St James's. To a city person this distance might seem long, but to a country walker it is merely a short stroll. Actually this walk through the parks makes London feel quite small, uncrowded, and integrated, a feeling contrary to that one gets along the congested sidewalks and streets. Hence, just a walk through the parks rather than along the sidewalks brings welcome relief to urban weary visitors and Londoners alike.

My stroll in St James's Park, the oldest of the eight Royal Parks, leaves no doubt that this place, like the others, has an identity of its own. Certainly the lake, which covers a sizeable part of the park's 93 acres, is responsible for much of its character. Although Henry VIII started this Royal Park like so many others, it was Charles II who had the lake dug, though in his day it was considered a canal with its 100-foot width and 2,800-foot length. Charles wanted this body of water, along with formal flower beds and straight walks, to resemble a miniature Versailles which he greatly admired during his exile in France before the Restoration. Being extremely fond of all exotic animals, but especially birds, he also wanted a place to build a series of aviaries, which he did on the south side of the park near what is known as Birdcage Walk today. Perhaps the park's various birds, most importantly its famous pelicans, do more today than even the lake itself to define the character of the park.[59]

Historically, the first pelicans were given to Charles in 1684 by the Russian ambassador, and other birds, including storks, swans, geese and cranes were soon added. Today there are so many varieties of waterfowl in the park that identification boards have been erected to help visitors sort things out. Altogether some 1,000 birds are forcibly resident in the park because they have had their flight wings clipped, but they are joined by numerous wild birds, making the totals much higher. Perhaps the importance of the waterfowl to the park's identity is also seen in the part known as Duck Island, which is not quite an island but a peninsula that extends out into the water of the lake. It is a bird sanctuary with only limited public access.[60]

When John Nash redesigned the park early last century, he converted the rather narrow canal into the present lake, surrounding it with the winding paths and lawns broken by clumps of trees seen today. He also built a bridge across the lake which divides it almost in half. Although the present bridge dates only from the 1950s, Davies believes that it is the 'nicest part of the whole Park.' What he means is not the bridge, per se, but the views from it.[61] I find it hard to disagree with him but for additional reasons.

The views are not only spectacular but also help to define the character of the park in human terms. Consider the view to the east in the direction of Horse Guards Parade. It is a total surprise because the British Government buildings that stand out have their skylines dominated by strange-looking turrets and minarets causing the observer to believe that he has been momentarily transported into the heart of Moscow or Istanbul. As the mind comes back to London, the fact that those buildings are filled with government workers is verified by morning and evening foot traffic through the park and by midday lunchers scattered about the lawns. Like Hyde Park, the location of St James's helps to define what it is in human terms.

The view from the bridge in the other direction is just as instructive. It is Buckingham Palace with the massive Queen Victoria Memorial in front. If one times things correctly, the Changing of the Guard may also be seen. So, like Kensington Gardens, not only the history of St James's Park but also its nearby palace and memorial give it a royal feeling.

Thus, these sights and feelings suggest the coming together there of elements which symbolize what the British Government is: a parliamentary constitutional monarchy. While this is national rather than local government, certainly the sense of face-to-face contact that Londoners have here with what are usually called faceless officials in a modern democracy must have a positive effect on public morale. In facilitating such contact, St James's Park ideally serves the same function as the agora, the public square in ancient Greek cities, where the people and their governors could assemble and interact – a critical element in Aristotle's notion of people as political beings. On a lighter note, perhaps the park's fame this century as the setting for spy stories is even more indicative of its importance in the political process of today's world!

## *Victoria Embankment Gardens*

Crossing only the third street since entering Kensington Gardens, I departed St James's Park at the corner where Birdcage Walk and Horse Guards Road merge into Great George Street. With Parliament Square just ahead, the sense of park is not completely lost during this short walk to Victoria Embankment Gardens. I do have to cross over one more major road, Parliament Street, but can go under another, Victoria Embankment, through a subway to reach the River Thames. Were I to choose, as I have done often in the past, to follow along the entire length of the Embankment river walkway, I could stroll into the City of London – past the Temple and Blackfriars Bridge, among other landmarks – without having to cross over another road. This is an incredible experience for a walker in such a huge, sprawling city.

As they walk along the Embankment, probably most users are not aware that a magnificent feat of engineering skill lies beneath their feet. This is a sewer network along the Thames, one of the major reasons for the Embankment's construction. Started in 1864, the project involved the draining of tidal mudflats and the construction of a wall to prevent flooding. Like the building of a newer London Bridge many years before, the completed Embankment speeded the flow of river water, which helps to explain why the Thames no longer freezes in winter as it once did. In terms of the past – at least after the Great Fire of London in 1666 – Sir Christopher Wren first proposed narrowing the Thames in this way to gain additional space for the rebuilt city, but his plan was not adopted, partly because the necessary technical skills were not yet available and partly because of opposition from wharf owners and other interests, the successors of whom finally lost out in the nineteenth century.[62]

Since most visitors to the Embankment probably focus on the river, they often miss the Gardens which lie rather unobtrusively across the busy road on a narrow strip of land some 20 acres in size. Actually, they stretch from the Ministry of Defence Building to the back of the Savoy Hotel, though they are divided into three parts by streets that run perpendicular to the river. The first part almost seems like it belongs to the Ministry of Defence alone because the Gardens here are so small while the building is so huge. As might be expected this part seems to take on the character of its location with the kind of emphasis it has. Two themes dominate – military and royal – with the first being represented by statues on plinths of military men of this and last century: Trenchard and Portal of the RAF and General Gordon killed at Khartoum in 1885. Royalty is represented more indirectly by what is left of curving steps onto which Tudor monarchs once stepped from the Royal Barge en route to the then standing Whitehall Palace nearby.[63]

The second part is very different in style, wider and more open, with formal plantings and flower beds on larger areas of grass, things absent in the first part. Yet, like that part statues again seem to be the focus of attention, only this time it is a standoff between the military and the religious. Hence one statue is that of General Sir James Outram of the last century and the other is that of William Tyndale, who completed the first translation of the Bible into English in 1525.[64]

The third part is not only the largest but also the most interesting with the Savoy Hotel suggesting what I like to call its true identity: 'Gilbert and Sullivan Park.' Actually it can be said that the Gardens here are sandwiched between Gilbert's monument beside the Hungerford Bridge and Sullivan's bust at the park's opposite end. The latter is located near a small, hedged garden enclosure with a sundial commemorating Gilbert and Sullivan's operas written between 1871 and 1890 and the riverside entrance to the Savoy Hotel. Near the Hungerford Bridge end of the park, a further attempt is made to promote the theatrical feeling of this part of the Gardens by a small stage for dance, poetry readings and music during summer lunchtimes and evenings.[65]

Although other monuments are to be found here, including a massive statue to the famous Robert Burns, perhaps sights of a different nature do much more to characterize this part of the Gardens. Among these are a lily pond with a little fountain, a formal pool with waterlilies and a small sunken garden. Beds of flowers and trees, one of which commemorates the coronation of Elizabeth II in 1953, scattered throughout the park help to give a sense of seclusion and serenity from the busy traffic along the road and the pedestrian activity along the river walkway. In short, this part of the Gardens is a wonderful place to rest and relax on the last leg of a journey through splendid parks from Kensington to the City.

## The Special Relationship

Given my background, perhaps it is not surprising that the last three chapters are tied together by walks. My love of walking probably began when I started delivering newspapers as a young boy. Although I also used my bicycle, I usually walked during the winter months when snow and ice covered the ground. Now I hasten to add that the actual delivery of papers themselves had little to do with the love of walking because the process itself was very boring. Yet perhaps because this was the case, my walks became an enjoyable time for thought, reflection and much day-dreaming. Indeed, there were times when I was so 'out of it' I couldn't remember delivering the papers at all. This, of course, was often very embarrassing when I returned home with extra papers I should not have had. At any rate, I learned from my experiences walking that the mind is often stimulated to think creatively. During an academic career, many lectures and articles had their beginnings while walking my dog at 6 in the morning. In fact much of this book was written after walks on my treadmill, around the block, and on a trail nearby. Having never taken a poll to determine whether this exercise works for others as well, I'll not try to provide an explanation but simply urge readers to try it for themselves.

With walking so important to stimulate my thought processes, it seemed appropriate to search for the Special Relationship in Britain in this way with the caveat, of course, that my conclusions would probably be highly impressionistic and even somewhat mystical. I imagine most readers have found these characteristics in the last three chapters. Solid evidence and logical conclusions have often been absent. Again, as stated above, I can only urge others to have the same walking experiences and institutional encounters along the way to determine whether those processes will produce similar results for them. I think they will.

Of course, part of the problem as discussed near the book's beginning is that our concepts – even our words generally – are inadequate to describe the essence of the phenomena, including the Special Relationship itself. Therefore, metaphors have often been employed, such as the Helper figure to get at the essence of the Special Relationship. So I have used that figure because of my belief that the configuration of values and attributes associated with her are at the heart of the Special Relationship.

Now in the course of my walks as described in the last three chapters I have felt that I have encountered many of those values and attributes in both Sussex and London. Obviously there are, of course, significant differences between rural walks along pathways, through villages, and into churches that are often rather isolated and urban strolls through parks, around villages, and into churches and theaters. The sights, sounds, bustle, and countless other things present two very different worlds. At times the huge, sprawling city seems so overpowering and oppressive that many if not most people want to escape to the countryside where things seem much more on a human scale, where there is a sense of community among inhabitants, and where meaningful contacts can be made with an environment that has helped to make us whom we are. I well remember the reply of a former colleague of some academic note who when asked about the problem of the city said: 'The only solution is to abandon it and to return to the rural villages.'

Given the nature of things today, this is not a solution. On the other hand, something may be done in the opposite direction that is not a solution either but can mitigate some of the worst aspects of city life. In short something of the rural can be brought to the urban. That is what I believe London has done with its churches, theaters, villages and parks. Obviously many of these in the city may appear rather artificial or like images rather than reality. Certainly the parks often seem like idealized copies of the countryside, and the villages appear to be, as noted before, images people have in their heads. Yet they seem to work rather well, and London is better for that. So, at their best, these institutions have Helper values and attributes at their cores, and therefore they have helped to make London liveable and workable.

# *Notes*

1. *The London Encyclopaedia*, s.v. 'Bloomsbury.'
2. Roger Hudson, *The London Guides: Bloomsbury, Fitzrovia, & Soho* (London: The Haggerston Press, 1996), 33.
3. *Encyclopaedia*, s.v. 'Bloomsbury.'
4. Ibid.
5. Ibid.
6. Ibid.
7. Ibid.
8. Hudson, 54.
9. *Encyclopaedia*, s.v. 'Bloomsbury.'
10. Mary Kenny, 'Bloomsbury,' in Peter Crookston (ed.), *Village London* (London: Arrow Books Ltd., 1978), 24.
11. *Encyclopaedia*, s.v. 'British Museum.'
12. *Encyclopaedia*, s.v. 'Bedford Square.'
13. Kenny, 24.
14. *Encyclopaedia*, s.v. 'University College,' 'University of London.'
15. Ibid.
16. Hudson, 50.
17. Ibid., 58, 60.
18. *Encyclopaedia*, s.v. 'Hospital for Sick Children.'
19. Ibid.
20. Ibid.
21. Andrew Duncan, *Village London* (London: New Holland, 1997), 63.
22. *Encyclopaedia*, s.v. 'Kensington.'
23. Ibid.
24. Ibid. See also Neil Grant, *Village London: Past and Present* (London: Pyramid Books, 1990), 15.
25. *Encyclopaedia*, s.v. 'Kensington.'

26. Ibid.
27. Ibid.
28. Ibid.
29. David Piper, *The Companion Guide to London* (London: Fontana Books, 1970), 187.
30. Harold P. Clunn, *The Face of London*. Revised by E. R. Wethersett. (London: Spring Books), 425.
31. Emma Tennant, 'Notting Hill,' in Crookston, 135.
32. Ibid.
33. *Encyclopaedia*, s.v. 'Holland House and Park.'
34. Ibid.
35. *Encyclopaedia*, s.v. 'Commonwealth Institute.'
36. Hunter Davies, *A Walk Round London's Parks* (London: Hamish Hamilton, 1983), 221.
37. Geoffrey Young, *Walking London's Parks and Gardens* (London: New Holland, 1998), 49; Davies, 49.
38. Davies, 49.
39. Ibid., 52.
40. Quoted in Robert Cameron and Alistair Cooke, *Above London* (London: The Bodley Head, 1980), 74.
41. Davies, 52–3.
42. Ibid., 63–4.
43. Young, 53.
44. Davies, 65.
45. Ibid., 57.
46. Ibid., 40; Grant, 25.
47. Young, 61–2.
48. Ibid., 57.
49. Quoted in Davies, 36.
50. Ibid., 25–7.
51. Young, 60.
52. Ibid., 62.
53. Ibid., 59; Davies, 38–9.
54. Young, 109–11; Grant, 69.
55. Young, 110.
56. Ibid.
57. Davies, 17–18.
58. Ibid., 17.
59. *Encyclopaedia*, s.v. 'St. James's Park'; Davies, 10.
60. Young, 120.
61. Davies, 15.
62. Young, 97.

63. Ibid., 102.
64. Ibid.
65. Ibid.

# Conclusion

> What then is the American, this new man?
>> J. Hector St John Crevecoeur in
>> *Letters From An American Farmer*, 1782

*F*irst published near the end of the American Revolutionary War, Crevecoeur's book is a classic in the literature of American character and culture. For students of that literature, his famous question, one of the most important raised, has served as a guide for their studies down through the years. Many have tried to answer it for themselves, but perhaps most have felt compelled to accept at least some of Crevecoeur's response to his own question. With his emphasis noted, he said in part:

> *He* is an American, who leaving behind him all his ancient preju-
> dices and manners, receives new ones from the new mode of life
> he has embraced, the new government he obeys, and the new rank
> he holds. He becomes an American by being received in the broad
> lap of our great *Alma Mater.*[1]

So Crevecoeur sees the American as a new and different person who has rejected his Old World past and who is being molded by his New World fostering mother.

For Henry Nash Smith, a noted scholar of American civilization, the problem with Crevecoeur's interpretation is that it significantly informed many subsequent writers of American history, above all Frederick Jackson Turner, to develop the doctrine that the United States is a continental nation of its own making rather than 'a member with Europe of an Atlantic community.' Despite much professional criticism of Turner, his famous 1893 essay, 'The Significance of the Frontier in American History,' influenced – Smith believes – a whole generation of American historians to rewrite the country's history. They did so in terms of the frontier, the lands in the West, making it the most familiar and possibly the most accepted interpretation in America.[2]

I think Smith is correct in arguing that this questionable, nationalistic interpretation of American history has had a significant impact on

Americans. Certainly, this was true when Smith wrote in the late 1940s. For me today, as my book suggests, my major problem with Crevecoeur centers on his choice of metaphors: the foster mother (America, for him) only and not the natural mother (Britannia, for me) too. In making this choice, he predicates the American identity on the present and future – America as a new nation in the making – and not at all on the past – the British heritage. Additionally, as I see it, when Crevecoeur's book was published during the Revolution, America was not a Helper – either foster or natural – but a Rebel, a young son in the process of rejecting his parents. Therefore Crevecoeur is wrong on two counts: excluding the natural mother altogether and identifying America as a foster mother rather than a rebellious son. Unfortunately, like the previous case with Turner and other historians, Crevecoeur's ideas have had a significant impact.

As indicated at the outset of my book, American history, especially American diplomatic history, makes the most sense to me when America is viewed as a Rebel – certainly not a Helper – well into the twentieth century. Given America's many favorable circumstances throughout the nineteenth century, a prolonged period of rebelliousness was possible, but the unfavorable consequences of this began to appear when America came on the world scene at the turn of the twentieth century and tried to become a leader. Unfortunately, desirable leadership characteristics had not been acquired, and America, the Rebel – still rejecting nurturing and other female qualities – continued with his 'protest masculinity' until the 1940s. The results, as I mentioned, showed immaturity and irresponsibility.

My belief is that at least part of America's problem in foreign affairs stems from the willingness of Americans down through the years to accept an interpretation like Crevecoeur's. By so doing we did not mature properly, for a major dimension in the maturation process, the past, was undervalued and the present and future overvalued instead. We did this because we accepted Crevecoeur's notion that *Alma Mater*, his foster Helper, could be a substitute for the natural one. What we failed to understand was that Crevecoeur had a limited role for this Helper – that of looking to the present and future only. Perhaps, as indicated above, his own failure lay in selecting the wrong metaphor for the situation at hand: the Helper rather than the Rebel. The latter, by definition, rejects the past and focuses on the present and future, and the America of the 1780s seems to fit that definition.

At any rate, as indicated in my book, the Helper's role is much larger. Standing in the present, she connects the future and the past like a link in a chain. She is Janus-like: she looks in both directions, like the law. (No wonder Richard Hooker personified the law as a woman for Elizabethans.) She does so because she picks and chooses from the past the important values of the entire cultural experience and passes them on to the next generation. Hence she does not reject the past but embraces it as a major source of values, including the Helper values mentioned throughout this book.

The consequence of undervaluing the past in the enculturation or socialization process is to produce someone lacking a fully-developed personality and character, essentially a rudderless individual without leadership qualities. My belief is that the same thing can happen to nations and something of this nature happened to America in foreign affairs.

My answer for this problem, as argued throughout the book, is for America to reconnect with Britain through the Special Relationship. Based on my experience, the way to do this is for Americans to connect with important traditional institutions of culture in Britain: family, university, church and government, and others like the theater, parks, pathways, and the media. In them can be found many values, but especially those Helper values, which were rejected and lost in international relationships as a consequence of the American Revolution. Out of this loss American isolationism evolved.

It is significant, I believe, that an isolationist tradition did not develop among Britain's other 'children' – only within the United States. Even Canada, so like the United States in many respects and certainly influenced greatly by its huge southern neighbor, has had a history of responsible internationalism, not isolationism. The main difference vis-a-vis Britain is that Canada's movement towards independence was evolutionary rather than revolutionary in nature – no violent rejection occurred. Hence important Helper values in international relations, such as cooperation, accommodation, and larger community interests – the basis for internationalism as opposed to isolationism – were retained by Canada.

Certainly since the late 1940s America has shown evidence of developing maturity and responsibility in international relations. Beginning with such policies as the Marshall Plan and NATO, the United States has moved in the direction of seeing itself – in Henry Nash Smith's words – as 'a member with Europe of an Atlantic community.' Isolationism has moved to the fringes, and connections with Britain and other countries have increased dramatically. Yet with the recent ending of the Cold War, it remains to be seen whether these changes are permanent or whether they are only temporary consequences of President Truman's 'scaring hell' out of the American people at the beginning of that war. Obviously one hopes for the former, but one needs to be prepared for the latter given the deeply ingrained American isolationist tradition. Hence the Special Relationship must continue with more rather than fewer connections between Britain and the United States. My hope for the future is that Britons and other non-Americans will feel less inclined to ask that most important question out of my past: 'Is America going isolationist again?'

# *Notes*

1. J. Hector St John Crevecoeur, *Letters From An American Farmer* (Garden City, New York: Doubleday & Company, Inc.), 49.
2. Henry Nash Smith, *Virgin Land: The American West as Symbol and Myth* (New York: Vintage Books, 1950), 3–4.